THE PEOPLE'S REPUBLIC OF CHINA:

A BASIC HANDBOOK

Fourth Edition


Steven M. Goldstein
China Council, Asia Society


Kathrin Sears
China Council, Asia Society


Richard C. Bush
House Committee on Foreign Affairs

Published in cooperation with

THE CHINA COUNCIL OF THE ASIA SOCIETY

by the

COUNCIL ON INTERNATIONAL AND PUBLIC AFFAIRS

1984


Distributed by

LEARNING RESOURCES IN INTERNATIONAL STUDIES
777 United Nations Plaza
New York, NY  10017

Cover Art:  John Kaljee, Artwork Unlimited, Inc.

Map Credits:  pages 15, 16, and 18 — Frederic M. Kaplan, Julian M. Sobin, and Stephen Andors, Encyclopedia of China Today (New York: Eurasia Press, 1979), pp. 157, 181, 10.  Reprinted with permission.

TABLE OF CONTENTS

## VII. MATERIAL WELFARE, EDUCATION, AND PUBLIC HEALTH

## VIII.  DAILY LIFE

FOREWORD

As Harold Isaacs has reminded us in the preface of the last
edition of Scratches on Our Minds, the American people have long
exhibited a mercurial attitude towards China. Rarely indifferent, the
dominant mood has shifted, like a vast pendulum, from one extreme to
the other.

These rapid changes in American perceptions of China are, at least
in part, a reflection of the limited knowledge which most Americans
have of the world's largest country, its contemporary institutions, and
its rich cultural heritage. Until we are able to broaden the base of
informed understanding of China, it will be difficult to supplant the
mercurial American attitude with one rooted in realistic knowledge and
sympathetic, but not uncritical, awareness of Chinese society.

The last four decades of US-China relations reflect all too
vividly these swings of the pendulum. From the warm friendship and
support accorded a wartime ally fighting bravely to repulse a totali-
tarian invader in the first half of the 1940s, the American posture
towards China had changed, by the end of that decade, to one of extreme
hostility. Americans even had the temerity of accusing one another of
"losing" China, as though another sovereign country was ours to keep or
lose under any circumstances.

There followed two decades of isolation, during which the extreme
hostility of the early 1950s gradually mellowed to the point of cold
indifference. Then followed President Nixon's dramatic journey to
Beijing in 1972, and the pendulum began a downward swing in the other
direction.

At first the pendulum moved slowly -- indeed to some observers
(both Chinese and American), almost imperceptibly, the bold and hopeful
language of the Shanghai Communique notwithstanding. But gradually it
began to gather momentum and was greatly accelerated by the normalization of US-China relations in December 1978.

In an effort to diminish these mercurial swings in national mood,
both education and the mass media have much to contribute to more
informed public understanding of China by the American people. The
media, with their enormous capacity for outreach, communicate to tens
of millions of Americans an awareness of those volcanic peaks of
activity when the media's threshold of "excitability" has been crossed.
The task of education is to provide that deeper understanding of the
events, processes, and institutions which connect these volcanic peaks
and cause them to erupt from time to time.

This handbook reflects a confluence of both streams of public
understanding of China. In 1975 the China Council of The Asia Society
assembled a set of briefing materials to assist the media in covering
President Ford's December 1975 visit to the People's Republic. It soon
became apparent to the Council that the biographies of Chinese leaders,
maps, several chronologies, glossary, and judiciously selected bibliography would have usefulness to those who wanted to enlarge their

knowledge of contemporary China much beyond the transitory attention generated by a presidential visit. This publication was widely distributed and used in college and university courses on China, US foreign policy, and international relations, as well as secondary school and adult education courses and programs.

The wisdom of this judgment was soon confirmed. The first edition of People's Republic of China: Press Briefing Materials was exhausted, and a second revised edition — updated to reflect subsequent leadership shifts and political developments — was issued in the latter part of 1976. This edition likewise soon became exhausted.

The basic idea by then having been validated, we decided to move to a greatly increased coverage and a more substantial handbook format. The first edition of the handbook appeared in the spring of 1979. The present handbook is an expanded and updated version of the earlier publications but its purpose remains the same — to provide in concise form authoritative information, based on the latest scholarship, to assist representatives of the media, teachers, students, business executives, government officials, and anyone else interested in increasing their understanding of the world's most populous country.

We are glad to have the opportunity to publish The People's Republic of China: A Basic Handbook in cooperation with the China Council of The Asia Society. The Council on International and Public Affairs is committed to the Jeffersonian principle that when the people are fully informed, they will reach right decisions on the great public questions of the day, and toward that end CIPA maintains an active interest in strengthening American mass media coverage of international affairs. Reflecting a similar commitment, the China Council conducts an extensive program of high quality to increase public understanding of China, both nationally and locally through its regional affiliates across the country. A central element in this program is its work with the mass media, electronic as well as print, in helping to improve media coverage of China.

The China Council has been a major factor in preparing the American people for the new phase in US-China relations into which we have now entered. The durability of this phase of US-China friendship and cooperation will depend in no small measure on the extent to which the China Council and the educational institutions and media organizations with which it works are able to replace the vacillating American attitudes of the past with those based on knowledge and realistic understanding of China and the Chinese people.

Ward Morehouse, President
Council on International and
Public Affairs

New York City
March 1984

PREFACE

The China Council of The Asia Society was established in 1975 to foster greater American understanding of China and US-China relations. Since then it has created across the country a network of regional councils which develop programs to meet local needs. It has also sponsored a number of educational materials for general and specialized audiences. This handbook is among them, and we hope that college students, high school teachers, business executives, and journalists among others will find it useful. The National Endowment for the Humanities, The Henry Luce Foundation, The Mellon Foundation, The Exxon Corporation, ARCO, and The Rockefeller Foundation provide generous support for the Council's efforts.

Though relatively young as organizations go, the China Council is both part and beneficiary of a long tradition. For many years, China specialists both inside and outside universities have made public education one of their primary professional responsibilities. Probably because of the special and sometimes tragic role China has played in American life, they have contributed uncommon energy to enlighten rather than heat public attitudes. Their compensation has never done justice to their sacrifice.

Such a commitment is certainly not absent in other fields of international studies. The China field is somewhat unusual in that public education work has taken more overt organizational forms -- first the National Committee on US-China Relations and now the China Council. Moreover, this effort has had a regional dimension, addressing the educational needs of local audiences. Still, the voluntary contributions of specialists have been crucial to this organizational process.

James Townsend is but one example of China specialists' commitment to public education. Long active in public education work in the Washington area, he supported the China Council from its inception and played a seminal role in the creation and active work of the Seattle Regional China Council. This handbook was developed from materials he prepared for his students at the University of Washington. And he went several extra miles in preparing them for publication in the handbook's first edition. Whatever the worth of this publication, it is due in large measure to him.

The China Council depends heavily on other international education organizations. By collaborating with them, it multiplies the effects of its own efforts. In this regard, the Council is deeply grateful to Ward Morehouse and the Council on International and Public Affairs and its affiliated organizations. Without them, it would be impossible to make this handbook available in a usable format and at a reasonable price. Special thanks go to Cynthia Morehouse for her consistently valuable editorial skills, to Gordon Woodside of Pageprint Systems, and to Milton Buschhoff of Learning Resources in International Studies.

- ix -

There are other individuals whose efforts should not go unrecognized. Harlan Jencks, Robert Weiss, Dorothy Margolis, and Arlene Cavanaugh assisted Jim Townsend in the selection and preparation of many materials included herein. Jonathan Daen of the China Council staff was indispensable in the compilation and preparation of this edition. Other colleagues at The Asia Society's Washington Center -- Robert Oxnam, Terry Lautz, Margaret Sullivan, Daisey Kwoh, Judith Sloan, Elizabeth Nichols, and Lisa Swanberg, all helped in a multitude of ways. Harry Harding suggested a number of improvements. I alone am responsible for any errors that remain.

Richard C. Bush
China Council of The Asia Society

Washington, D. C.
December 1980

## PREFACE TO THE THIRD EDITION

This edition of the Handbook is not a radical departure from its predecessor. However, it has been possible to update much of the material, take advantage of new material released by the Chinese government, and correct a number of errors. New or remaining mistakes continue to be my responsibility.

I wish to acknowledge the assistance provided by Christopher Albrecht, Nai-ruenn Chen, Robert Michael Field, Carol Lee Hamrin, Jennifer Little, Cynthia and Ward Morehouse, Leo Orleans, and Susan O'Sullivan. Robert B. Oxnam and James R. Townsend continue to be generous in their support.

Richard C. Bush
China Council of The Asia Society

Washington, D. C.
December 1981

# PREFACE TO THE FOURTH EDITION

The publication of this fourth edition coincides with the appointment of a new staff at the China Council. However, although some fresh names appear on this handbook, we would like to begin by acknowledging the debt which we owe our predecessors. In particular, so much of this handbook remains the work of James Townsend. In addition, Goldstein and Sears would like to acknowledge the contribution of Richard Bush. In this publication, as well as in his work at the China Council in general, he maintained an extremely high standard which we will endeavor to continue. Dr. Bush's work on this handbook was completed before he joined the staff of the House Committee on International Affairs. Naturally, his work reflects his own views and not those of the United States Congress.

Professors Carl Riskin and Martin Whyte read parts of this Handbook and offered valuable advice. Finally, we thank Tzu-lin Li who has provided not only good humor, but essential editorial assistance.

Steven M. Goldstein
China Council

Kathrin Sears
China Council

Richard C. Bush
House Committee on
   International Affairs

New York City
March 1984

A NOTE ON ROMANIZATION


        Chinese proper names in this volume are rendered in the pinyin
system of romanization (the only exceptions are the conventional ren-
derings for Sun Yat-sen and Chiang Kai-shek). The People's Republic of
China has used this system in its foreign language publications since
January 1, 1979, and most American publishers subsequently adopted it.
        Many readers will be more familiar with renderings of the tradi-
tional systems — Postal Atlas for place names and Wade-Giles for personal names and other words. To reduce confusion, the old forms of the
best known names appear parenthetically in the text at appropriate
places. The appendix (pages 166-167) gives old and new forms for all
words. Below are guidelines on how to pronounce words rendered in
pinyin (Wade-Giles equivalents are in parentheses).


a (a):        as in far
b (p):        as in baby
c (ts):       as "ts" in its
ch (ch'):     as "ch" in church, strongly aspirated
d (t):        as in do
e (e):        1)  as "er" in her, the "r" being silent
              2)  as in yes in the "ie" dipthong
              3)  as in way in the "ei" dipthong
f (f):        as in foot
g (k):        as in go
h (h):        as in her, strongly aspirated
i (i):        1) as in eat
              2) as in sir in syllables beginning with c, ch, r, s, sh,
                 z, zh
j (ch):       as in jeep
k (k'):       as in kind, strongly aspirated
l (l):        as in land
m (m):        as in me
n (n):        as in no
o (o):        as "aw" in law
p (p'):       as in par, strongly aspirated
q (ch'):      as "ch" in cheek
r (j):        as "r" but not rolled, or like "z" in azure
s (s,
  ss, sz):    as in sister
sh (sh):      as "sh" in shore
t (t'):       as in top, strongly aspirated
u (u):        1)  as in too
              2)  as in the French "u" in "tu" or the German umlauted "u"
                  in "Muenchen"
w (w):        as in want
x (hs):       as "sh" in she
y (y):        as in yet
z (ts,tz):    as in zero
zh (ch):      as "j" in jump

ABBREVIATIONS

The following abbreviations are used for frequently cited sources:

BN                    U.S. Department of State, Bureau of Public
                      Affairs. Background Notes: China. Washington,
                      DC: Government Printing Office.

BR                    Beijing Review (before 1982 known as Peking
                      Review)

CBR                   The China Business Review

China Facts           John L. Scherer, ed. China Facts and Figures
                      Annual, 1983, vol. 6. Gulf Breeze, FL: Academic
                      International Press, 1983.

China Report          1982/83 China Offical Annual Report. Hong Kong:
                      Hong Kong Kingsway International Publications
                      Limited, October 1982.

CQ                    The China Quarterly

I.  LEARNING MORE ABOUT CHINA


Anyone wishing to learn more about China is blessed with an excess of riches.  Extensive and varied materials exist on most subjects; each type of source has its strengths and weaknesses.  Succeeding chapters provide suggestions for further reading on the topic concerned.  This chapter outlines how to get access to the general categories of information available.


## 1.  Current Events -- External Sources

Newspapers and newsmagazines are a basic source of information on contemporary China.  The national press -- The New York Times, The Washington Post, the Christian Science Monitor, The Wall Street Journal, Time, and Newsweek -- all have correspondents in Beijing who provide regular coverage of Chinese politics and social life for their own publications and, through their news services, a number of other newspapers as well.  However, their coverage is inevitably thin on certain subjects, and should be supplemented with periodicals focusing on Chinese and Asian affairs, such as the following:

Asian Survey.  Published monthly by the University of California Press, Berkeley.  Contains frequent articles on China.  The January issue each year surveys events in China during the previous year.

Asia Week.  Published weekly in Hong Kong.  An excellent weekly newsmagazine of current developments in Asia.

The China Business Review.  Published bimonthly by the National Council for US-China Trade, Washington, DC.  Provides an exhaustive review of developments in the Chinese economy and Chinese trade with the US and other countries, plus articles on topics of interest to business people.

China Exchange News.  Formerly China Exchange Newsletter.  Published quarterly by the Committee on Scholarly Communication with the People's Republic of China, Washington, DC.  Comprehensive review of scholarly developments in China and of US-China academic exchanges.  Includes an excellent bibliography of recent articles and books on contemporary China.

The China Quarterly.  Published quarterly in London.  The leading Western journal of contemporary China studies, with scholarly articles and book reviews.  Each issue contains a valuable chronology and documentary review of the previous quarter.

CIA Reference Aids. Unclassified Central Intelligence Agency charts, statistical compendia, directories, and reports on the Chinese economy and other topics, published on an occasional basis. Information about items dated before February 1, 1979 is available from the Documents Expediting Project, Exchange and Gifts Division, Library of Congress, Washington, DC  20540; photocopies are available from the Library of Congress's Photo Duplication Service.  Items dated after February 1, 1979 can be ordered from the National Technical Information Service, 5285 Port Royal Road, Springfield, VA  22161.

Far Eastern Economic Review. Published weekly in Hong Kong.  Similar to an American weekly newsmagazine, but with an emphasis on economic affairs.  Very good for up-to-date reporting on China. Publishes an annual Yearbook with survey articles and forecasts, accompanied by considerable statistical data.

Issues and Studies. Published monthly in Taipei by the Institute of International Relations, National Political University.  Features articles, biographies and documents said to have been acquired by Nationalist agents on the Chinese mainland.

Modern China. Published quarterly in Beverly Hills, CA.  A scholarly journal, more historically oriented, but with many articles on current affairs

Notes from the National Committee. Published quarterly by the National Committee on United States-China Relations, Inc., New York, NY.  A review of US-China exchanges as well as new developments in US-China relations.


2.  Current Events -- Materials from China in English

An enormous amount of material from the PRC is available in English translation, most of it falling into two categories: publications in English from the Foreign Languages Press in Beijing; and English translations of Chinese radio broadcasts, newspaper and periodical articles, books, and so on.  Publications from China have a public relations purpose, but in the last few years, even these have been remarkably candid about some of China's problems.  Other translations are voluminous but very useful, and constitute one major source for scholars and journalists analyzing developments in China.

What follows are the most prominent examples of each type of source:

a)  Publications of Foreign Languages Press.  China Books and Periodicals, Inc., the PRC's US distributor for publications, is the easiest point of access for this material.  Periodic catalogues of books, pamphlets, maps, tourist guides, posters, and other items, and subscriptions for periodicals are available from CB&P's three offices:

East Coast Center
125 Fifth Ave.
New York, NY  10003
212/677-2650

Midwest Center
37 South Wabash St.
Chicago, IL  60603
312/782-6004

West Coast Center
2929 24th Street
San Francisco, CA  94110
415/282-2994

China publishes a large number of periodicals in English, with more expected in the future. The most prominent are:

Beijing Review (weekly; formerly Peking Review). Extremely valuable for anyone interested in contemporary China. Includes translations of major articles, editorials, documents, and government statements that have appeared in the Chinese press, plus feature articles on important issues and controversies in Chinese society.

China Daily. The only English language daily newspaper from China available in the US.

China Pictorial (monthly). Color photography and short articles.

China Reconstructs (monthly). Feature articles and photos on life in the PRC.

Chinese Literature (monthly). Short stories, poems, and novellas from both the traditional and modern periods.

b) English Language Translation Services. The major serial translations of Chinese materials are voluminous and expensive. Their titles, coverage, and distribution patterns have changed frequently. Most users must consult them -- preferably with the help of a librarian or experienced user -- in libraries that maintain special collections of such materials. However, the sources listed below open many windows on the entire history of the PRC. Consequently, they are indispensable to anyone desiring a deeper understanding of contemporary China.

US Consulate-General, Hong Kong. From the 1950s to October 1977, the Hong Kong consulate offered four principal translation series, with varying titles:

Current Background (irregular topical document collections)
Survey of People's Republic of China Magazines (formerly Survey of Chinese Mainland Magazines)
Survey of People's Republic of China Press (formerly Survey of Chinese Mainland Press)
Index (to the above items)

These series were discontinued in 1977, but much of the material covered was divided among the various serials of the next two translation services. Their distribution is handled by the National Technical Information Service, US Department of Commerce, 5285 Port Royal Road, Springfield, VA 22161.

Foreign Broadcast Information Service. Daily Report: People's Republic of China. Distributed every working day; contains translations of Chinese radio broadcasts and some newspaper and periodical articles.

Joint Publications Research Service. Has distributed several serial and monograph translations under various titles since 1957. Two of the most important are Translations on the PRC and Red Flag

Magazine. (Red Flag [Hongqi] is the official theoretical journal of the Chinese Communist Party Central Committee.)

M. E. Sharpe, Inc., 901 No. Broadway, White Plains, NY 10603. Publishes several quarterly journals of Chinese documents in translation, and initiates many other documentary and book translation projects. The journals are:

Chinese Economic Studies
Chinese Education
Chinese Law and Government
Chinese Sociology and Anthropology

Chinese Studies in History
Chinese Studies in Literature
Chinese Studies in Philosophy

## 3. Bibliographies for Scholarly Resources

The past 15 years have seen a flood of scholarly works on China. These draw on archives of Chinese-language sources, translated material, interviews with emigres in Hong Kong, and travel and field research in China. Maintaining control over this avalanche is not easy, even for the specialist. Most of the items listed below are already dated; information about current books and periodicals is most easily found in Focus on Asian Studies (see section 6 below), in the bibliography section of China Exchange News, and in the book review and book received sections of The China Quarterly (see section 1 above). For recent books on Chinese history, see the book review section of Journal of Asian Studies, published by the Association for Asian Studies.
Major bibliographies include:

Association for Asian Studies. Bibliography of Asian Studies. Annual comprehensive citation of publications (books, articles, monographs) in Western and Asian languages, organized by country and topics with extensive entries on China.

Blair, Patricia. Development in the People's Republic of China: A Selected Bibliography. Washington, DC: Overseas Development Council, 1976. A topically organized list of about 400 publications on political, economic, and social developments in the PRC, most written in the early 1970s. Includes an introductory essay on Chinese development strategies by A. Doak Barnett.

Nathan, Andrew J. Modern China, 1840-1972: An Introduction to Sources and Research Aids. Ann Arbor: University of Michigan Center for Chinese Studies, 1973. Designed as a guide for graduate student research, but generally useful for all advanced students of China.

Posner, Arlene, and Arne J. deKeijzer, eds. China: A Resource and Curriculum Guide. 2nd revised edition. Chicago: University of Chicago Press, 1976. An excellent guide for the general teacher or student. Contains essays on teaching about China, an annotated review of curriculum units and audio visual materials, and a selective annotated bibliography organized by topic.

Shulman, Frank J., and Leonard H.J. Gordon, eds. Doctoral Dissertations on China, 1945-70. Seattle: University of Washington

Press, 1972. And Shulman, Frank J. <u>Doctoral Dissertations on</u>
<u>China, 1971-75</u>. Seattle: University of Washington Press, 1978.

The above items identify other bibliographies and reference works.
There are two specialized bibliographies which are particularly useful
for background on contemporary Chinese affairs and US-China relations
prior to 1973:

McCutcheon, James M. <u>China and America: A Bibliography of Interac-</u>
<u>tions, Domestic and Foreign</u>. Honolulu: University Press of
Hawaii, 1972.

Oksenberg, Michel C., et al. <u>A Bibliography of Secondary E n g l i s h</u>
<u>Language Literature on Contemporary Chinese Politics</u>. New York:
Columbia University East Asian Institute, 1970.


## 4. Handbooks

Several handbooks exist that provide comprehensive surveys of the
PRC. They are:

Bunge, Frederica, and Rinn-Sup Shinn. <u>China: A Country Study</u>.
Washington, DC: Government Printing Office, 1984.

Hinton, Harold. <u>The People's Republic of China: A Handbook</u>. Boulder, CO: Westview Press, 1979.

Hook, Brian, ed. <u>The Cambridge Encyclopedia of China</u>. Cambridge:
Cambridge University Press, 1982.

Kaplan, Frederic M., and Julian M. Sobin, eds. <u>Encyclopedia of China</u>
<u>Today</u>. 3rd edition. New York: Harper & Row, 1981.

Scherer, John L., ed. <u>China Facts and Figures Annual</u>. Gulf Breeze,
FL: Academic International Press. Published every year since
1978. Available from P.O. Box 555, Gulf Breeze, FL 32561.

<u>1982/83 China Official Annual Report</u>. Hong Kong: Hong Kong Kingsway
International Publications Ltd., October 1982.


## 5. Travel Guides

Going to China is an obvious way of learning more. A variety of
guidebooks are now available:

China Travel and Tourism Press, ed. <u>The Official Guidebook of China</u>.
New York: Hippocrene Books, 1982.

deKeijzer, Arne J., and Frederic M. Kaplan. <u>China Guidebook: 1980/81</u>
<u>Edition</u>. New York: Eurasia Press, 1980. Very thorough; espe-
cially good on the problems and opportunities of China travel.

Fodor's. <u>Beijing, Guangzhou, Shanghai, 1984</u>. New York: Fodor's
Travel Guides, 1984. Pocket-sized guide to the three cities,

notable for providing Chinese characters for restaurants and menu items.

Fodor's People's Republic of China. New York: Fodor's Travel Guides, 1984.

Nagel's Encyclopedic Guide to China. Geneva: Nagel Publishers, 1982. Quite expensive, but very useful for those interested in history, museums, monuments, and palaces.

More specialized travelers, especially those engaged in business, should consult:

China Directory. Tokyo: Radiopress, Inc., 1983.

The China Phone Book & Address Directory. Hong Kong: The China Phone Book Company Ltd., 1982.

China's Provinces: An Organizational and Statistical Guide. Washington, DC: National Council for US-China Trade, 1982.

Clarke, Christopher M., and Kathryn L. Dewenter, compilers. China Business Manual 1981. Washington, DC: National Council for US-China Trade, 1981.

## 6. For the Teacher

China: A Resource and Curriculum Guide, edited by Posner and deKeijzer, is the best published guide for teachers (see entry in section 3 for details). Already eight years old, it should be supplemented by consulting one or more of the resource centers around the country. Among them are (listed in zip code order):

Harvard University East Asian Educational Project, Children's Museum, 300 Congress St., Boston, MA 02210 (617/426-6500).

Council on East Asian Studies, Yale University, 85 Trumbell Street, Box 13A, Yale Station, New Haven, CT 06520 (203/432-4029).

East Asian Studies, Princeton University, 211 Jones Hall, Princeton, NJ 08544 (609/452-4276).

The Education Department of The Asia Society, 725 Park Avenue, New York, NY 10021 (212/288-6400). Publishes Focus on Asian Studies, a resource journal for elementary and secondary school educators that includes articles, book reviews, model curricula, multimedia teaching resources, graphics, and a calendar of major cultural events across the country. Subscription: $5.00 for three issues a year (single copy price, $3.00). The Education Department has also embarked on a comprehensive survey of recent scholarship on China useful to upper elementary and secondary school educators. The ultimate product will consist of an annotated bibliography, selected readings, and suggested classroom strategies, all designed to bridge the gap between the textbook picture of China and current reality.

East Asian Curriculum Project, Columbia University, 420 West 118th Street—9th Fl., New York, NY 10027 (212/280-4278).

The Center for Teaching About China, 2025 I Street, Suite 715, Washington, DC 20006 (202/296-4147). A national clearinghouse for teaching materials for all ages. Publishes a catalogue, China in the Classroom.

East Asian Language and Area Center, University of Virginia, 1644 Oxford Road, Charlottesville, VA 22903 (804/295-1808).

East Asian Outreach Program, Indiana University, Goodbody Hall 348, Bloomington, IN 47405 (812/335-3767).

Project on East Asian Studies in Education, University of Michigan, 108 Lane Hall, Ann Arbor, MI 48109 (313/764-5109).

Midwest China Center, 308 Gullixson Hall, 2375 Como Avenue West, St. Paul, MN 55108 (612/614-3238). Publishes China Update, a monthly newsletter that reviews recent events in China.

Outreach Educational Project, University of Chicago, Foster Hall, 1130 East 59th Street, Chicago, IL 60637 (312/962-3635).

Center for East Asian Studies, University of Kansas, Lawrence, KS 66045 (913/864-3849).

Texas Program for Educational Resources, University of Texas, Center for Asian Studies, SSB4.126, Austin, TX 78712 (512/471-5811).

East Asian Studies Center, University of Arizona, Tucson, AZ 85721 (602/626-5463).

East Asia Resource Center, School of International Studies DR-05, 302 Thomson Hall, University of Washington, Seattle, WA 98195 (206/543-1921).

II.  THE LAND AND THE PEOPLE

1.  Introduction and Suggested Readings

Chinese leaders throughout the 20th century have shared the goal of building a strong and prosperous country.  And sooner or later they have had to come to grips with the limits to economic growth posed by China's physical environment and human population.  Past episodes of visionary optimism have given way to the recognition that geography and demography dictate a "Chinese-style" modernization strategy, characterized by a moderate pace and moderate expectations.

The Physical Environment  The Chinese land mass (3,692,244 square miles) descends from the Himalayan highlands to the sea in a series of steps: the first is the Tibetan plateau, the second the western uplands, and the third a vast and fertile agricultural plain (see map [II.2] on page 13).  The lower the elevation, the more suitable for human habitation.  This land mass is subject to a variety of climates, ranging from continental in the west to maritime in the east, and from subpolar in the north to subtropical in the south.  As the map (II.3) on page 13 suggests, rainfall is sparse in the far west, low-to-moderate in the northeast, and heavy in the south.

A number of major river systems cut their way through the land mass, carrying water and silt necessary for agriculture (see map and table [II.4] on page 14).  But the rivers can be a mixed blessing: inadequate flow reduces the area under cultivation; silting raises the level of the river and produces deltas as the rivers near the sea.  Water resource management -- facilitating irrigation and preventing floods -- has thus been an age-old Chinese problem.  Because of the uneven rainfall distribution, irrigation is the primary water management task in the north, flood control in the south.

A comparison with the American physical environment is instructive.  China is slightly larger than the US, and the two countries are roughly comparable in north-south range and in extent and diversity of topography and climate.  But China has greater extremes of climate and larger areas that are unproductive and uninhabitable; cultivated land area in China is only 70% that of the US.

Economic Potential  China's physical environment influences profoundly its economic potential.  In agriculture there are three very general land-use patterns (see map [II.5] on page 15).  A diagonal line drawn from northeast to southwest would halve the country.  In the high and dry land to the west of the line, stock raising and oasis cultivation predominate.  The eastern half contains the other two regions, north and south of the Jinling mountains/Huai valley dividing line.  In the relatively dry northern zone, single cropping of grains like wheat and millet is the rule, although summer rice is common in some areas.  With its wetter and warmer climate the southern zone supports multiple cropping of rice and commercial crops.

Well endowed with mineral and energy resources, China has great
industrial potential.    Before 1949, industrial development took place
in major coastal and riverine centers that had higher population
densities, better transportation and financial facilities, and some
foreign presence.    Particularly important were southern Manchuria, led
by Shenyang and Dalian (Dairen), and the lower Yangzi (Yangtze) valley,
dominated by Shanghai.    Once order and central control were restored in
1949, industrialization began in a number of other centers (see map
[II.6] on page 16).    Nevertheless, development of both extractive and
manufacturing industries still requires hard choices among competing
priorities:    accommodating regional diversification, minimizing investment in transportation facilities (already available in older centers),
and promoting national security.

Human and Political Geography    China's population is the largest
in the world, but how large is still a question.    After years of providing only rounded figures, the Chinese government is again announcing
specific estimates.    The 1 billion mark was broken in mid-1980, and a
detailed census was taken in 1982, the first in 29 years.    Chinese
government population figures from the census are presented in the
table (II.7) on page 17.

China's population is not only large, it is also distributed
unevenly over the landscape.    It is concentrated in the area east of
the diagonal line referred to above, concentrated in fertile, low-land
agricultural areas, and along rivers and transportation arteries (see
map [II.8] on page 18).    Thus, one-fifth of the globe's population must
support itself on land that is about 12% arable.    (Again, there is an
interesting contrast with the United States:    China has many rural
areas just as densely populated as urban America.)

At present, the age distribution of the population also poses
problems.    As the table (II.9) on page 19 indicates, approximately 46%
of the population is under 20 years of age, consuming much more than
they are producing.    Moreover, the percentage of women in the 20-50
childbearing years -- now about 38% -- will grow over the rest of the
century.    Chinese population specialists have estimated that the
population could quadruple in the next century if each fertile woman
bore three children.

In view of these factors -- high absolute numbers and uneven age
and spatial distribution -- the PRC government has intensified its
already vigorous birth control program.    The previous policy --
encouraging late marriage and distributing free contraceptives -- did
reduce birth rates when it was strictly implemented, but it did not
reduce population growth enough in the eyes of the present leadership.
In 1980 the "one-child family" policy was introduced along with a
system of benefits and penalties to encourage compliance.    One-child
families are given priority in housing, medical care, and education.
Working mothers who pledge to have only one child are given longer
maternity leaves.    And intense social pressure is often brought to bear
on couples to comply with the one-child family program.    The birth of a
second child can result in lack of access to nursery schools, salary
reductions, or fines.    Despite these measures, resistance to the
one-child family program is common, especially in rural China.
Traditional preference for male children has resulted in instances of
female infanticide in some areas.    Perhaps more significant for the
ultimate success of the one-child family policy, is the disincentive
provided by the introduction, in 1979, of the responsibility system in
the countryside (see chapter 8).    The greater freedom given to the

household to produce for its own use encourages peasant families to have more, rather than fewer, children as a way to increase the number of individuals contributing to total family income. Compliance with the one-child family program is thus stymied not only by traditional values but also, ironically, by the current economic reforms.

Although over 80% of the population lives in the countryside, China has many large cities, more in fact than the United States. To guarantee food supplies Chinese municipalities include rural areas within their jurisdiction. Cities have both an economic role, as centers of manufacturing and distribution, and a political function, as links in the administrative chain of command.

The province is the most important subnational administrative unit. The PRC has 29 provincial-level units, most of them of substantial area and population (see map [II.10] on page 20 and table [II.11] on page 21). There are two special categories. One is the autonomous region, of which there are five. These have large minority populations who have received at least nominal guarantees that certain aspects of their culture will be preserved. The other special category is the centrally administered city, of which there are three: Beijing (Peking), the national capital; Tianjin (Tientsin), its port; and the great industrial and commercial metropolis of Shanghai. Like other municipalities, these units consist of the dominant city and the surrounding suburban and rural hinterland. At times during the PRC's history six regional units composed of several provinces have played an important role; over the long term, the central government, fearing the emergence of "independent kingdoms," has let power flow to the regional level only in special circumstances.

The people of China are ethnically and linguistically diverse. Although ethnic Chinese (Han) constitute 94% of the population, the 55 "national minorities" recognized by the government constitute 60 million people. Thirteen have populations exceeding 1 million (see table [II.12] on page 22). Minority peoples live mainly in a belt that surrounds the core Han population on the south, west, and north. They vary greatly in degree of integration with Chinese society and culture, though the pace of integration is faster now than in the past. As noted above, some minorities have "autonomous" provincial-level units; lower level units have been created for smaller concentrations.

Linguistic divisions occur not only between the Han and minorities, but also among the Chinese speakers themselves (see map [II.13], page 23). The basic division in spoken Chinese is between the Mandarin dialect of north and central China and the numerous non-Mandarin dialects of the southeast. These "dialects" are really different languages, as different, say, as Italian and Spanish. Mandarin itself divides into different dialects, which are sufficiently dissimilar in pronunciation to cause some communication problems. The written language is the same for all these Chinese language groups, and a single national spoken language (called pu'tonghua [common speech]) is taught in all schools. Eventually, all PRC citizens will be able to converse in this official dialect, which is based on northern Mandarin. For the foreseeable future, however, pu'tonghua will remain a second language for close to 40% of the population.

## Suggested Readings

Aird, John S. "Recent Demographic Data from China: Problems and Prospects." U.S. Congress, Joint Economic Committee. China Under the Four Modernizations: Retrenchment, Reform and Reappraisal. Washington, DC: Government Printing Office, 1982. Reviews and evaluates recently released information on the world's most populous country.

_____. "The Preliminary Results of China's 1982 Census," The China Quarterly, no. 96 (December 1983), pp. 613-640.

China: A Geographical Sketch. Beijing: Foreign Languages Press, 1974. A collection of articles on various aspects of China's geography and resources.

Dryer, June Teufel. China's Forty Millions: Minority Nationalities and National Integration in the People's Republic of China. Cambridge, MA: Harvard University Press, 1976. A comprehensive discussion of Beijing's policies towards its many national minorities and the problems and process of implementation.

Fullard, Harold, ed. China in Maps. London: Denoyer-Geppert, 1968. An annotated collection of maps covering China's history, geography, climate, industry, agriculture, and communications networks.

An Illustrated Atlas of China. New York: Rand McNally, 1972. An excellent map collection, illuminating many aspects of China's material and human resources.

Lewis, John W., ed. The City in Communist China. Stanford: Stanford University Press, 1971. An anthology of articles on aspects of the post-1949 Chinese city.

Nickum, James E., ed. Water Management Organization in the People's Republic of China. White Plains, NY: M. E. Sharpe, Inc., 1981. Case-study analysis of China's irrigation and flood control problems.

Orleans, Leo A. "China's Urban Population: Concepts, Conglomerations, and Concerns." U.S. Congress, Joint Economic Committee. China Under the Four Modernizations: Retrenchment, Reform and Reappraisal. Washington, DC: Government Printing Office, 1982. Describes China's effort to control urbanization while promoting modernization.

_____. Every Fifth Child: The Population of China. Stanford: Stanford University Press, 1972. A general discussion of China's population growth and problems, including chapters on urban population, population distribution, and national minorities. An excellent introduction.

Shabad, Theodore. China's Changing Map: National and Regional Development, 1949-71. Revised edition. New York: Praeger, 1972. A comprehensive survey of China's physical, political, and administrative geography, with detailed chapters on each region of the country.

Skinner, G. William, ed. The City in Late Imperial China. Stanford: Stanford University Press, 1979. A scholarly anthology on the traditional Chinese city and its relations to the rural hinterland.

____, and Mark Elvin, eds. The Chinese City Between Two Worlds. Stanford: Stanford Univerity Press, 1974. A collection of scholarly essays on the process of modernization and urbanization of a range of Chinese cities.

2.  <u>Elevation (in meters)</u>

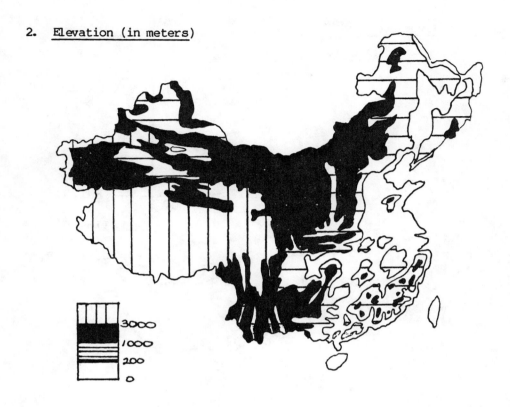

3.  <u>Precipitation (in inches)</u>

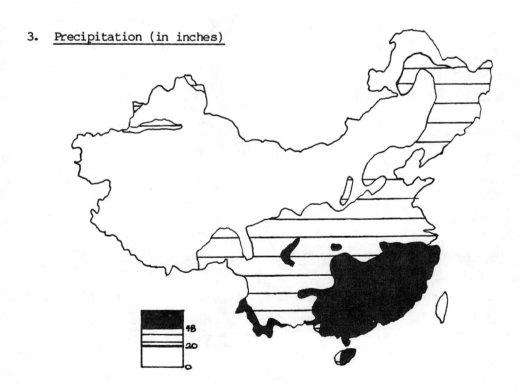

4. <u>Major River Systems</u>

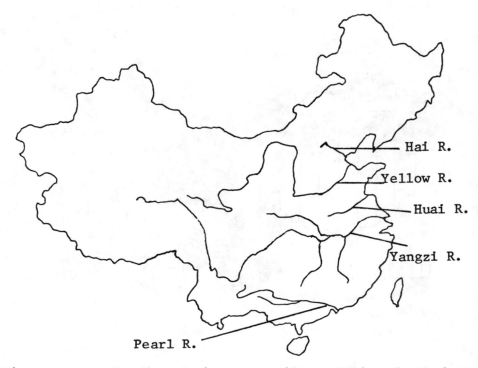

| River | Length (1000 km.) | Drainage Area (billion sq. km.) | Silt Dischage (cu. m. per year) | Cultivated Area (mn. ha.) | Irrigated Area (mn. ha.) |
|---|---|---|---|---|---|
| Yangzi (Yangtze) | 5800 | 1,800 | 1,020 | 27 | 13 |
| Yellow | 5464 | 750 | 48 | 20 | 3.2 |
| Pearl | 2200 | 420 | 356 | -- | -- |
| Hai | 1090 | 265 | 15 | 12 | — |
| Huai | 1000 | 260 | 42 | 13 | 4.7 |
| China | | | 2,600 | 107 | 43.7 |

Source: James E. Nickum, <u>Hydraulic Engineering and Water Resources in the People's Republic of China</u> (Stanford: US-China Relations Program, 1974), p. 10. Abbreviations: km. = kilometers; sq. km. = square kilometers; mn. = million; cu. m. = cubic meters; ha. = hectares.

## 5. Agricultural Regions

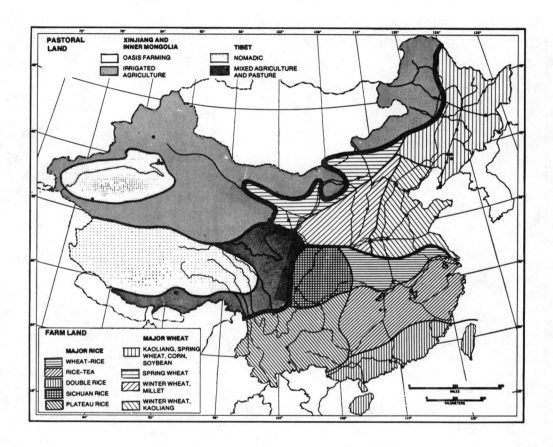

Source: Frederick M. Kaplan, et al., Encyclopedia of China Today (New York: Eurasia Press, 1979), p. 157. Reprinted with permission.

6.  <u>Industrial Zones</u>

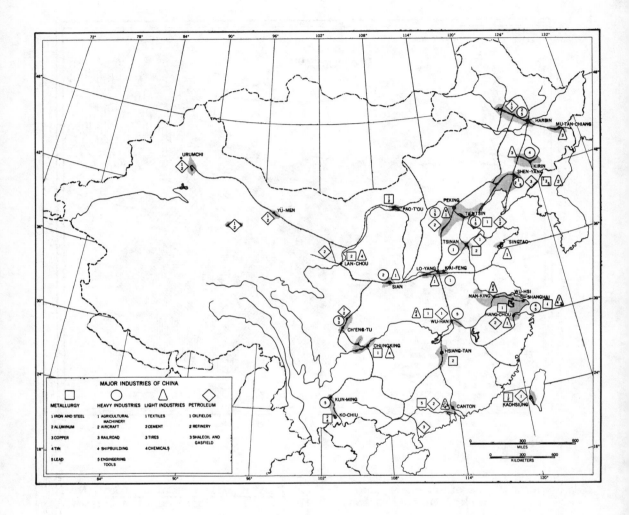

Source: Frederick M. Kaplan, et al., <u>Encyclopedia of China Today</u> (New York: Eurasia Press, 1979), p. 181. Reprinted with permission.

## 7. Population and Vital Rates

| Year | Thousand Persons | Natural Increase | Births | Deaths |
|------|------------------|------------------|--------|--------|
| | | Vital Rates/1,000 Persons | | |
| 1949 | 541,670 | 16.0 | 36.0 | 20.0 |
| 1950 | 551,960 | 19.0 | 37.0 | 18.0 |
| 1951 | 563,000 | 20.0 | 37.0 | 17.0 |
| 1952 | 574,820 | 20.0 | 37.0 | 17.0 |
| 1953 | 587,960 | 23.0 | 37.0 | 14.0 |
| 1954 | 602,660 | 24.8 | 38.0 | 13.2 |
| 1955 | 614,650 | 20.3 | 32.0 | 12.3 |
| 1956 | 628,280 | 20.5 | 31.9 | 11.4 |
| 1957 | 646,530 | 23.2 | 34.3 | 10.8 |
| 1958 | 659,940 | 17.2 | 29.2 | 12.0 |
| 1959 | 672,070 | 10.1 | 24.8 | 14.5 |
| 1960 | 662,070 | -4.6 | 20.9 | 25.4 |
| 1961 | 658,590 | 3.8 | 18.1 | 14.4 |
| 1962 | 672,950 | 27.1 | 37.2 | 10.1 |
| 1963 | 691,720 | 33.5 | 43.6 | 10.1 |
| 1964 | 704,990 | 27.8 | 39.3 | 11.6 |
| 1965 | 725,380 | 28.5 | 38.1 | 9.5 |
| 1966 | 742,060 | 26.3 | 35.2 | 8.9 |
| 1967 | 760,320 | 25.6 | 34.1 | 8.5 |
| 1968 | 781,980 | 27.5 | 35.7 | 8.2 |
| 1969 | 803,350 | 26.2 | 34.2 | 8.1 |
| 1970 | 825,420 | 26.0 | 33.6 | 7.6 |
| 1971 | 847,790 | 23.4 | 30.7 | 7.3 |
| 1972 | 867,270 | 22.3 | 29.9 | 7.6 |
| 1973 | 887,610 | 20.1 | 28.1 | 7.1 |
| 1974 | 904,090 | 17.6 | 25.0 | 7.4 |
| 1975 | 919,700 | 15.8 | 23.1 | 7.4 |
| 1976 | 932,670 | 12.7 | 20.1 | 7.3 |
| 1977 | 945,240 | 12.1 | 19.0 | 6.9 |
| 1978 | 958,090 | 12.0 | 18.3 | 6.3 |
| 1979 | 970,920 | 11.7 | 17.9 | 6.2 |
| 1980 | 982,550 | 12.0 | n/a | n/a |
| 1981 | 996,220 | 14.0 | n/a | n/a |
| 1982 | 1,008,175 | 14.5 | 20.9 | 6.3 |

Source: China Report, pp. 834-835, and John S. Aird, "The Preliminary Results of China's 1982 Census," CQ, no. 96 (December 1983), p. 614.  n/a = not available.

8. <u>Population Distribution</u>

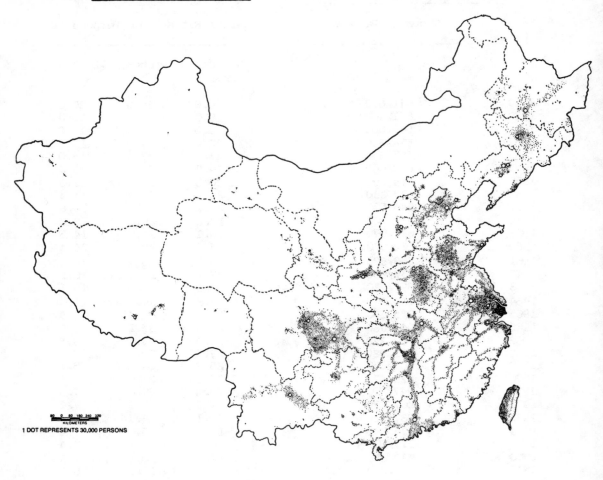

1 DOT REPRESENTS 30,000 PERSONS

Source:  Frederick M. Kaplan, et al., <u>Encyclopedia of China Today</u> (New York:   Eurasia  Press,  1979),  p.  10.    Reprinted  with permission.

9. Estimated Age and Sex Distribution, 1982

| Age range | Thousand Persons | | | Percent | | | M/100 F |
| | Total | Males | Females | Total | Males | Females | |
|---|---|---|---|---|---|---|---|
| All | 1,003,790 | 515,221 | 488,568 | 100.0 | 100.0 | 100.0 | 105.46 |
| 0–4 | 94,716 | 48,992 | 45,724 | 9.40 | 9.50 | 9.35 | 107.15 |
| 5–9 | 110,731 | 57,040 | 53,690 | 11.03 | 11.07 | 10.98 | 106.24 |
| 10–14 | 131,802 | 67,861 | 63,940 | 13.13 | 13.17 | 13.08 | 106.13 |
| 15–19 | 125,312 | 63,747 | 61,564 | 12.48 | 12.37 | 12.60 | 103.55 |
| 20–24 | 74,312 | 37,855 | 36,456 | 7.40 | 7.34 | 7.46 | 103.84 |
| 25–29 | 92,591 | 47,781 | 44,809 | 9.22 | 9.27 | 9.17 | 106.63 |
| 30–34 | 72,957 | 37,906 | 35,051 | 7.26 | 7.35 | 7.17 | 108.15 |
| 35–39 | 54,203 | 28,545 | 25,657 | 5.39 | 5.54 | 5.25 | 111.26 |
| 40–44 | 48,381 | 25,792 | 22,588 | 4.81 | 5.00 | 4.62 | 114.18 |
| 45–49 | 47,364 | 25,046 | 22,317 | 4.71 | 4.86 | 4.57 | 112.23 |
| 50–54 | 40,850 | 21,560 | 19,289 | 4.06 | 4.18 | 3.95 | 111.77 |
| 55–59 | 33,909 | 17,499 | 16,409 | 3.37 | 3.39 | 3.36 | 106.64 |
| 60–64 | 27,382 | 13,714 | 13,667 | 2.73 | 2.66 | 2.80 | 100.34 |
| 65–69 | 21,267 | 10,175 | 11,092 | 2.12 | 1.97 | 2.27 | 91.73 |
| 70–74 | 14,348 | 6,439 | 7,909 | 1.43 | 1.25 | 1.62 | 81.40 |
| 75+ | 12,658 | 5,260 | 8,396 | 1.36 | 1.02 | 1.72 | 62.65 |

Source:  BR, January 16, 1984.

10.  Political and Administrative Map

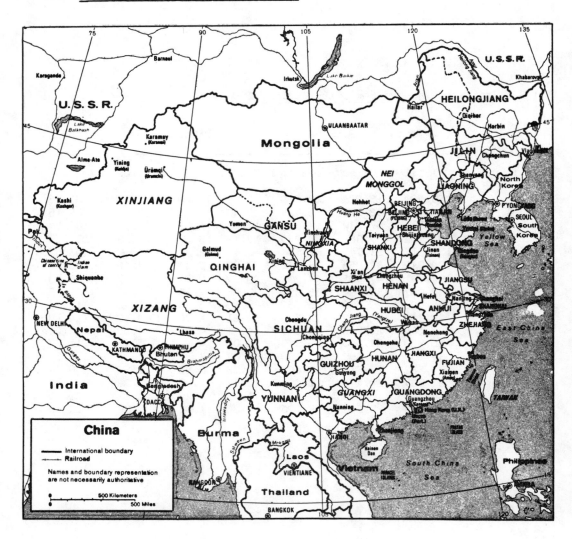

Source:  BN, March 1980.  The dotted line denotes the July 1, 1979
expansion of Inner Mongolia (Nei Monggol), whereby the
autonomous region received the western portions of Heilongjiang and Jilin provinces, and the northern portions of
Liaoning and Gansu provinces and of the Ningxia Hui Autonomous
Region.  This change restored the borders existing before July
1969.

## 11. Provincial-Level Units:  Area and Population

| Unit | Capital City | Area* | Population (in thousands) 1953 | 1965 | 1982 |
|---|---|---|---|---|---|
| **Provinces:** | | | | | |
| Anhui | Hefei | 54 | 30,663 | 37,442 | 49,665 |
| Fujian | Fuzhou | 48 | 13,143 | 17,823 | 25,873 |
| Gansu | Lanzhou | 142 | 11,291 | 15,200 | 19,569 |
| Guangdong | Guangzhou | 83 | 34,770 | 42,684 | 59,299 |
| Guizhou | Guiyang | 67 | 15,037 | 19,302 | 28,552 |
| Hebei | Shijiazhuang | 72 | 33,181 | 41,428 | 53,005 |
| Heilongjiang | Ha'erbin | 179 | 12,681 | 21,320 | 32,665 |
| Henan | Zhengzhou | 65 | 43,911 | 54,829 | 77,422 |
| Hubei | Wuchang | 72 | 27,790 | 35,221 | 47,804 |
| Hunan | Changsha | 81 | 33,227 | 40,563 | 54,008 |
| Jiangsu | Nanjing | 40 | 38,329 | 48,523 | 60,521 |
| Jiangxi | Nanchang | 64 | 16,773 | 22,271 | 33,184 |
| Jilin | Changchun | 72 | 12,609 | 17,177 | 22,560 |
| Liaoning | Shenyang | 58 | 22,269 | 32,403 | 35,721 |
| Qinghai | Xi'ning | 280 | 1,677 | 2,664 | 3,895 |
| Shaanxi | Xi'an | 76 | 15,881 | 20,800 | 28,904 |
| Shandong | Ji'nan | 60 | 50,134 | 63,257 | 74,419 |
| Shanxi | Taiyuan | 61 | 14,314 | 18,349 | 25,291 |
| Sichuan | Chengdu | 220 | 65,685 | 81,634 | 99,713 |
| Yunnan | Kunming | 168 | 17,473 | 22,120 | 32,553 |
| Zhejiang | Hangzhou | 39 | 22,866 | 28,918 | 38,884 |
| **Autonomous Regions:** | | | | | |
| Guangxi Zhuang | Nanning | 91 | 19,561 | 24,776 | 36,420 |
| Inner Mongolia | Huhehaote | 457 | 3,532 | 5,778 | 19,274 |
| Ningxia Hui | Yinchuan | 25 | 1,637 | 2,253 | 3,895 |
| Tibet (Xizang) | Lhasa | 470 | 1,274 | 1,458 | 1,892 |
| Xinjiang Uighur | Urumqi | 640 | 4,874 | 7,119 | 13,081 |
| **Centrally Administered Cities:** | | | | | |
| Beijing | | 6 | 4,591 | 7,730 | 9,020 |
| Shanghai | | 2 | 8,808 | 10,966 | 11,630 |
| Tianjin | | 4 | 4,622 | 6,686 | 7,630 |
| total | | 3,700 | 583,603 | 750,394 | 996,220 |

* in thousand square miles; approximate 1980 figures

Source:  Population figures for 1953 and 1965 from CIA, National Foreign Assessment Center, China: Economic Indicators (ERTH0508, October 1977), p. 9.; figures for area and 1979 population from Zhongguo Kaiguang; figures for 1982 population are from John S. Aird, "The Preliminary Results of China's 1982 Census," CQ, no. 96 (December 1983), pp. 616-617.

## 12. China's 13 Largest National Minorities

| Minority | Language Group | Primary Location | Population (in thousands) | | |
|---|---|---|---|---|---|
| | | | 1953 | 1965 | 1978 |
| Zhuang | Zhuang-Thai | Guangxi Yunnan | 7,030 | 7,780 | 12,090 |
| Hui | Chinese | Ningxia Gansu | 3,559 | 3,930 | 6,490 |
| Uighur | Turkic | Xinjiang | 3,640 | 3,900 | 5,480 |
| Yi | Tibeto-Burmese | Sichuan Yunnan | 3,254 | 3,260 | 4,850 |
| Tibetan | Tibeto-Burmese | Tibet Qinghai Sichuan | 2,776 | 2,770 | 3,450 |
| Miao | Miao-Yao | Guizhou Hunan | 2,511 | 2,680 | 3,920 |
| Manchu | Tungus-Manchurian | Liaoning Jilin Heilongjiang | 2,419 | 2,430 | 2,650 |
| Mongol | Mongolian | Inner Mongolia Xinjiang | 1,463 | 1,640 | 2,660 |
| Bouyei | Zhuang-Thai | Guizhou | 1,248 | 1,310 | 1,720 |
| Korean | Korean | Jilin | 1,120 | 1,250 | 1,680 |
| Yao | Miao-Yao | Guangxi Hunan | 666 | n/a | 1,240 |
| Dong | Zhuang-Thai | Guizhou Hunan | 713 | n/a | 1,110 |
| Bai | Tibeto-Burmese | Yunnan | 567 | n/a | 1,050 |

Source: Adapted from Leo A. Orleans, Every Fifth Child: The Population of China (Stanford: Stanford University Press, 1972), p. 101. Figures for 1965 from Renmin Shouce (Beijing: Dagongbaoshe, 1965), p. 115. Data for 1978 from China Report, pp. 18-27. n/a = not available.

## 13. Ethnolinguistic Distribution

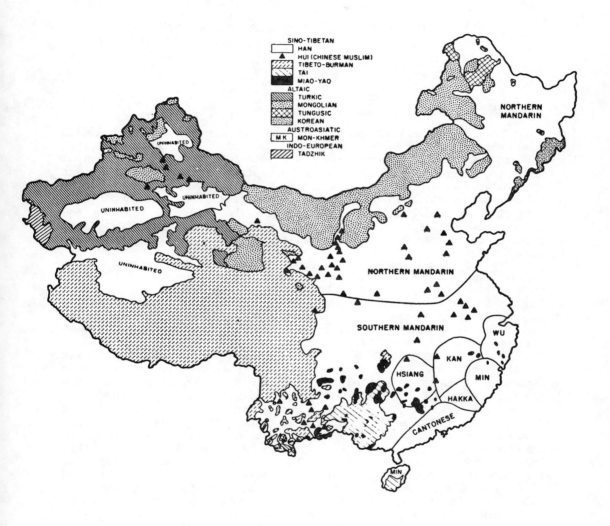

Source: Area Handbook for the People's Republic of China (Washington, DC: Government Printing Office, 1972), p. 89.

III. HISTORY OF THE CHINESE REVOLUTION

## 1. Introduction and Suggested Readings

There is general agreement that the Chinese Communist Revolution was a major event of the contemporary world. But unlike previous "great revolutions," which took place within a fairly short span of time, the Chinese Revolution spanned more than a century. It brought the collapse of one of the world's great traditional empires under the weight of internal revolts and foreign penetration. For nearly 50 years competing political forces contended for the right to shape a new China. The ultimate victor, the Chinese Communist Party (CCP), found great challenges in deciding how far and how fast to change the Chinese social order.

The End of the Empire   The Qing (Ch'ing) dynasty, established by invading Manchu armies in 1644, was the last in a series of dynasties that governed the empire from its first unification in 221 B.C. China flourished for a century and a half under its new non-Chinese emperors, but domestic problems (especially growing population pressure) and revolts (most notably the Taiping Rebellion of 1850-64) were a common feature of the 19th century.

The Opium War of 1839-42 marked the beginning of imperialist penetration. The Western powers, and later Japan, forced increasing demands on a Manchu regime already weakened by domestic problems. The growing package of foreign exactions included territorial acquisitions and leases, trading and manufacturing rights, special privileges for foreign residents and missionaries, war indemnities, and other financial obligations. All these were secured by treaty and backed by the threat of military force. Scholars disagree on how much this foreign penetration actually hurt China; what was important was that the Chinese, themselves, believed increasingly that their country was in dire straits. The alternatives proposed ranged from conservative renewal to liberal reformism to anti-Manchu revolution. By the turn of the century, the revolutionary approach was winning the day.

National Disintegration   The Revolution of 1911 was in some ways the result of the Manchu court's imperfect reform effort. The government had begun building modern armies, but could not prevent revolutionary propaganda from reaching the young officers recruited. It had started China down the road of parliamentary institutions, but not fast enough to suit local and provincial elites. It had also initiated a program of economic development, but at the expense of the projects begun by those same elites. Out of this combustible mix erupted a transformation that went far beyond the removal of the Manchus. The imperial structure was dismantled and a republican form of government proclaimed.

But the new parliamentary institutions were soon subverted because military power was dispersed among a number of political forces, none of which wished to allow its rivals to dominate the civil government. Thus military strongmen, dubbed "warlords," dominated the first phase of the republican period -- up until 1928. From their regional bases they contended for control of the major transportation arteries and for the capital city of Beijing (Peking). At lower levels of the political hierarchy, and in areas not reached by the grid of major rivers and railways, minor militarists carved out spheres of control.

The first major challenge to the shifting warlord balance of power came from the Nationalist Party (also known as the Kuomintang [KMT]). Sun Yat-sen founded the movement and, after his death in 1925, Chiang Kai-shek led it for the next five decades (see biographies [III.2a] on pages 28-29). In the 1920s, supported by the Soviet Union and allied with the nascent Chinese Communist Party (CCP), the Nationalists established a base in Guangdong province and tried building political institutions and military forces simultaneously. Chiang Kai-shek led a "Northern Expedition" during 1926-28 that gave his party a place on the river-railway grid and international recognition as the government of China, with its capital in Nanjing (Nanking).

Over the next nine years Chiang tried and failed to establish more than nominal control over the rest of China. He had to contend first with warlords not eliminated during the Northern Expedition, and made moderate progress against them. Then, in 1931, Japan invaded the northeastern provinces (called Manchuria), and subsequently extended its political and economic penetration into north China. The Communists posed a very different challenge from their remote base areas. Chiang's continuing preoccupation with military matters stunted the growth of political institutions and limited reform in the economic sector. War broke out with Japan in 1937, and the invaders soon took control of major cities and transportation arteries. The Nationalist defenders retreated to the southwest, where their movement fell into decline.

The Rise of the CCP   The Chinese Communist Party, founded in 1921 amid the political and intellectual ferment following the May Fourth Movement of 1919, only gradually developed a formula for achieving political dominance. In the early years, under the guidance of the Soviet-dominated Communist International (Comintern), the CCP joined the Nationalists in a united front against the warlords and imperialist powers and pursued the conventional Bolshevik strategy of mobilizing and organizing urban workers. But conflicts with the Nationalists grew, and Chiang Kai-shek led an assault on the Communists in the spring of 1927. The CCP's two founding fathers left the scene: a northern warlord executed Li Dazhao (Li Ta-chao) and the Comintern purged Chen Duxiu (Ch'en Tu-hsiu) for his role in the failure of the united front. (see section [III.2b], pages 29-34, for biographies of CCP leaders, including those mentioned in this introduction.)

Remnants of the outlawed, but surviving, Communist forces turned to the countryside, where Mao Zedong (Mao Tse-tung) and Zhu De (Chu Te) led the formation of a Red Army based in scattered rural "soviets" in south-central China. Simultaneously, the CCP began looking to the peasantry as a source of political support. But Nationalist military pressure in the early 1930s forced the CCP's main units to undertake the "Long March" of 1934-35. The leadership established a new head-quarters at Yan'an (Yenan), in the remote northwestern province of Shaanxi. It was during the Long March that Mao established his primacy in the CCP.

With the beginning of the War of Resistance in 1937, the Communists and the Nationalists formed a second united front for the purpose of resisting the Japanese. The actual cooperation was minimal, but the CCP took advantage of reduced Nationalist pressure to expand its forces by guerrilla mobilization against the Japanese. By the end of the war in 1945, it had grown into a formidable political and military movement, as the table on CCP growth (III.3, page 35) indicates. The Party governed large parts of north China. Moreover, Mao and other CCP leaders had enriched their policy repertoire for promoting social, economic, and political change. Complementing the approach of "class struggle" was that of "new democracy" -- peaceful co-optation from a position of Communist strength of neutral or sympathetic elements of the existing order, particularly members of the capitalist class. Marxism-Leninism had been adapted to the Chinese Revolution.

After the war's end, only the Communists and Nationalists remained as serious contenders for power. Through American-sponsored mediation the two parties attempted to negotiate a coalition government but to no avail. Both sides seemed bent on civil war. The Communists began that war on the defensive, but proved their superiority faster than even they expected. They had won the struggle by late 1949, and declared the new People's Republic of China government on October 1, 1949. The Nationalists retreated to the island of Taiwan, which, along with several offshore islands, they have controlled ever since.

China under Mao    Establishing military control was only the first step for the victors. A long agenda of new issues had to be addressed: determining the balance of power between central and regional governments, building new political institutions, rehabilitating and collectivizing the economy, formulating a strategy of economic development, remolding social values and institutions, and engineering a method of political succession. As time passed, the leadership became increasingly divided on all these issues. Mao Zedong, who once termed himself a "left centrist," tended to favor periodic shake-ups of social and political institutions ("class struggle") in order to prevent the emergence of new patterns of domination and inequality ("revisionism," or "capitalist restoration"). His opponents, who tended to coalesce around such figures as Liu Shaoqi (Liu Shao-ch'i), Deng Xiaoping (Teng Hsiao-p'ing), and, to an extent, Zhou Enlai (Chou En-lai), favored a more gradual approach that emphasized the building of a technological and human foundation under the leadership of the Party bureaucracy (see chronology of the PRC under Mao [III.4] on pages 36-37).

During the early years (1949-57), Soviet-style economic planning and Soviet aid were the order of the day. But Mao and his colleagues became increasingly disenchanted with this approach and launched the Great Leap Forward 1958-60 (see chapter 6). A combination of weather and human failures brought serious economic disruption, damaging Mao's reputation and strengthening the hand of moderate elements. Their pragmatic rehabilitation of the economy only made Mao even more suspicious that fundamental political principles were being discarded. By political maneuver and mobilization of substantial social discontent, he engineered a vast social movement -- the "Great Proletarian Cultural Revolution" -- to attack his opponents and the political institutions through which they ruled.

The origins and consequences of the Cultural Revolution remain the subject of deep controversy both inside and outside China. Following its most convulsive period (1966-69), which shattered most institutions and destroyed many individuals' lives and careers, there ensued seven years of intense political conflict. The first phase pitted Mao and Zhou against Lin Biao (Lin Biao -- Minister of Defense, one of Mao's Cultural Revolution allies, and his heir apparent). Lin died in a plane crash in Mongolia in 1971 after allegedly conspiring to assassinate Mao. From that point till his death, Mao presided over an uneasy alliance between a moderate coalition led by Zhou Enlai and Deng Xiaoping (rehabilitated in 1973, see next chapter for biography), and a radical coalition led by the "gang of four," which included Mao's wife Jiang Qing. This conflict between the two groups made policymaking extremely difficult and reached a climax with Zhou's death in January 1976. In April there were massive demonstrations in support of the moderates and Deng Xiaoping's purge in the same month. However, a month after Mao's death in September, the "gang of four" and other radicals were arrested.

## Suggested Readings

a) General works:

Bianco, Lucien. *Origins of the Chinese Revolution 1915-1949*. Stanford: Stanford University Press, 1971. A synthesis of differing interpretations of the revolution, emphasizing its social origins.

Clubb, O. Edmund. *Twentieth Century China*. Revised edition. New York: Columbia University Press, 1978. An exhaustive factual history, from the fall of the Imperial system to the death of Mao.

Fairbank, John K. *The United States and China*. 4th edition. Cambridge, MA: Harvard University Press, 1979. Describes the fall of the Imperial system, the rise of the Communist Party, and American evolving relationship with China.

Frolic, B. Michael. *Mao's People*. Cambridge, MA: Harvard University Press, 1981. Mao's China as viewed through the lives of 16 Chinese.

Harrison, James P. *The Long March to Power: A History of the Chinese Communist Party, 1921-1972*. New York: Praeger, 1972. Focuses on the Party's effort to mobilize and organize the Chinese masses.

Meisner, Maurice. *Mao's China: A History of the People's Republic*. New York: Free Press, 1977. A careful, detailed history of the PRC from 1949 to 1976.

Spence, Jonathan D. *The Gate of Heavenly Peace: The Chinese and Their Revolution 1895-1980*. New York: Viking, 1981. Elegantly recounts almost a century of revolutionary upheaval, as experienced and interpreted by some of China's most prominent intellectuals.

Wakeman, Frederic, Jr. *The Fall of Imperial China*. New York: Free Press, 1975. A comprehensive analysis of late traditional China and the causes -- domestic and foreign -- of its collapse.

b) Books by and about Mao Zedong

Mao Tse-tung. Selected Works of Mao Tse-tung. Five vols. Beijing: Foreign Languages Press. The selections in volumes 1-4, from a 1960 edition, were written before September 1949. Volume 5, released in 1977, offers selections from the September 1949-November 1957 period.

Schram, Stuart. Mao Tse-tung. New York: Simon & Schuster, 1967.

____, ed. Chairman Mao Talks to the People: Talks and Letters: 1956-1971. New York: Pantheon, 1974. A good supplement to the Selected Works, bringing together many of Mao's later works, many of which are informal talks and conversations.

Snow, Edgar. Red Star Over China. New York: Grove, 1971. First published in 1938, this is a classic journalistic account of the Communist movement. Snow's interviews with Mao remain a primary source of information on Mao's early life and career. Snow's The Long Revolution (New York: Random House, 1971), contains interviews with Mao and Zhou Enlai much later in their careers.

Terrill, Ross. Mao: A Biography. New York: Harper & Row, 1980.

Wilson, Dick. Mao: The People's Emperor. New York: Doubleday, 1980.

____, ed. Mao Tse-tung in the Scales of History. Cambridge: Cambridge University Press, 1977. Twelve scholars offer diverse and provocative essays on the significance of Mao's career.


2. Biographies of Revolutionary Leaders


a) the Nationalist Party

Sun Yat-sen (1866-1925)   The Chinese Nationalists regard Sun as "father of the country" and founder of their party. The CCP honors him as a leader of the Chinese Revolution. Born near Canton, he received most of his education in Western schools in Hong Kong and Hawaii. After joining the reform movement of the 1890s, he became a leader of the revolutionary forces seeking to overthrow the Manchu dynasty. Sun lost out to military leader Yuan Shikai in the struggle for the presidency of the new Republic of China after the 1911 revolution, but he continued to head the major republican party and, at least abroad, was China's best known revolutionary leader. In the early 1920s, after establishing a Nationalist-led government in Guangzhou, Sun sought and received Soviet advice and materials in building a party-army to challenge the northern warlords. At the same time, he accepted a united front with the Communists. Sun died in Beijing in 1925. His "Three Principles of the People" (Nationalism, Democracy, and People's Livelihood) remain the guiding tenets of the Nationalist Party.

Chiang Kai-shek (1887-1975)   Chiang was a native of Zhejiang province. He studied in military academies in both China and Japan, and became one of Sun's principal military advisers in the late 1910s.   When Sun began building a party-army under Russian guidance in the early 1920s, he picked Chiang to be commandant of the Whampoa Military Academy.   After Sun died in 1925, Chiang outmaneuvered his more prominent rivals and led the Northern Expedition (1926-28) against the northern warlords. Until 1949 he was locked in periodic struggles with a variety of military opponents (remnant warlords, the Japanese, and the CCP) and opponents within his own party.   His power and prestige began to decline during World War II, as did the effectiveness of the Nationalist regime.   Because of military blunders, political corruption, hyperinflation, and alienation of political support, Chiang's forces lost the 1945-49 civil war to the CCP.   He retreated to the island of Taiwan, which, now under the leadership of his son Chiang Ching-kuo, has enjoyed a remarkable economic prosperity.   Chiang Kai-shek died in April 1975.


b) the Chinese Communist Party

Chen Duxiu (Ch'en Tu-hsiu) (1879-1942)   Chen was the founder of New Youth magazine, a leader in the literary and cultural revolution which culminated in the May Fourth Movement, and a founder of the Chinese Communist Party.   He headed the Party from 1921 to 1927, after which he was expelled on charges of being too friendly with the Nationalists during the united front.

Hua Guofeng (Hua Kuo-feng) (1920-    )   Born in Shanxi Province, Hua worked in Mao Zedong's native province of Hunan for over two decades after 1949.   He served as Party secretary at the county and special district level in the early 1950s, and became a provincial vice governor and a member of the provincial Party committee in 1958.   He survived the Cultural Revolution to become a vice chairman of the Hunan revolutionary committee in 1968 and first Party secretary in 1970.

Hua was transferred to Beijing in 1971, working initially in the State Council staff office under Zhou Enlai and on a special body investigating the Lin Biao affair.   He was elected to the Politburo in 1973 and became a vice premier and minister of public security in 1975.   He was also responsible for agriculture and science policy.

After the January 1976 death of Zhou Enlai, Hua was named acting premier, leapfrogging the two leading contenders, Deng Xiaoping and Zhang Chunqiao.   After Deng's purge in April 1976, Hua became premier and first vice chairman of the Party Central Committee, reportedly on Mao's proposal.   Following Mao's death in September, the "gang of four" sought to block Hua's accession to the Party chairmanship.   He played an important role in their arrest in October, and the Politburo named him chairman of the Party's Central Committee and Military Commission.

But the very fact that Hua was Mao's chosen successor made him the target of Deng Xiaoping and other victims of the Cultural Revolution. After 1977 Deng successfully advocated policies, personnel changes, and evaluations of the past that went against the Maoist grain. Increasingly isolated, Hua's own political position deteriorated markedly during 1980. February saw the purge of four Politburo members (Wang Dongxing, Chen Xilian, Ji Dengkui, and Wu De) who, like Hua, had had close ties to Mao and rose during the Cultural Revolution. In September Hua gave up the post of premier to Zhao Ziyang. Under fire for "leftist" mistakes and fostering a "cult of personality," Hua resigned his top Party posts at the end of the year. It was formally announced in late June 1981 that Hu Yaobang was the new Party chairman and that Hua had been demoted to vice chairman. In September of 1982, the position of vice chairman was abolished and Hua was dropped from the ruling Politburo.

<u>Jiang Qing (Chiang Ch'ing) (1913 -    )</u>    Jiang Qing was Mao's third wife and a member of the "gang of four." She gained national visibility in 1966 as a leader of the militant elements in the Cultural Revolution. She was born in Shandong and was a Shanghai film actress before moving to Yan'an to join the Communists in the late 1930s. She married Mao in the early 1940s, generating hostility from many Party veterans. Jiang became head of the film office of the CCP Central Committee's propaganda department in 1948, but for the most part remained in the background over the next decade. In the early 1960s, as Mao began mobilizing allies for his attack on the Party bureaucracy, Jiang launched a revolutionary reform movement in ballet and Beijing opera, provoking some opposition from the cultural establishment. During the Cultural Revolution, she became first vice chairman of the Cultural Revolution Group and also directed much of the cultural work in the military. In the early 1970s, she was one of the most implacable foes of Deng Xiaoping and his moderate colleagues. In October 1976, one month after Mao's death, she was arrested and subjected to virulent criticism in the mass media. She and other members of the "gang of four" were brought to trial in November 1980. She received a suspended death sentence which was changed to life imprisonment in January 1983.

<u>Li Dazhao (Li Ta-chao) (1888-1927)</u>    Li was another influential leader of the May Fourth Movement. Along with Chen Duxiu, he was one of the founding fathers of the Chinese Communist Party. He led the CCP's organizational and propaganda activities. In adapting Marxism to the Chinese situation, he stressed the importance of the peasants and nationalism. These elements later became part of Mao's formula for revolution. Li was executed by warlord Zhang Zuolin in 1927.

<u>Lin Biao (Lin Piao) (1907-1971)</u>    Lin was a veteran Red Army military commander who played important roles in battles against the

Japanese and Nationalist forces. He rose rapidly in political rank in the mid-1950s and replaced Peng Dehuai as defense minister in 1959. He soon undertook a campaign to emphasize Maoist principles and the study of Mao's thought within the military. One of the most fervent "Maoists" in the Cultural Revolution, he was officially designated Mao's "successor" and "closest comrade-in-arms." Then in 1971 he was charged with deviations from Mao's policies and with plotting a coup against Mao. He died in a plane crash in Mongolia in September 1971, allegedly trying to escape to the Soviet Union.

Liu Shaoqi (Liu Shao-ch'i) (1898-1969)    Liu was an early labor leader and one of the first Chinese Communists to study in the Soviet Union. He emerged during the 1940s as a major Party theoretician and specialist in organization, ranking second only to Mao. In 1959 he replaced Mao as chief of state (Mao remained Party chairman), and was regarded as Mao's successor. With Deng Xiaoping and others, Liu guided the retrenchment from the Great Leap Forward, and his pragmatic approach increasingly offended Mao. Liu therefore became the chief target of the Cultural Revolution. He was labeled "China's Khrushchev" and stereotyped as China's leading proponent of Soviet-style "revisionism." Liu was formally expelled from all government and Party posts in 1968 and died of pneumonia in Kaifeng in 1969. As one element in the post-Mao leadership's judgment on the Cultural Revolution, Liu's "good name" was completely restored in February 1980. Since then, his selected works have been published and, in December 1983, a memorial room for him was opened in Mao's mausoleum.

Mao Zedong (Mao Tse-tung) (1893-1976)    Born in Hunan, Mao was one of the historic figures of the 20th century. A founder of the CCP, he played a major role in the establishment of the Red Army and the development of a defensible base area in Jiangxi province during the late 1920s and early 1930s. He consolidated his rule over the Party in the years after the Long March and directed overall strategy during the Sino-Japanese War and the civil war. He formally assumed the post of Party chairman in 1945. His reliance on the peasantry (a major departure from prevailing Soviet doctrine) and dependence on guerrilla warfare in the revolution were essential to the Communist triumph in China.

Following the establishment of the PRC in 1949, Mao was responsible for many of the political initiatives that transformed the face of China. These included land reform, the collectivization of agriculture, and the spread of medical services. In particular, this leader of the revolution remained alert to what he saw to be new forms of oppression and sensitive to the interests of the oppressed. In 1958 he advocated a self-reliant "Great Leap Forward" campaign in rural development. The failure of the Leap led Mao to turn many responsibilities over to other leaders (Liu Shaoqi, Deng Xiaoping, etc.) and to withdraw from active decision making.

During the early 1960s, Mao continued his restless challenge of what he perceived as new forms of domination (in his words, "revisionism" or "capitalist restoration"). In foreign policy he led China's divorce from the Soviet Union. Domestically, he became increasingly wary of his subordinates' approach to development, fearing that it was fostering deep social and political inequalities. When Liu, Deng, and others seemed to be ignoring his call to "never forget class struggle," Mao in 1966 initiated the "Great Proletarian Cultural Revolution," exploiting discontent among some students (the "Red Guards") and others. The Cultural Revolution was successful in removing many who opposed his policies but led to serious disorder, forcing Mao to call in the military to restore order in 1967.

In 1969 Mao designated Defense Minister Lin Biao, a Cultural Revolution ally, as his heir apparent. But Mao came to have doubts about Lin and soon challenged him politically. One of the issues of debate was the opening to the United States, advocated by Mao and Zhou Enlai as a counter to the Soviet Union. In 1971 Lin was killed in a plane crash while fleeing China after an alleged assassination attempt on Mao.

Until his death, a failing Mao refereed a struggle between those who benefited from the Cultural Revolution and defended its policies, and rehabilitated veterans who believed that the Cultural Revolution had done China serious harm. It seemed for a while that the veterans, led by Deng Xiaoping, had won the day. But the radicals, either by manipulating Mao or by appealing to his basic instincts, regained momentum after Zhou Enlai's death in January 1976. Mao chose the more centrist Hua Guofeng to carry on his vision. Four weeks after Mao's death, Hua led the arrest of major radical figures, who -- Zhang Chunqiao, Jiang Qing, Wang Hongwen, and Yao Wenyuan -- were dubbed the "gang of four."

The post-Mao era has seen a reversal of much that Mao stood for and the eclipse of many individuals, living and dead, that he stood behind. His leadership, especially the Cultural Revolution initiative, has been hotly debated. In June 1981 the Party Central Committee approved a resolution that criticized Mao's rule after 1958, but affirmed his place as a great leader and ideologist of the Chinese Communist Revolution (see pages 67-69 for an extract).

Peng Dehuai (P'eng Te-huai) (1898-1974)    Peng was an important Communist military commander, beginning in the Jiangxi Soviet period. He took part in the Long March, was deputy commander under Zhu De during the Sino-Japanese War, commanded the Chinese forces which fought in the Korean War (1950-53), and was named minister of defense in 1954. He was purged in 1959 after attacking Mao's Great Leap policies and urging more emphasis on military modernization. Peng's case remained a controversial issue for almost two decades. Maoists used him as a symbol of Chinese "revisionism"; other leaders tried to reinstate him because they believed his challenge to have been correct. Once Deng Xiaoping got the political upper hand in December 1978, Peng was posthumously rehabilitated, four years after his death.

Wang Hongwen (Wang Hung-wen) (1935 -     )    A native of Zhejiang province, Wang was a worker in a cotton mill in Shanghai when the
Cultural Revolution began in 1966.  He became a leader of the
offensive against the municipal establishment, and was· promoted to high Party and governmental posts in Shanghai.  Wang
became a member of the Party Central Committee in 1969, and a
Party vice chairman and member of the Politburo's Standing
Committee in 1973.  He was purged and labeled a member of the
"gang of four" in October 1976, and put on trial in November
1980.  He received a life sentence.

Yao Wenyuan (Yao Wen-yuan) (1931 -     )    Born in Jilin province, Yao
was a literary critic and ideologue, and a close confidant of
Mao's wife Jiang Qing.  His 1965 articles attacking the anti-
Mao drama, "Dismissal of Hai Rui," signalled the start of the
Cultural Revolution.  He was a member of the Cultural Revolution Group and entered the Politburo in 1969.  He had substantial influence over the mass media, and served as chief
editor of the key Party journal Hongqi (Red Flag).  He was
purged in October 1976 and named a member of the "gang of
four."  Tried in November 1980, he received a life sentence.

Zhang Chunqiao (Chang Ch'un-ch'iao) (1917 -     )    Zhang, a native of
Shandong province, got his start in the leftist literary and
art circles of Shanghai, and moved steadily up in the municipal Party structure.  In 1966 he was catapulted into national
prominence, becoming deputy chief of the Cultural Revolution
Group.  A capable theoretician and propagandist, he was a
leading candidate to succeed Zhou Enlai as premier when the
latter died a year later, but like Deng Xiaoping was passed
over in favor of Hua Guofeng.  In October 1976 Hua led the
purge against Zhang and other members of the "gang of four."
They were tried in November 1980; Zhang received a life
sentence.

Zhou Enlai (Chou En-lai) (1898-1976)    Zhou Enlai was for decades one
of the most prominent and respected leaders of the Communist
movement.  Born into an upper class family, he was drawn into
the vortex of Chinese politics during the May Fourth Movement.
In 1920 he traveled to Europe on a work-study program in which
he met a number of future CCP leaders.  He joined the Party in
1922 and returned to China in 1924, becoming the political
commissar of the Whampoa Military Academy in Canton during the
first united front with the Nationalists.  He was in charge of
labor union activity in Shanghai when Chiang Kai-shek attacked
the CCP in April 1927 and helped to plan the Nanchang Uprising
against the Nationalists in August -- the event now celebrated
as the founding of the CCP's Red Army.
        But Zhou was always most prominent during periods in
which the CCP reached out to otherwise hostile political
forces.  He played an important role in securing Chiang
Kai-shek's release during the Xian (Sian) Incident of December
1936.  Once the Nationalists and CCP had formed a second
united front to oppose Japanese imperialism, it was Zhou who
headed the CCP liaison team.  Similarly, Zhou represented the
CCP in negotiations with the Nationalists during the mediation

effort of US General George Marshall.

After the founding of the People's Republic in 1949, Zhou became premier of the Government Affairs (later State) Council and foreign minister. In 1955 he acted as China's bridge to the non-aligned world at the Bandung Conference, and in the same year helped engineer initial contacts with the United States. He passed the foreign minister portfolio to Chen Yi in 1958, but continued to play an active role in foreign policy.

Zhou supported Mao Zedong in the latter's Cultural Revolution attack on the entrenched Party bureaucracy, and subsequently played a critical role in rebuilding political institutions and mediating numerous political quarrels. With the Soviet invasion of Czechoslovakia, Zhou advocated an opening to Japan and the West to counter the Russian threat. Zhou welcomed President Nixon to China in February 1972 and signed the historic Shanghai Communique for the PRC. That same year Zhou was diagnosed as having cancer, and he began shedding some of his responsibilities, especially to Deng Xiaoping who was rehabilitated in April 1973. Zhou was also a strong advocate of modernization, particularly at the Fourth National People's Congress in January 1975. Amid radical attacks on him during the Anti-Confucius Campaign during 1974, Zhou entered the hospital and died on January 8, 1976.

Zhou continued to affect Chinese politics even after his death. In April 1976 the removal of memorial wreaths placed in Tiananmen Square sparked riots that led to the second ouster of Deng Xiaoping. With the purge of the "gang of four" in October 1976, his policy of "four modernizations" received the full endorsement of the new leadership. His selected works were published in December 1980 and three years later a memorial room for him was established in Mao's mausoleum.

Zhu De (Chu Te) (1886-1976)    Zhu was the major Communist military commmander during the revolutionary period. In 1928 he joined with Mao to form the Red Army and was primarily responsible for much of its organization and tactics. Zhu was on the Long March and commanded the Communist armies in the Sino-Japanese War and civil wars. From 1950 to 1959 he was vice chairman of the Beijing government. He became less active thereafter but continued to serve as an elder statesman of the Party. He, too, has been honored with a memorial room in Mao's mausoleum.

### 3. Growth of the Chinese Communist Party

| Period and Year | Number of Members | Years Covered | Average Annual Increase |
|---|---|---|---|
| **1st Revolutionary Civil War** | | | |
| 1921 (1st Congress) | 57 | – | – |
| 1922 (2nd Congress) | 123 | 1 | 66 |
| 1923 (3rd Congress) | 432 | 1 | 309 |
| 1925 (4th Congress) | 950 | 2 | 259 |
| 1927 (5th Congress) | 57,967 | 2 | 28,508 |
| 1927 (after Nationalist purge) | 10,000 | – | – |
| | | | |
| **2nd Revolutionary Civil War** | | | |
| 1928 (6th Congress) | 40,000 | 1 | 30,000 |
| 1930 | 122,318 | 2 | 41,159 |
| 1933 | 300,000 | 3 | 59,227 |
| 1937 (after the Long March) | 40,000 | 4 | -65,000 |
| | | | |
| **Anti-Japanese War** | | | |
| 1940 | 800,000 | 3 | 253,333 |
| 1941 | 763,447 | 1 | -36,533 |
| 1942 | 736,151 | 1 | -27,296 |
| 1944 | 853,420 | 2 | 58,635 |
| 1945 (7th Congress) | 1,211,128 | 1 | 357,708 |
| | | | |
| **3rd Revolutionary Civil War** | | | |
| 1946 | 1,348,320 | 1 | 137,192 |
| 1947 | 2,759,456 | 1 | 1,411,136 |
| 1948 | 3,065,533 | 1 | 306,077 |
| 1949 | 4,488,080 | 1 | 1,422,547 |
| | | | |
| **Under the PRC** | | | |
| 1950 | 5,821,604 | 1 | 1,333,524 |
| 1951 | 5,762,293 | 1 | -59,311 |
| 1952 | 6,001,698 | 1 | 239,400 |
| 1953 | 6,612,254 | 1 | 610,556 |
| 1954 | 7,859,473 | 1 | 1,247,219 |
| 1955 | 9,393,394 | 1 | 1,533,921 |
| 1956 (8th Congress) | 10,734,384 | 1 | 1,340,990 |
| 1957 | 12,720,000 | 1 | 1,985,616 |
| 1959 | 13,960,000 | 2 | 620,000 |
| 1961 | 17,000,000 | 2 | 1,520,000 |
| 1973 (10th Congress) | 28,000,000 | 12 | 916,666 |
| 1977 (11th Congress) | more than 35,000,000 | 4 | 1,750,000 |
| 1980 | 38,000,000 | 3 | 1,000,000 |
| 1981 | 39,000,000 | 1 | 1,000,000 |
| 1984 | nearly 40,000,000 | 3 | 333,333 |

Source: 1921-1963: adapted from John W. Lewis, Leadership in Communist China (Ithaca: Cornell University Press, 1963); 1973: Zhou Enlai's "Report" to the CCP 10th Congress, found in 10th National Congress of the Communist Party of China (Documents) (Beijing: Foreign Languages Press, 1973), p. 8;

1977: PR, August 26, 1977, p. 6; 1980: Foreign Broadcast Information Service, Daily Report: China (Springfield, VA: National Technical Information Service, March 11, 1980, Supplement), p. 24; 1981: BR, July 13, 1981, p. 22; 1984: Richard D. Nethercut, "Leadership in China: Rivalry, Reform, and Renewal," Problems of Communism, vol. XXXII (March-April 1983), p. 34.

## 4. Chronology of China Under Mao

1949:      The Communist Red Army defeats the Nationalists in a civil war. The People's Republic of China (PRC) is established on October 1. Chiang Kai-shek and the Nationalists retreat to the island of Taiwan.

1950:      Signing of Sino-Soviet Treaty (See Sino-Soviet chronology [V. 2]). China enters the Korean War; Marriage Law promulgated, providing freedom of marriage and divorce.

1952:      Basic land reform completed after a five-year campaign. All land deeds destroyed and land redistributed (roughly two million landlords executed).

1953:      Korean War armistice. Inauguration of PRC's First Five-Year Plan, relying on Soviet model of industrial development.

1954-55:   Zhou Enlai plays a major role at the Geneva Convention and the Bandung Conference, establishing a new diplomatic prominence for the PRC. First constitution of the PRC is promulgated. Collectivization of agriculture is stepped up.

1956-57:   In the wake of Khrushchev's denunciation of Stalin and political explosions in Poland and Hungary, Mao calls for a "Hundred Flowers Movement" to improve the relationship between the CCP and the people. Critics soon attack the legitimacy of CCP rule. The Party responds with an "anti-rightist campaign," suppressing the opposition.

1958-59:   Mao promotes a "Great Leap Forward" in economic development, relying on mass mobilization, the commune system, and indigenous methods. The effort fails for the most part because of administrative weakness aggravated by bad weather. PRC attacks offshore islands under Nationalist control (September 1958). In August 1959 Defense Minister Peng Dehuai ousted after he criticizes Mao's sponsorship of the Great Leap Forward; replaced by Lin Biao.

1960:      Withdrawal of the Soviet technical advisors, widening the Sino-Soviet rift (see Sino-Soviet chronology [V.2]). Return to more conventional economic development policies to deal with the post-Great Leap Forward depression.

1961-65:   The polity and economy recover, but the CCP becomes increasingly divided over how to pursue economic development, with Mao and his more radical associates pitted against Liu Shaoqi, Deng Xiaoping, and other moderate leaders. Lin Biao, defense minister and one of Mao's allies, leads campaigns to increase political consciousness in the military by stressing the study of Mao's thought. China detonates its first nuclear device (1964).

1966-69:   Mao leads the "Great Proletarian Cultural Revolution" to attack the Party bureaucracy that was frustrating his initiatives and to revive revolutionary commitment. Millions of youths (the Red Guards) are mobilized, the Party-state machinery is crippled, and a host of Party veterans -- most notably Liu Shaoqi and Deng Xiaoping -- are purged. Mao is forced to call the army in to end the resultant disorder.

1969:   The Ninth National Congress of the CCP issues a new Party Constitution that names Lin Biao as "Comrade Mao Zedong's close comrade-in-arms and successor."

1971:   The beginning of Sino-American rapprochement (see Sino-American chronology [V.4]). Death of Lin Biao after alleged coup attempt (September). PRC succeeds to China's seat in the United Nations (October).

1972:   Nixon visits the PRC. Shanghai Communique (see [V.5]) signed.

1973:   Deng Xiaoping reappears in public for the first time since the Cultural Revolution (April). In August the CCP's Tenth Congress issues a new Party Constitution, eliminating the clause naming Lin Biao as Mao's successor.

1974:   Zhou Enlai, Deng Xiaoping, and other moderate leaders chip away at policies introduced during the Cultural Revolution. Radical forces mount a campaign to "criticize Confucius," ostensibly to eliminate feudal ways of thought but actually to defend the Cultural Revolution and indirectly attack Zhou.

1975:   Fourth National People's Congress is convened. Zhou Enlai outlines an economic modernization plan for the PRC, but radical opposition is apparent. Deng Xiaoping is elected to Politburo Standing Committee. However, his approach to economic development, education, and science comes under increasing attack by Mao's more radical followers.

1976:   Zhou Enlai dies (January 8). Hua Guofeng is named acting premier (February 7) amid expectations that Deng Xiaoping would succeed Zhou. A mass demonstration occurs in Beijing's Tiananmen Square over the removal of wreaths honoring Zhou Enlai (April 5). The Politburo strips Deng of all his posts and names Hua Guofeng full premier and first vice chairman of the CCP (April 7). Zhu De dies (July 6). The northern city of Tangshan is struck by a massive earthquake (July 28) that kills close to a million people. Mao Zedong dies (September 9). Four weeks later (October 6), Hua

Guofeng leads the arrest of leading radicals, including Jiang Qing, Zhang Chunqiao, Wang Hongwen, and Yao Wenyuan (soon labeled the "gang of four"). Hua, already Premier, now becomes chairman of the CCP and chairman of its Military Affairs Commission, thus officially succeeding Mao.

IV.  CHINA AFTER MAO


## 1.  Introduction and Suggested Readings

Mao Zedong died on September 9, 1976.   On October 6 veterans of
the revolution arrested a number of Mao's radical adherents and dubbed
the leading figures the "gang of four" (the biographies of Jiang Qing,
Zhang Chunqiao, Yao Wenyuan, and Wang Hongwen appear in section
III.2b).   Those Politburo members remaining named Hua Guofeng the new
Party chairman (biography begins on page 29).

But like the Chinese Revolution as a whole, political succession
in China should be seen not as a single event -- a change in the
occupant of the nation's supreme office.   Rather it is a process that
goes through stages, beginning with key leadership positions and
bodies, extending to policies and institutions, and culminating in the
society as a whole.   It is a process that must deal with the past as
well as the present and the future.   And it is a process that takes
years rather than days, one that in fact began well before Mao died and
continues today (see chronology [IV.2] on pages 44-48).

The Leadership    Since Mao's death Deng Xiaoping and his
associates have gradually eclipsed Hua Guofeng and others who rose to
power during the Cultural Revolution.   Even in the mid-1970s, Deng had
emerged as the leader of the moderate coalition, buoyed by broad
political support in the government, Party, and military hierarchies.
His vigorous advocacy in 1975 of policies that would reverse the
Cultural Revolution precipitated his second purge at the hands of the
radicals in 1976.   And in that year, Mao picked Hua Guofeng as his
successor.   Yet, Deng's support in the Chinese political system had
greater depth and breadth than that of Hua.   In July of 1977, he
returned to active political life.   Since that time he has sought to
reshape the central Party and state leaderships by removing those who
opposed him and transferring power to individuals whom he could trust
to perpetuate his policies.

By 1979 Deng's imprint on China's post-Mao politics was evident.
In 1980 and 1981, he won decisive victories on the personnel front --
at least at the top leadership level.   In February of 1980, his protege
Hu Yaobang became Party general secretary and the "little gang of four"
(Maoist holdovers who had frustrated Deng's efforts) was purged.   In
April of the same year, another close ally Zhao Ziyang took charge of
day-to-day government administration, and in September he formally
replaced Hua Guofeng as premier.   Mao's chosen successor was stripped
of his remaining post when in June of 1981 Hu Yaobang replaced him as
chairman of the CCP.

China's ruling elite -- and Deng's paramount position within that
elite -- was confirmed at the Twelfth Congress of the Communist Party,
held in September of 1982.   At that meeting Hua was removed from the
Politburo, the post of Party chairman was abolished with Hu taking the

newly enhanced office of general secretary, and many of Deng's opponents were dropped from the Party's Central Committee. The leading policymaking body for the nation became the Politburo, with its Standing Committee of six representing the apex of political power.

Deng is clearly the dominant member of that Standing Committee. His importance is bolstered by his immense prestige, his chairmanship of the bodies within the state and Party which control the army, and the fact that his two proteges, Hu Yaobang and Zhao Ziyang, also sit on the committee. But Deng is no dictator. Hu and Zhao have been known to hold and express their own views. Moreover, the other members of the committee are powerful Chinese politicians in their own right. Chen Yun is a skilled economist who did not shrink from opposing Mao during the Great Leap Forward. Li Xiannian, also an economist and member of the Party's old guard, has opposed Deng in the past and is now China's head of state. Finally, although he is probably too old to actively participate in decision making, Ye Jianying has a strong following in the Chinese military. Moreover, outside the Standing Committee, Politburo members Peng Zhen, Deng Yingchao, and Nie Rongzhen exercise considerable influence (see biographies on pages 53 and 55). These are the powerful, but ageing (the average age of the Standing Committee is about 76), men and one woman who dominate the policymaking process in China.

Institutions    To implement its policies the Chinese leadership chooses to rely on a Soviet-style dual structure of Party and state hierarchies that reach from Beijing to every city and township. It is within this huge, complex bureaucracy that the fate of the new leadership's policies will be determined. Victory at the Politburo level by no means assures implementation in the villages. Deng Xiaoping and his colleagues have quickly come to realize that they must gain control of this bureaucracy if they are to change the nation's agenda.

The formal Party structure (see chart [IV.6] on page 64) is modeled on the Soviet Communist Party. It combines two different types of institutions: members' meetings and representative congresses on the one hand, and leaders (called secretaries) and executive committees on the other. Despite attempts to enhance the power of the representative bodies, the latter institutions are more important than the former. In addition, power has flowed from the top down rather than the other way. Formally, Party congresses -- held at national, provincial, and county levels -- and general membership meetings of primary organizations elect the committees and secretaries to be the executive bodies at that level. In practice, they meet infrequently, largely to ratify the work of their committees. Moreover, higher levels have a large say in the scheduling of congresses, their composition, and the election of the committees and secretaries.

At the national level, for example, the Central Committee of the Party, the most important representative body in China, delegates key decision-making powers to its Politburo, whose power is further centralized in the Standing Committee. The Politburo exercises its executive power through a central Party bureaucracy consisting of the Central Committee Secretariat -- reestablished in 1980 -- and its various specialized departments. This body, headed by Hu Yaobang, is thus second only to the Politburo as the most powerful institution in China. Central Committee departments play a dual role. They supervise state ministries and also oversee local level state organs and CCP organizations that conduct the daily work of the Party. The Party runs

China.  But the Secretariat, under Hu Yaobang, runs the Party.

Underlying this Party structure is the basic organizational principle of "democratic centralism."  This principle combines "inner-Party democracy" in the discussion of issues and election of leading bodies, and "centralist discipline" once a decision is made, subordinating the individual to the organization, the minority to the majority, the lower level to the higher, and the entire Party to the Central Committee.

The state structure (see chart [IV.7] on page 65) roughly parallels that of the CCP in two respects.  First, there is a similar division of administrative units among central, provincial, county, and basic levels, facilitating Party supervision of state organs at the same level.  Second, there is a similar distinction between representative and executive/administrative hierarchies.  Representative congresses possess formal constitutional authority, but the administrative organs have the actual power.  The representative bodies are called people's congresses; administrative bodies are known as governments (a change from the Cultural Revolution era when they were known as "revolutionary committees").  At the central level, the key administrative unit is the State Council, a sort of large cabinet.  With an array of commissions and ministries under its control, it is an important agency of the centralized governmental structure, even though it is subordinate to central Party directives and subject to Party supervision.

As suggested earlier, this immensely complex bureaucracy was copied from the Soviet Union where Lenin believed that only Party supervision of government at all levels could assure loyal service by former Czarist officials.  In theory, the Party is to simply decide broad policy guidelines and supervise their implementation.  The government is expected to do the actual day-to-day governing.  In practice, these functions have never been easily separated.  Bureaucratic expansion, overlapping jurisdictions, and complaints of Party meddling are endemic to the Chinese system.

The post-Mao leadership has, to some degree, tried to deal with these problems.  It has sought to define the role of the Party, to allow greater freedom from bureaucratic interference for certain institutions, and to streamline the number of Party-government offices.  However, in recent years organizational changes have largely taken a backseat to attempts at personnel change.

Put simply, it has become clear that Deng and his colleagues doubt that the Party-state bureaucracy as currently staffed is either willing or able to implement the new economic policies.  In part, the problems are those common in any large bureaucracy:  caution, neopotism, corruption, exploitation of privilege, etc.  But there are also problems peculiar to China.  The sudden reversals of past years suggest to many bureaucrats that caution in implementing new policies might be advised.  The bureaucracy is also ageing.  The old revolutionaries do not have the vitality or the skills to rule a China undergoing rapid economic transformation.  Moreover, of the nearly 40 million party members, perhaps 18 million joined during the Cultural Revolution.  This group is poorly trained and generally considered to be ill-disposed toward much of the post-Mao platform pursued by Deng and his colleagues.

Deng and his supporters have pursued a number of tactics in their effort to discipline the bureaucracy and infuse it with new blood.  Both the carrot and the stick are being used.  Older cadres are provided with pensions, nominal posts on advisory commissions, and are in other ways encouraged/pressured to make way for younger, better trained men and women. Disciplinary commissions and formal trials are used to deal with corrupt or more recalcitrant cadres.

Since the Twelfth Party Congress in the fall of 1982, efforts have been stepped up. Observers of China have noted that while the top leadership has stayed in the hands of the old guard, a new technocratic leadership has shown signs of emerging at the middle levels. Since the Twelfth Congress, pressure has been intensified for the recruitment of younger, better trained cadres. The launching of an important Party "consolidation" campaign in the fall of 1983 suggests that Deng and his colleagues are intent on rooting out those unwilling or unable to implement their policies.

What the results of all this will be is hard to say. There is evidence that a corps of younger, more skilled bureaucrats is emerging in China. However, the problems of reforming the Chinese bureaucracy are immense. Bureaucrats, after all, are notorious footdraggers when it comes to implementing new policies; and they can become even more so when their jobs are at stake.

Policy and Society     In later chapters we will discuss the specific content of the policies pursued by the post-Mao leadership. In general, one can say that since Mao's death there has been a sweeping reversal of Cultural Revolution policy in almost every field. Where Mao had advocated a policy of growth with equality, Deng Xiaoping and his colleagues have advocated rewarding expertise and performance that contribute to economic growth. Prosperity not politics, they believe, will end inequality. In the countryside, this has meant de facto de-collectivization. In the cities, differential wages for the workers are now commonplace and small-scale private enterprise is encouraged. Where Mao had preferred to open China's doors only slightly to the outside world rather than risk "bourgeois" contamination, the new leadership, while not unconcerned about social and intellectual influences from abroad, has opened the door rather widely. Whereas the late Maoist era saw close political supervision of all aspects of life, the new leadership is experimenting with allowing relatively more autonomy to economic enterprises, peasants, writers and artists, the legal system, religious believers, scientists, educators, and political critics. However, the boundaries between freedom and control will, for the near future, be a subject of continual negotiation and flux -- and uncertainty. This, at least, was a very important lesson of the "anti-spiritual pollution" campaign of 1983-1984 which exposed some of the opposition to the regime's current "open door" policy.

Yet, one should not overdo the question of discontinuities from the Maoist period. As the appended documents suggest, although Mao's behavior during the Cultural Revolution has been consistently criticized since 1981, his importance as a unifying symbol of the Party's authority has precluded any "de-Maoification." While recognizing the contributions of other revolutionaries to its corpus and carefully selecting its content, the current leadership has placed "the thought of Mao Zedong" at the ideological center of the regime.

Thus, Mao's continued presence represents, in part, a belief on the part of the present leadership that it needs, and can use, a properly sanitized Mao to serve their ends. However, the presence is also the result of pressures from forces in the political system that genuinely adhere to Maoist principles. It is these forces -- in the

Party as well as the army -- which pose the greatest threat to the continuance of the bold reversals instituted after Mao's death. As noted above, the succession process in China has by no means run its course.


## Suggested Readings

Barnett, A. Doak. Cadres, Bureaucracy, and Political Power in Communist China. New York: Columbia University Press, 1967. Based on research in the early 1960s, it provides a wealth of detail on the political system that the post-Mao leadership is to some extent trying to restore.

Garside, Roger. Coming Alive!: China After Mao. New York: McGraw-Hill, 1981. Political life in post-1976 China, focusing on the democracy movement in late 1978.

Harding, Harry. Organizing China: The Problem of Bureaucracy 1949-1976. Stanford: Stanford University Press, 1981. A detailed study of the impact and role of bureaucratic organization on politics.

Hsu, Immanual. China Without Mao. New York: Oxford University Press, 1983. A brief history of post-Mao China with discussion of Sino-US relations.

Kallgren, Joyce, ed. The People's Republic of China After Thirty Years: An Overview. Berkeley: University of California at Berkeley Center for Chinese Studies, 1979. Includes chapters on political institutions, political development, foreign policy, the economy, and public policy.

Ma Hong. New Strategy for China's Economy. Beijing: Foreign Languages Press, 1983. The influential president of the Chinese Academy of the Social Sciences discusses the economic reform movement.

Oxnam, Robert B., and Richard C. Bush, eds. China Briefing, 1980. Boulder, CO: Westview Press, 1980. Short reviews on developments in China from late 1978 to early 1980 in the fields of politics, economics, foreign affairs, and culture.

_____, eds. China Briefing, 1981. Boulder, CO: Westview Press, 1981. Short reviews on developments in China during 1980 in the fields of politics, economics, foreign affairs, society, and culture.

"Resolution on Certain Questions in the History of Our Party Since the Founding of the People's Republic of China." Beijing Review, July 6, 1981, pp. 10-39. The current official verdict on Mao, his thought, and the Cultural Revolution.

Townsend, James R. Politics in China. 2nd edition. Boston: Little, Brown, 1980. A general survey of the Chinese political system, focusing on institutional development.

2.  Chronology of Post-Mao China (Much of what follows is drawn from
    the "chronicles" section of The China Quarterly.)

1976:   September 9  Mao Zedong dies.
        October  Premier Hua Guofeng leads the arrest of the leading
        "radicals," including Jiang Qing, Zhang Chunqiao, Wang Hongwen,
        and Yao Wenyuan who are dubbed the "gang of four." Hua Guofeng
        succeeds Mao as Chairman of the Communist Party and of its
        Military Affairs Commission. It is announced that a mausoleum
        will be constructed for Mao.
        November  The new leadership reinstates the "four moderniza-
        tions" as the central focus of economic policy. Jiang Qing is
        attacked for her "nitpicking" in assessing artistic works. The
        slogan "let a hundred flowers bloom, let a hundred schools of
        thought contend" is raised once more.

1977:   January  The Anti-Confucius Campaign of 1974 is denounced as a
        political plot by the "gang of four" against Zhou Enlai and
        other moderate leaders. Beijing wall posters call for the
        rehabilitation of Deng Xiaoping.
        March  A Party central work conference considers the rehabili-
        tation of Deng Xiaoping.
        April  The fifth volume of the Selected Works of Mao Zedong
        (covering the years 1949-57) is published.
        July  The CCP Central Committee confirms Hua Guofeng's Party
        posts, returns Deng Xiaoping to Party and state posts, and
        expels the "gang of four."
        August  The Eleventh Party Congress is held, a new Central
        Committee and Politburo are selected, and Hua Guofeng announces
        the end of the "first Cultural Revolution."
        Fall  During the fall, 60% of  Chinese  industrial  workers
        receive wage increases, and bonuses reemerge to spur produc-
        tivity. Academic entrance examinations are restored, and high
        school graduates no longer have to work before entering
        college.

1978:   February-March  The Fifth session of the Fifth National
        People's Congress is held. Hua Guofeng announces an ambitious
        program of industrial, agricultural, and scientific moderni-
        zation. A new state constitution is promulgated. At a national
        science conference in March, Deng Xiaoping proposes an enhanced
        role for science in economic development and less political
        restrictions for scientists.
        April  A national education work conference is held amid
        continuing controversy over educational reforms.
        June  At an army political work conference, Deng proposes
        "seeking truth from facts" rather than taking Mao Zedong's
        ideas too literally.
        Fall  China modifies its foreign economic policies to permit
        more liberal credit arrangements, compensation trade, and
        direct foreign investments. Negotiations proceed with foreign
        corporations on a broad array of projects.
        October  The verdict on the Tiananmen Incident is reversed; it
        is now termed a "revolutionary act." Wu De, the mayor of

Beijing during the incident and an alleged ally of the "gang of four," is removed from his position.

November  Amid contentious Party meetings on a broad range of issues, a vigorous "wall poster" campaign begins, attacking the Cultural Revolution and policies of Mao Zedong.

December  The normalization of US-China relations is announced. From December 18 to 25, the third plenum of the CCP Central Committee meets.  It calls for a focus on "socialist modernization," liberalizes agricultural policies, exonerates Deng Xiaoping of charges made against him in 1976, approves of the Tiananmen Incident as a "revolutionary" action, rehabilitates Peng Dehuai (see page 32), calls for a strengthening of the legal system and Party discipline, and promises an evaluation of the Cultural Revolution.

1979:  January  China enunciates a new policy on the "reunification" with Taiwan, whereby much of the status quo on the island could continue in return for Nationalist acceptance of PRC sovereignty.  Deng Xiaoping visits the United States.

February  China invades Vietnam and begins a reevaluation of the scope of the modernization program.

March  Wall posters are restricted and leading dissidents arrested.

April-May  Deng Xiaoping comes under attack on a range of issues (modernization, political dissidence, social unrest, the opening to the US, the Vietnam war, and his views on Mao).

June  Deng and his allies counterattack and regain the political momentum.  The second session of the Fifth National People's Congress endorses an economic "readjustment," abolishes the revolutionary committee structure, and passes laws on the criminal legal system and joint ventures with foreign firms.

September  Fourth plenum of the Central Committee elevates Zhao Ziyang and Peng Zhen to the Politburo, approves more flexible agriculture policies, and endorses a review of the history of the PRC that criticizes the Cultural Revolution.  Ye Jianying delivers the review as a speech celebrating the 30th anniversary of the People's Republic of China.

October  Wei Jingsheng, a leading dissident, is sentenced for 15 years.  Cultural Congress convenes, the first in 19 years; calls for greater freedom of artistic expression.

November  China admitted to the Olympics.

December  Beijing "Democracy Wall" moved from downtown area and tighter curbs enacted.

1980:  January  New laws governing local governments and the legal system go into effect.  On the 16th Deng Xiaoping gives a major speech on China in the 1980s and recommends that the display of wall posters no longer be constitutionally protected.

February  Deng resigns his position as army chief of staff. The fifth plenum of the Central Committee fully rehabilitates Liu Shaoqi, Mao's principal Cultural Revolution target; removes the "little gang of four," Wang Dongxing, Chen Xilian, Ji Dengkui, and Wu De (all beneficiaries of the Cultural Revolution) from the Politburo; restores the Party Secretariat; and elevates Deng's supporters Hu Yaobang and Zhao Ziyang to the Politburo Standing Committee.

March  The CCP issues a set of "principles for internal Party political life" in an effort to revive institutional vitality.

April  Zhao Ziyang becomes a vice premier and Deng suggests that he "is now in charge of the day-to-day work of the State Council."  China is admitted to the International Monetary Fund.

May  China is admitted to the World Bank.  Memorial meeting for Liu Shaoqi is held and an exhibition opened in his honor.

August  Most public portraits of Mao are ordered removed.

September  At the third session of the Fifth National People's Congress, Hua Guofeng resigns the premiership and is replaced by Zhao Ziyang.  Peng Zhen reports on major revisions of the country's legal system.

November  The "gang of four" and former military figures associated with Lin Biao go on trial for their activities.

December  Hua Guofeng reportedly resigns his position as Party chairman; Deng Xiaoping replaces him as chairman of the Party's Military Commission.  Growing inflation forces the government to reduce spending through canceling or postponing capital construction projects and reducing military spending.

1981:  January  The trial of the "gang of four" and other Cultural Revolution leaders ends.  Jiang Qing and Zhang Chunqiao receive the harshest sentences -- execution, suspended for two years.

A movement is begun to improve the work style of the Party and strengthen "ideological and political work."  Bureaucratic behavior is attacked and the Party is called upon to cultivate "spiritual civilization" among the nation's youth.  All of this suggests that Deng and his colleagues are becoming concerned that the new economic policies are promoting materialism and corruption.

February  The Standing Committee of the National People's Congress hears a report by Yao Yilin, chairman of the State Planning Commission.  Problem areas identified are financial deficits, emphasis on heavy industry, and inflation.

April  Fears of a new cultural crackdown are rekindled as the campaign promoting "socialist morality" and opposing the filmscript Bitter Love continues.

June  The Party Central Committee holds its sixth plenary session.  Hu Yaobang replaces Hua Guofeng as Party chairman, and Deng Xiaoping is confirmed as chairman of the Party Military Commission.  A major resolution on the 30 years of Communist Party rule is released.  It commends Mao for his contributions to the Chinese revolution, but asserts that he increasingly lost touch with reality, causing the country great harm (see pages 67-69).

July-August  The campaign against "bourgeois liberalization" continues as Deng makes a strong speech and several cultural figures are criticized.

October  Ye Jianying announces a nine-point plan for Taiwan's reunification with the mainland.

November-December  At the fourth session of the Fifth National People's Congress, Zhao Ziyang outlines the ten principles for future economic construction.  Peng Zhen announces a postponement in the unveiling of a revised state constitution.

1982:    February  Standing Committee of the Fifth National People's
         Congress endorses a decision on the punishment of criminals who
         damage the nation's economy.  A campaign against crime and
         corruption begins.
         April  Draft version of the new state constitution published
         for discussion.  It reflects two important themes of the
         post-Mao leadership:  administrative streamlining, and the
         creation of a more articulated legal system.  Major changes are
         the return of the office of head of state, a new Civilian
         Military Council and the abolishing of the commune as a
         political unit.
         July  National census held.  Campaign against economic crime
         continues with the dismissal of a vice minister of the chemical
         industry.
         September  Twelfth National Congress of the CCP held, the first
         in five years.  Major structural changes include:  abolishing
         the posts of chairman and vice chairman of the Party and the
         establishment of a Central Advisory Committee for older party
         veterans.  Most of the higher ranking older cadres remain at
         their posts, but there is some infusion of new blood into the
         Central  Committee.  Party  policy  is  affirmed  and  a
         rectification campaign announced which would run over the three
         years, beginning in late 1983.
         November  Fifth session of the NPC held which approves new
         state constitution and hears Zhao's report on the Sixth
         Five-Year Plan.

1983:    March-April  Movement begins for reorganization of provincial
         Party and state offices.  It is intended to streamline
         administration and bring in younger, better educated cadres.
         Central Committee issues statement affirming the responsibility
         system.
         June  Sixth Congress of the National People's Congress is held.
         Li Xiannian is elected president of the PRC, replacing the aged
         Ye Jianying who had earlier resigned.  Peng Zhen is elected
         chairman of the National People's Congress and Deng Xiaoping
         becomes  chairman  of  the  government's  Central  Military
         Commission.  In his speech Premier Zhao announces the creation
         of a new Ministry of State Security, presaging a crackdown on
         crime.
         July  The Selected Works of Deng Xiaoping are published and
         become the subject of a nationwide study campaign.
         August-September  Anti-crime  campaign  intensifies  with
         executions and deportations to the countryside.
         October  CCP issues a decision on Party "consolidation" which
         seems to be aimed at bringing forth a younger, better trained
         group of cadres, while purging older and corrupt cadres as well
         as those promoted during the Cultural Revolution.  In the
         cultural sphere, a campaign against "spiritual pollution" gains
         momentum.
         December  Mao's 90th birthday celebrated.  His mausoleum is
         reorganized with additional rooms commemorating Zhou Enlai, Zhu
         De, and Cultural Revolution victim, Liu Shaoqi.

1984:    January  "Anti-spiritual pollution" campaign loses momentum and
         seems to come to an end.  However, efforts to reduce government

bureaucracies and raise the quality of personnel continue as does the nationwide Party consolidation campaign.

<u>March</u> The Standing Committee of the National People's Congress approves a patent law for China.

<u>April</u> Rumors circulate that Deng Liqun, chief of the Party's Propoganda Department, had been removed because of his overzealous management of the campaign against "spiritual pollution." The Chinese government issues an official denial.

<u>May</u> At the second session of the National People's Congress, Premier Zhao Ziyang announces that in the fourth quarter of 1984 all enterprises would adopt a system of paying taxes to the state rather than handing over a share of their profits. He also announces that regulations in effect in the special economic zones would be extended to 14 coastal cities.

## 3.  <u>Leadership of the CCP</u>

### <u>The Politburo</u>

| | | |
|---|---|---|
| Chen Muhua** | Ni Zhifu | Xi Zhongxun |
| Chen Yun* | Nie Rongzhen | Xu Xiangqian |
| Deng Xiaoping* | Peng Zhen | Yang Dezhi |
| Deng Yingchao | Song Renqiong | Yang Shangkun |
| Fang Yi | Ulanhu | Ye Jianying* |
| Hu Qiaomu | Wan Li | Yu Qiuli |
| Hu Yaobang* | Wang Zhen | Zhang Tingfa |
| Li Desheng | Wei Guoqing | Zhao Ziyang* |
| Li Xiannian* | | |

### <u>The Secretariat</u>

General Secretary:  Hu Yaobang

Members:                                          Alternates:

| | | |
|---|---|---|
| Chen Pixian | Wan Li | Hao Jianxiu |
| Gu Mu | Xi Zhongxun | Qiao Shi |
| Hu Qili | Yao Yilin | |
| Deng Liqun | Yu Qiuli | |

 * members of the Politburo's Standing Committee
** alternate (non-voting) member

Biographical Sketches of Politburo Members of the CCP   This appendix to IV.3 includes those individuals who were elected to the Politburo following the Twelfth Party Congress in September 1982.  The Wade-Giles form of their names is given parenthetically at the beginning of each entry.  PLA = People's Liberation Army.

MEMBERS OF THE STANDING COMMITTEE (in formal rank order)

## Hu Yaobang (Hu Yao-pang)

Hu Yaobang was born in 1915 in Mao's home province of Hunan.  Early in his career he specialized in youth work, and participated in the Long March.  After war broke out with Japan in 1937, he worked in the military's commissariat.  In 1941 Hu became a subordinate of Deng Xiaoping, and the two have worked together ever since.  From 1949 to 1952, years that Deng Xiaoping worked in Sichuan, Hu was a key official in the province's northern region.

Then in 1952 he returned to his original field, becoming head of the Communist Youth League.  He entered the Central Committee in 1956, and generally spent the next decade in Beijing, except for a brief interlude in Shaanxi province in early 1965 as acting first Party secretary.  During the Cultural Revolution, Hu was denounced as a follower of Liu Shaoqi, and had to undergo a period of "reeducation."  In 1975, during Deng's short-lived return to power, Hu worked on science policy.

With Deng's rehabilitation in mid-1977, Hu began his climb to the top.  Late that year he became director of the Party's organization department.  At the third plenum of the Eleventh Central Committee in December 1978, he became a Politburo member, Party secretary general, and third secretary of the Central Commission for Inspecting Discipline.  At about this time, he moved from the Party organization department to its propaganda department.  At the February 1980 fifth plenum, Hu was elevated to the standing committee of the Politburo and was named head of the newly reconstituted Party Secretariat, with the title of general secretary.  (He gave up his post as director of the Party propaganda department.)

In late 1980 rumors began circulating that Hu would replace Hua Guofeng as Party chairman — rumors confirmed in June 1981 at the sixth plenum of the Central Committee.  At the Twelfth Party Congress (September 1982), the post of chairman was not retained, and Hu resumed his position of general secretary.  That reflected no diminution of Hu's power.  He has the power to convene the Politburo, oversees the work of the Secretariat, and has begun an overhaul of the central Party bureaucracy, placing trusted associates in leading positions.  In 1983 Hu projected his image abroad with a highly publicized trip to Japan.  In early 1984 he played a prominent role in the return visit of Prime Minister Nakasone and met with President Reagan.

## Ye Jianying (Yeh Chien-ying)

Born in 1898, Ye was a major military figure during the revolution and a close collaborator of Zhou Enlai.  He was on the Long March and served as chief of staff of the PLA in the late

1940s. After 1949 he served as mayor of Guangzhou and governor of his native Guangdong Province. With the reorganization of the PLA after the Korean War, Ye was named director of the PLA inspectorate and was elected to the Party's Military Commission. During the mid-1950s, he was an outspoken advocate of military modernization. He was elected to the Politburo in January of 1967 and became a Party vice chairman in 1973. After the purge of Lin Biao in 1971, Ye was placed in charge of military affairs and was formally named minister of defense in 1975. He was instrumental in the arrest of the "gang of four" in October 1976 and was a strong supporter of Hua Guofeng becoming Party chairman.

Since that time Ye has shed many of his responsibilities and played the role of Party elder. In early 1978 he turned over the national defense portfolio to Xu Xiangqian in February and became chairman of the Standing Committee of the National People's Congress (equivalent to head of state). In late September 1979, on the leadership's behalf, Ye delivered a major address marking the 30th anniversary of the founding of the People's Republic. In it he rejected Mao's definition of revisionism, thus eroding the ideological justification of the Cultural Revolution. In September 1981 Ye announced a PRC offer to the Nationalist regime on Taiwan for "peaceful reunification."

However, Ye has resisted other initiatives of Deng Xiaoping. He reportedly opposed the 1980 posthumous rehabilitation of Liu Shaoqi, the demotion of Hua Guofeng, and heavy criticism of Mao Zedong. At the time of the Twelfth Party Congress, Ye continued on the Politburo Standing Committee despite his advanced age and obvious poor health. In June of 1983, his purported ally Li Xiannian succeeded him as the president of China. His declining health makes it unclear whether or not he is still able to act as the supporter, among the upper elite, of Party conservatives — especially in the army.

## Deng Xiaoping (Teng Hsiao-p'ing)

Born in Sichuan in 1904, Deng joined the Chinese Communist Party in 1924 while on a work-study program in France. A veteran of the Long March, he assumed important posts in the political commissariat in the Red Army, eventually becoming the political commissar of the Second Field Army under Liu Bocheng. After 1949 Deng served for three years in southwest China, but was transferred to Beijing in 1952, becoming a vice premier and serving briefly as minister of finance. In 1954 he became secretary general of the Central Committee, where he was responsible for the day-to-day work of the Party. The following year he was elected to the Politburo, and in 1956 his title was changed to general secretary, reflecting an increase in his power.

Deng held both those positions until the Cultural Revolution and was considered to be one of the most powerful men in China, along with Mao, Zhou, and Liu Shaoqi. But during the Cultural Revolution he was accused of following "Liu Shaoqi's revisionist line" and was dismissed from office.

Deng was rehabilitated in April 1973 and resumed his vice premiership. He was returned to the Politburo in late 1973, and in early 1975 became a vice chairman of the Party and chief of staff of the military. He also took charge of the day-to-day work of the Party. Soon, however, his criticism of Cultural Revolution programs and his plans for China's economic development aroused the opposition of Mao's radical followers. In April 1976 they succeeded in having him purged for a second time. After Mao's death and considerable discussion within the Polit- buro, Deng was restored to his various posts at the third plenum of the Tenth Central Committee in July 1977. Gradually thereafter, he achieved a preeminent political position by facilitating a nearly total reversal of the verdict on the Cultural Revolution and its victims (including his former ally Liu Shaoqi).

Deng has been the prime mover in China's post-Mao "great leap outward." In the fall of 1978, he himself traveled to Japan to sign the Sino-Japanese Treaty of Peace and Friendship, and to Southeast Asia to shore up China's diplomatic position against Vietnam. The following January he came to the US to celebrate the normalization of relations.

As part of the transfer of power to younger leaders, Deng gave up his army chief of staff post in April 1980 and his vice premiership in September of the same year. With Hua Guofeng's resignation from his top Party posts in late 1980, Deng took over the duties of Party Military Commission chairman. His protege Hu Yaobang formally became Party chairman in June 1981, replacing Hua Guofeng. In February 1982 it was announced that Deng had moved to the leadership's "second line."

At the Twelfth Party Congress in September, Deng further secured the position of his successors and policies. At that time he became chairman of the Central Advisory Commission, a body of Party elders. He remained on the Politburo Standing Committee, though the post of vice chairman was abolished. He was also confirmed as chairman of the Party's Military Commission. In June of 1983 he was elected chairman of the government's Central Military Commission. In July of the same year, his selected works were published and became the object of nationwide study.

## Zhao Ziyang (Chao Tzu-yang)

Born in 1919 in Henan Province, Zhao is a veteran Party cadre with extensive experience in south China. Between 1951 and 1955 he was secretary general of the Party's south China bureau, responsible for Guangdong and Guangxi Provinces. He rose gradually in the Guangdong provincial Party apparatus, finally becoming first Party secretary in 1965.

Purged during the Cultural Revolution as a "revi- sionist," Zhao was rehabilitated in 1971 and sent to Inner Mongolia to serve on the provincial Party committee. By March 1972 he was back in Guangdong and was named first secretary in April 1974. In December 1975 he was transferred to Sichuan, China's most populous province, to become first Party secretary, chairman of the provincial revolutionary committee, and first political commissar of the Chengdu Military Region.

Since Deng Xiaoping's July 1977 rehabilitation, Zhao has rapidly gained political prominence. He made Sichuan a pacesetter in a number of policy areas, particularly economic management and population control. He was elected an alternate member of the Politburo at the Eleventh Party Congress (August

1977), a full member at the Central Committee's fourth plenum
(September 1979), and a member of the Standing Committee at the
fifth plenum (February 1980).

In early 1980 Zhao moved from the provinces to the
center. Having relinquished his posts in Sichuan, he became a
vice premier in April, and it was soon revealed that he had taken
charge of the day-to-day work of the State Council, previously
Deng Xiaoping's responsibility. He became premier in September
1980, replacing Hua Guofeng, and Party vice chairman in June 1981
(the latter post was eliminated at the Twelfth Party Congress).
In early 1982 he sponsored a major streamlining of the government
bureacracy through a reduction in the number of agencies and
retirement by older officials. At the September 1982 Party
Congress, his Politburo status was confirmed and he made a major
speech on the work of the government. He has made important state
visits to Africa (1983) and the United States (1984).

## Li Xiannian (Li Hsien-nien)

Born in Hubei Province about 1905, Li was a
commander in the Red Army before 1949 and a veteran of the Long
March. In the early 1950s, he was governor of his native province
and held several other important positions in the central-south
region. Li became finance minister in 1954, succeeding Deng Xiaoping. He was soon promoted to vice premier, with responsibility
for all financial and trade matters. He entered the Politburo in
September 1956.

Li was one of the few high-ranking economic
planners to remain in office throughout the Cultural Revolution,
and he became a Party vice chairman at the Eleventh Party Congress
in August 1977. He was chiefly responsible for drafting the
Ten-Year Plan, unveiled in February 1978, which called for rapid
growth of heavy industry and the importation of whole plants from
abroad. Since early 1979 that policy has been attacked for
neglecting the material needs of the Chinese people. In September
1980 Li gave up his vice premiership, and, late in the year,
reportedly made a self-criticism of his economic leadership. Some
of his proteges lost their positions in the government reshuffling
in early 1982. Li remains a member of the Standing Committee of
the Politburo but his post of vice chairman was abolished at the
Twelfth Party Congress in September 1982. His fortunes changed
somewhat when, in June 1983, he became China's president, a
prominent but largely ceremonial position as head of state. This
position provided him much public exposure during the Reagan
visit.

## Chen Yun (Ch'en Yun)

Chen was born around 1900 (some sources say 1905)
in Jiangsu Province. He participated in part of the Long March,
and spent time in Russia in the mid-1930s. In 1945 he was elected
to the Politburo and made a member of its inner circle. With the
founding of the PRC in 1949 he became one of four vice premiers,
and worked closely with Zhou Enlai to rehabilitate the economy.
He became a Party vice chairman in 1956.

In the debates surrounding the Great Leap Forward,

which Mao initiated in the late 1950s, Chen continually called for measured, steady, and systematic growth, to be stimulated by material incentives rather than mass mobilization. Thus in the early 1960s, he played a significant role in bringing the economy out of its post-Leap depression. But because of Mao's growing fears that such pragmatism was leading China down the road of revisionism, Chen was politically inactive from 1962 until Mao's demise and the purge of the "gang of four" in 1976. (Formally, Chen lost his major positions during the 1966-69 period.)

At the Eleventh Central Committee's third plenum, Chen was catapulted back onto the Politburo and its standing committee. Also, he was named first secretary of the Commission for Inspecting Party Discipline, created to restore the Party's organizational vitality. In mid-1979 he was also named a vice premier, but gave up the post a year later as part of an effort to elevate younger officials. The post of vice chairman was abolished at the Twelfth Party Congress of September 1982, but Chen remained a standing committee member and was confirmed as head of the Discipline Inspection Commission, which leads the Party rectification campaign.

FULL MEMBERS (in alphabetical order)

## Deng Yingchao (Teng Ying-ch'ao)

Deng is the widow of former Premier Zhou Enlai. She was born in 1903, and is a revolutionary figure in her own right. Deng participated in the Long March and has always been an advocate of women's rights. During the late 1930s and early 1940s, she and Zhou were part of a Communist liaison group in the Nationalists' capital of Chongqing. After 1949 Deng specialized in social welfare policy, but her position was largely honorific, especially in the 1960s. She weathered the Cultural Revolution well, and in the 1970s played an active role in the National People's Congress, serving as a vice chairman and member of its Standing Committee. In December 1978 she became a Politburo member and was named second secretary of the Central Commission for Inspecting Discipline. In September 1982 she was confirmed in that office, and in June of 1983 was elected chairperson of the Chinese People's Political Consultative Conference, a body for consultation with non-Communists. She has also made some important statements regarding Taiwan. In a June 1983 interview with the American political scientist Parris Chang, Hu Yaobang identified her as part of the small group of high officials who "decided China's major policies."

## Fang Yi (Fang Yi)

Born in 1916, Fang's experience in administrative and economic affairs dates back to 1939. Between 1949 and 1953 he served in various posts in Fujian, Shanghai, and the east China region. He was transferred to Beijing in September 1953 and served for a year as vice minister of finance. Between 1956 and 1960 Fang served in Hanoi as the representative of the ministry of foreign trade. Upon returning to China, his principal position was director of the Commission for Economic Relations with Foreign Countries. Fang survived the Cultural Revolution, and returned to head the commission in January 1975.

Two years later he was transferred from economic affairs to science administration, becoming vice president of the Chinese Academy of Sciences. He was elected to the Politburo at the Eleventh Party Congress (August 1977) and was named minister in charge of the state Scientific and Technological Commission in October 1977. He became a vice premier in early 1978. Though named president of the Chinese Academy of Sciences in mid-1979, Fang resigned the post two years later, on the grounds that it should be held by a scientist rather than a government official. He lost his vice premiership in the government shake-up of early 1982, but was named to be an adviser to the State Council instead. In June of 1983 he became a state councillor.

### Hu Qiaomu (Hu Ch'iao-mu)

Hu Qiaomu is a leading Chinese Communist Party theoretician. He was born in Jiangsu Province in 1912, and became actively involved in revolutionary activities in Shanghai in the 1930s. Once war with Japan began in 1937, he moved to the Communist headquarters in Yan'an. In the early 1940s, he served as secretary for Mao Zedong and the Party Politburo.

After 1949, he assumed an important role in the Party apparatus. In 1956 he became an alternate member of the Secretariat headed by Deng Xiaoping, and played an important role in drafting important Party documents (including editing of Mao's Selected Works).

Hu was purged at the outset of the Cultural Revolution but Deng brought him back in the early 1970s to be a leader in his brain-trust. Then in 1977, after Deng's second return, Hu was named president of the Academy of Social Sciences, established to study policy-related issues. He became a member of the revived Secretariat in February 1980. Hu was in charge of drafting the resolution on Party history since 1949, which attacked Maoist dogmatism (issued in June 1981). Although he was removed from the Secretariat in 1982, he was elected to the Politburo. Replaced several months before as president of the Social Sciences Academy, he now serves as honorary president of the Chinese Academy of Sciences.

### Li Desheng (Li Te-sheng)

Li was a major beneficiary of the Cultural Revolution whose career has been in a holding pattern for some years now. Before 1966 he was commander of an army unit stationed in Anhui Province. Because of his early support of some of the more radical Red Guard groups in the province, Li became commander of the provincial military district in December 1967 and chairman of the provincial revolutionary committee in April 1968. He was named an alternate Politburo member in 1969 and transferred to Beijing the following year to become director of the general political department of the PLA, responsible for fostering ideological purity in the military.

Li's career peaked in 1973 when he became a full Politburo member and Party vice chairman. Then, late in the year, he was rotated out of Beijing, replacing Chen Xilian as commander of the Shenyang Military Region, his current post. Li lost his Party vice chairmanship in 1975, perhaps because of his ties to radical elements, but he has remained on the Politburo. Clearly though, his role is much diminished from that of 1973.

## Ni Zhifu (Ni Chih-fu)

The worker representative on the Politburo, Ni was born in 1933. Raised in Shanghai, Ni moved to Beijing soon after 1949 to work at a machine tool plant where he became a worker technician. Ni was active during the Cultural Revolution, and was a municipal official in Beijing from 1971 to 1976. He became an alternate member of the Politburo in 1973. After the fall of the "gang of four" in late 1976, Ni worked in their old bailiwick of Shanghai. He was raised to full Politburo membership at the Eleventh Party Congress in August 1977, and was transferred back to Beijing late in the year. In October 1978 Ni became chairman of the National Federation of Trade Unions. Despite allegations of links with the leftist leaders of the Cultural Revolution, his position was confirmed at the Twelfth Party Congress (September 1982).

## Nie Rongzhen (Nieh Jung-chen)

Nie, born in 1899, is a native of Sichuan. A veteran of the Long March, he was commander of the North China Field Army in the late 1940s. He served as mayor of Beijing in the early 1950s, after which he was acting chief of staff of the PLA until 1954. Around the late 1950s he was named a vice chairman of the Party's Military Commission.

In the mid-1950s Nie began to specialize in military science administration. He became a vice premier in 1956 and chairman of the Scientific Planning Commission in 1957. Although that body was abolished during the Cultural Revolution, it is likely that Nie has continued to have some responsibility for scientific matters, possibly through the National Defense Commission for Science and Technology. Nie served on the Politburo briefly at the beginning of the Cultural Revolution, but was criticized during the Red Guard movement and lost his formal posts. He was restored to the Party's Military Commission in 1974 and returned to the Politburo at the Eleventh Party Congress (August 1977). In 1982 he was reelected to the Politburo, and in June of 1983 became one of the vice chairmen of the state Central Military Commission. Hu Yaobang included him among the inner circle of policymakers in his 1983 interview (see Deng Yingchao).

## Peng Zhen (P'eng Chen)

Born in 1902, Peng is a long-time Party leader and was the first major purge victim of the Cultural Revolution. As early as 1943, he was head of the Party's powerful organization department, and was first elected to the Politburo in 1945. He became mayor of Beijing in 1951. In 1956 he was also named to the

Party Secretariat, ranking immediately behind Deng Xiaoping.
On the eve of the Cultural Revolution, Peng was one
of the strongest political figures in China, and some analysts
speculated that he might succeed Mao Zedong. But this prediction
proved erroneous: Peng was purged in May 1966 for protecting
subordinates who had made thinly veiled attacks against Mao. In
December of that year, he was personally subjected to humiliating
criticism at a mass rally in Beijing.
Peng was not rehabilitated until 1979, as the
post-Mao regime was openly rejecting the Cultural Revolution and
restoring to power its principal victims. He was named a vice
chairman of the National People's Congress Standing Committee at
mid-year and was elevated to the Politburo in September 1979. His
main responsibility has been the development of the legal system.
In 1983 he was elected chairman of the Standing Committee of the
National People's Congress -- China's legislature -- and in Hu's
1983 interview (see biography of Deng Yingchao), he was named as
one of the top policymakers. He is undoubtedly a very influential
-- and conservative -- voice on policy matters.

### Song Renqiong (Sung Jen-ch'iung)

Song was born in 1909 in Hunan Province, in Hu
Yaobang's native county. He joined the Communist movement in the
late 1920s and participated in the Long March. During the
anti-Japanese and civil wars he was a subordinate of Deng
Xiaoping. Deng's forces occupied China's southwest in 1949, and
Song worked there for five years. He was then transferred to
Beijing, where he successively held important positions in the
military, Party, and government hierarchies. In 1961 he was named
first secretary (leader) of the Party's newly revived bureau in
the northeast region (Manchuria). He was purged at the outset of
the Cultural Revolution.
Song was nominally rehabilitated in 1974 after Deng
returned to power, but he did not get an official position until
after the fall of the "gang of four." He headed the seventh
Ministry of Machine Building from 1977 to late 1978. He became a
member of the Party Secretariat when it was revived in February
1980 with Hu Yaobang at its head, but was removed from his post
when he became a Politburo member in September 1982.

### Ulanhu (Ulanfu)

A Mongol, Ulanhu was born in 1906. From 1949 to
1966 he held the leading Party, government, and military key posts
in Inner Mongolia. Concurrently, he was vice chairman and then
chairman of the nationalities affairs commission of the State
Council, and also a vice premier. In September 1956 he was named
an alternate member of the Politburo. During the Cultural
Revolution he was attacked by Red Guards and lost all his posts.
Ulanhu was rehabilitated in 1973, and was elected a
full member of the Politburo at the Eleventh Party Congress in
August 1977. At the same time, he became director of the Party's
united front work department, responsible for Party relations with
minority nationalities and with non-communist groups, particularly
intellectuals. He gave up that position in April 1982. In June

1983 he was elected vice president of the People's Republic of China.

## Wan Li (Wan Li)

Wan was born in 1916 in Shandong Province, and joined the Communist Party in 1936. He was active in guerrilla activities against Japan, and did political-military support work during the civil war.

After working with Deng Xiaoping in Sichuan Province from 1949 to 1952, Wan was transferred to Beijing where he worked in the field of urban construction. In 1958 he became a party secretary and vice mayor of the capital. Because the Beijing municipal government was one of Mao Zedong's principal targets at the outset of the Cultural Revolution, Wan was purged in 1966.

Wan was rehabilitated in early 1971 to work again in the Beijing municipal government. When Deng Xiaoping took over the work of the State Council from Zhou Enlai in January 1975, he picked Wan to end the disorder in China's railroad system. After achieving initial success, Wan disappeared from view when Deng was purged in April 1976. With the fall of the "gang of four" he was assigned to the Ministry of Light Industries. Then in June 1977, just before Deng's official reinstatement, Wan became the leading official in Anhui Province, which was plagued by continuing poverty and leftism. His liberalization of the agricultural system in Anhui was later applied nationwide. He was named a member of the Party's Central Secretariat in February 1980.

Wan became first vice premier late in the year and a subordinate of Premier Zhao Ziyang. In addition, Wan headed the State Agricultural Commission and the State Council's Economic Readjustment Office. Those bodies were abolished in the spring of 1982, but Wan's prominence did not abate. Only he and Yao Yilin retained their vice premierships at that time. Wan entered the Politburo at the time of the Twelfth Party Congress (September 1982). He was reelected vice premier in June 1983. In February 1984 he led the Chinese delegation to the funeral of the Soviet leader Yuri Andropov.

## Wang Zhen (Wang Chen)

Wang Zhen was born in 1909 in Mao Zedong's home province (Hunan) and Hu Yaobang's home county. He was on the Long March and spent much of his subsequent career as an army officer. Wang made a name for himself during the anti-Japanese war by having his troops engage in productive labor both to help the civilian populace and meet their own logistic requirements. From the early 1950s to the start of the Cultural Revolution, Wang was head of the railway corps of the PLA and minister of state farms and land reclamation. He became a vice premier in 1975, and a Politburo member in December 1978. He resigned his vice premiership in September 1980, but was named head of the Central Party School in April 1982, a position formerly held by Hua Guofeng. Wang is a member of the Standing Committee of the Party Military Commission.

## Wei Guoqing (Wei Kuo-ch'ing)

Born around 1914, Wei is a native of Guangxi Autonomous Region, a member of the Zhuang minority, and a veteran of
the Long March. He became governor of Guangxi in 1955, and first
Party secretary in 1961. Though heavily criticized by Red Guards
during the Cultural Revolution, he held on to both his posts. He
became a Politburo member in 1973. In October 1975 he was
promoted to first Party secretary of Guangdong province. He was
transferred to Beijing in September 1977 to serve as director of
the PLA's general political department. Since July 1981 he has
been a member of the Standing Committee of the Party Military
Commission. In September 1982 he was replaced as director of the
PLA's general political department, amid signs of conflict between
him and Deng Xiaoping. In June of 1983 he was elected a vice
chairman of the National People's Congress.

## Xi Zhongxun (Hsi Chung-hsun)

Xi was born in 1903 in Shaanxi Province, the
terminal point of the Communist Party's Long March. Both before
and immediately after the Communist victory of 1949, he worked in
China's northwest region and was associated with the famous
military commander Peng Dehuai. By early 1953, Xi had been
transferred to Beijing where he soon assumed the important
position of secretary general of the State Council, working with
Premier Zhou En-lai. He was named a vice premier in 1959. Then,
in the fall of 1962, Xi disappeared from public view, and formally
lost his position in January 1965.

It is believed that Xi's fall was due to his
relationship with Peng Dehuai, who, in the fall of 1959, crossed
Mao and was purged. That is confirmed by the fact that Xi did not
return to office until early 1979, just after Peng had been
posthumously rehabilitated. At that time, he assumed the leading
Party, government, and military commissar positions in Guangdong
Province. He returned to Beijing in 1980, and became a member of
the Party Secretariat in June 1981. He retained his position in
the Secretariat and entered the Politburo at the time of the
Twelfth Party Congress. It is thought that he is the Secretariat
member responsible for redefining the previously extensive role of
the public security forces.

## Xu Xiangqian (Hsu Hsiang-ch'ien)

Born in 1902, Xu is known primarily for his distin-
guished military career before 1949. He participated in part of
the Long March and, after war with Japan broke out in 1937, had
command responsibilities in the Eighth Route Army. In the late
1940s, he was a commander in the North China Field Army, led by
Nie Rongzhen. After 1949, Xu was named chief of staff of the PLA
but apparently never served actively in the position because of
ill health (Nie acted in his stead). Like Nie, Xu was on the
Politburo briefly during the Cultural Revolution. He was
reelected at the Eleventh Party Congress (August 1977), and became
minister of national defense and a vice premier in early 1978.
Because of his health he resigned both posts in September 1980.

He is still a vice chairman of the Party's Military Commission as well as vice chairman of the Central Military Commission on the state side. In his 1983 interview, Hu identified Xu as a part of the top policymaking group (see Deng Yingchao biography).

## Yang Dezhi (Yang Te-chih)

Yang was born in 1910 in Hunan, the home province of Mao Zedong and Hu Yaobang. He was drawn into the revolutionary movement in the late 1920s, and was a troop commander during the wars against the Japanese and Nationalists before 1949. Soon after the Communist victory, he became deputy commmander and later commander of Chinese forces in Korea.

Yang gave up his Korean command in 1955 and, after three years at the Nanjing Military Academy's staff college, he became commander of the Jinan Military Region, which is coterminous with Shandong Province. He was named first secretary of that province's Party committee in April 1971, evidence of the military's involvement in civilian politics after the Cultural Revolution.

Yang was part of a general shuffle of military region commanders in late 1973, and was transferred to Wuhan. In October 1979 Yang became commander of the Kunming Military Region. Five months later, in February 1980, Yang became the military representative on the reconstituted Party Secretariat in Beijing. At the same time, he replaced Deng Xiaoping as PLA chief of staff. He entered the Politburo in September 1982, and Yang Yong replaced him on the Secretariat.

## Yang Shangkun (Yang Shang-k'un)

Yang was born in Sichuan Province in 1907, and engaged in a wide range of revolutionary activities after 1925. He was one of the so-called "28 Bolsheviks" -- a group of Chinese Communist Party leaders trained in Moscow in the late 1920s, and distrusted by Mao thereafter because of their "dogmatic" adherence to foreign formulas for seizing power. Yang apparently made his peace with Mao, and held important positions in the Party before 1949. After victory, he served for over a decade as director of the Party's General Office, the nerve center of its operations. In a formal sense, Yang was a deputy of Party General Secretary Deng Xiaoping.

Like Peng Zhen, Yang was an early victim of the Cultural Revolution. He was rehabilitated in 1978, and took up several positions in Guangdong Province, working closely with Xi Zhongxun. In September 1980 he returned to Beijing serving first as secretary general of the National People's Congress's Standing Committee. In July 1981 he became also secretary general of the Party Military Commission, working on behalf of its chairman, Deng Xiaoping. He became a Politburo member in September 1982. In June 1983 he became vice chairman of the government's Civilian Military Commission.

## Yu Qiuli (Yu Ch'iu-li)

Born in 1912, Yu served as an army officer before

1949 and made a gradual transition into economic affairs thereafter. Immediately after the civil war Yu was part of the
military occupation forces in both the northwest and southwest.
In the mid-1950s he was transferred to Peking to serve as director
of the finance department of the PLA, and shortly thereafter
became political commissar of the PLA's general logistics department.

In 1958 he moved out of the army to become minister
of the petroleum industry, spending much of the early 1960s
opening up the Daqing oil field. In 1965 he was appointed a vice
chairman of the State Planning Commission, and was one of the few
ministers to receive Mao's repeated praise. Although he was severely criticized during the Cultural Revolution, Yu survived to
become chairman of the State Planning Commission in October 1972.
He became a vice premier in January 1975 and a Politburo member at
the Eleventh Party Congress (August 1977).

In 1980 Yu came under attack as a leader of the
"petroleum kingdom," a group of economic planners who allegedly
overemphasized the role of oil in China's economic development.
He lost his post at the State Planning Commission in August 1980.
At the same time he became head of the newly created State Energy
Commission, which itself was abolished in March 1982. Yu lost his
vice premiership at the same time and became instead an adviser to
the State Council. In September 1982 it was announced that he had
replaced Wei Guoqing as director of the PLA general political
department and had become a member of the Party's Central Military
Commission.

## Zhang Tingfa (Chang T'ing-fa)

Zhang is a relative newcomer to top-level Party
leadership. A professional air force officer, Zhang was named
deputy chief of staff of the air force in 1958 and then promoted
to become deputy commander in 1964. Dismissed during the Cultural
Revolution at the time when Lin Biao's supporters dominated the
air force, Zhang was rehabilitated as deputy air force commander
in July 1975. He became air force commander in April 1977 and
first secretary of the air force Party committee at about the same
time. Zhang became a Politburo member in August 1977, even though
he had never been a member of the Central Committee. He is a
member of the Party Military Commission's Standing Committee.

## ALTERNATE (non-voting) MEMBERS

## Chen Muhua (Ch'en Mu-hua)

Most of Chen's career was spent in the Commission
(later Ministry) of Economic Relations with Foreign Countries. A
middle-level official at the start of the Cultural Revolution, she
rose to vice minister in April 1971 and minister in 1977. Chen
became an alternate member of the Politburo at the Eleventh Party
Congress (August 1977), and became a vice premier in 1978. She is
one of two women on the Politburo, the other being Deng Yingchao.
In recent years Chen has also been responsible for the govern-

ment's work in family planning, and in March 1981, was named head of a newly created state commission for that field.

In May 1982 Chen's position became more prominent and more focused. She was named minister of a newly constituted Ministry of Foreign Trade and Economic Relations, which includes within its jurisdiction all central agencies involved in foreign economic relations. At the same time, she gave up her family planning portfolio and vice premiership, becoming an adviser to the State Council. In June 1983 she was elected a state councillor.

## Qin Jiwei (Ch'in Chi-wei)

Qin is a career military officer, born in 1914 in Hubei Province. He joined the Red Army in 1929, and, after Japan attacked China in 1937, was a commander in the forces for which Deng Xiaoping was the chief political commissar. He commanded troops in the Korean War. Subsequently he was assigned to China's southwest, which the Deng forces had occupied at the time of the Communist victory in 1949. Ultimately he rose to the post of commander of the Kunming Military Region. In August 1973 he took over as commander of the Chengdu Military Region, also in the southwest.

In late 1975 Qin was transferred to Beijing, where he was soon identified as second political commissar of the Beijing Military Region. In November 1978 he was promoted to first political commissar, as part of Deng's effort to isolate Chen Xilian, the military region commander. Qin replaced Chen in that position in February 1980. He was named an alternate member of the Politburo in September 1982.

## Yao Yilin (Yao Yi-lin)

Yao was born in Anhui Province in 1917. He became a Communist in the 1930s and engaged in resistance activities in north China during the war with Japan.

After the Communist victory in 1949, Yao held a number of positions in the economic sphere. He became minister of commerce in 1960, and also worked in the offices of the Central Committee and State Council which supervise finance and trade. In 1967, during the Cultural Revolution, Yao was stripped of all his posts.

Yao reemerged in 1973 and served as vice minister of foreign trade until mid-1978, when he again became minister of commerce. He gave up that position in early 1979 to become head of the Party Central Committee's General Office, a post he held until until May 1982. In February 1980 Yao became a member of the Party Secretariat, with responsibilities for planning. He has served as minister in charge of China's State Planning Commission, which is responsible for drafting long-range economic plans. Thought to be a close associate of Chen Yun, he is a vice premier. In September 1982, at the time of the Twelfth Party Congress, he became an alternate member of the Politburo.

## 4. Government Leadership

President: Li Xiannian
Vice President: Ulanhu

## National People's Congress Standing Committee

Chairman: Peng Zhen

## The State Council

Premier: Zhao Ziyang

Vice Premiers:

Li Peng          Wan Li
Tian Jiyun       Yao Yilin

State Councillors:

Chen Muhua
Fang Yi
Gu Mu
Ji Pengfei
Kang Shien
Song Ping
Wang Bingnan
Wu Xueqian
Zhang Aiping
Zhang Jingfu

## Commissions of the State Council

| | |
|---|---|
| Planning: | Song Ping |
| Economic: | Zhang Jingfu |
| Restructuring the Economic System: | Zhao Ziyang |
| Science and Technology: | Fang Yi |
| Science, Technology, and Industry for National Defence: | Chen Bin |
| Nationalities Affairs: | Yang Jingren |
| Physical Culture and Sports: | Li Menghua |
| Family Planning: | Qian Xinzhong |

5.  Government Biographies (Ministers of Defence and Foreign Affairs and Vice Premiers, based on China Directory, Tokyo: Radiopress, Inc., 1983.)

Zhang Aiping  Zhang was born in 1910 in Sichuan province.  He joined the Communist Party in 1928 and took part in the Long March.  During the anti-Japanese and civil wars, he served in various military posts.
     After 1949, he served as deputy chief of staff of the PLA and chairman of the Science and Technology Commission for National Defence of the PLA.  In November 1982 he succeeded Geng Biao as minister of defence, and the following year he hosted the American Secretary of Defence Casper Weinberger.

Wu Xueqian  Wu was born in 1921 in Shanghai.  He joined the Communist Party in 1939 and was active in front and underground organizations. After 1949, he was active in youth work and as a part of these duties traveled abroad to numerous international Communist front organization meetings.  He was then transferred to the Party's International Liason Department where he eventually became deputy director.  After a brief stint as vice foreign minister, he succeeded Huang Hua in November 1982 as foreign minister.


VICE PREMIERS

Li Peng  Li was born in 1928 in Sichuan province.  He joined the Communist Party in 1945.  His educational training is in engineering and he studied at the Moscow Power Institute after completing his education in China.  His bureaucratic experience has been primarily in the field of electric power generation.

Tian Jiyun  Tian was born in 1929 in Shandong province.  He joined the Party in 1945.  His experience since then has been almost exclusively in the field of finance and trade.  He appears to have been one of the administrators of Zhao Ziyang's Sichuan experiment.  His career is closely linked to the premier's.

Wan Li  See Politburo biographies.

Yao Yilin  See Politburo biographies.

## 6. Structure of the Chinese Communist Party

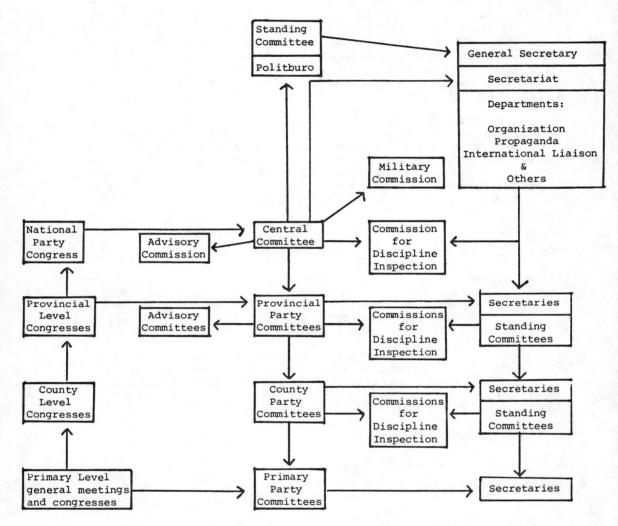

Note: County-level organizations include congresses and committees at the regimental level and above in the PLA. Primary-level organizations include branches, general branches, or committees which are set up in factories, mines and other enterprises, communes, offices, schools, shops, neighborhoods, PLA companies and other such units.

## 7. Structure of the PRC Government

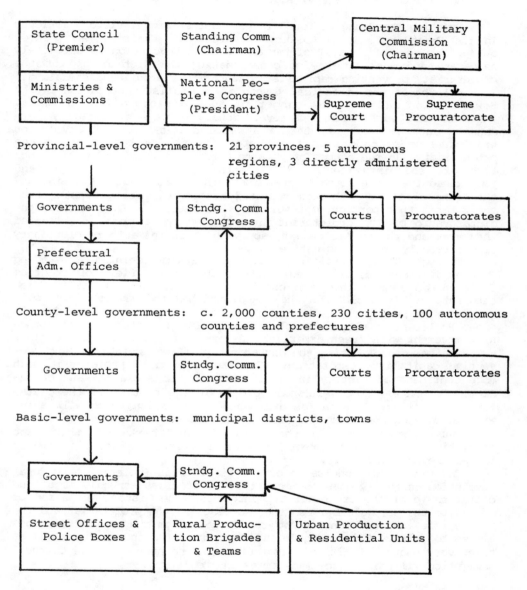

State Council (Premier)

Ministries & Commissions

Standing Comm. (Chairman)

National People's Congress (President)

Central Military Commission (Chairman)

Supreme Court

Supreme Procuratorate

Provincial-level governments: 21 provinces, 5 autonomous regions, 3 directly administered cities

Governments

Prefectural Adm. Offices

Stndg. Comm. Congress

Courts

Procuratorates

County-level governments: c. 2,000 counties, 230 cities, 100 autonomous counties and prefectures

Governments

Stndg. Comm. Congress

Courts

Procuratorates

Basic-level governments: municipal districts, towns

Governments

Stndg. Comm. Congress

Street Offices & Police Boxes

Rural Production Brigades & Teams

Urban Production & Residential Units

Note: Terms for people's congresses are five years at the national and provincial levels, three years at the county level, and two years at the basic level.

8. <u>Evaluations of the Cultural Revolution and Mao Zedong</u>

a) Hua Guofeng's Political Report to the Eleventh Congress of the
   Chinese Communist Party, August 12, 1977

Smashing the "gang of four" is yet another signal victory achieved in the Great Proletarian Cultural Revolution. Chairman Mao pointed out: "The current Great Proletarian Cultural Revolution is absolutely necessary and most timely for consolidating the dictatorship of the proletariat, preventing capitalist restoration and building socialism." In the light of the historical lesson of capitalist restoration in the Soviet Union and the real danger of such a restoration in China, Chairman Mao, with unmatched revolutionary courage and vision, personally launched and led the Great Proletarian Cultural Revolution which has no precedent in the history of the dictatorship of the proletariat. In the course of this momentous political revolution, our Party won the ninth, tenth and eleventh major struggles of line and demolished the three bourgeois headquarters of Liu Shaoqi, Lin Biao and the "gang of four." Through repeated battles our Party wrested from their hands that portion of power they had usurped. As a result, the dictatorship of the proletariat in our country is more consolidated than ever and the way is open to applying Chairman Mao's revolutionary line correctly and in its entirety. . . .
Through this political revolution Marxism-Leninism-Mao Zedong Thought has been disseminated, and in this great field of practice Chairman Mao's great theory of continuing the revolution under the dictatorship of the proletariat has been enriched and developed and been grasped more profoundly by the numerous cadres and the masses. China's Great Proletarian Cultural Revolution provides the international communist movement with fresh experience in combatting and guarding against revisionism, consolidating the dictatorship of the proletariat and preventing capitalist restoration. It makes the world proletariat much more confident of victory in their struggle for socialism and communism. Beyond any doubt, it will go down in the history of the dictatorship of the proletariat as a momentous innovation which will shine with increasing splendour with the passage of time. . . .
Thus, the smashing of the "gang of four" marks the triumphant conclusion of our first Great Proletarian Cultural Revolution, which lasted eleven years. . . .
The victorious conclusion of the first Great Proletarian Cultural Revolution certainly does not mean the end of class struggle or of the dictatorship of the proletariat. Throughout the historical period of socialism the struggle between the two classes, the proletariat and the bourgeoisie, and between the two roads, socialism and capitalism, continues to exist. This struggle will be protracted and tortuous and at times very sharp. Political revolutions in the nature of the Cultural Revolution will take place many times in the future.

b) Communique of the Third Plenum of the Eleventh Congress of the
   Chinese Communist Party, December 22, 1978

. . . Socialist modernization is . . . a profound and extensive revolution. There is still in our country today a small handful of counterrevolutionary elements and criminals who hate our socialist modernization and try to undermine it. We must not relax our class struggle against them, nor can we weaken the dictatorship of the proletariat. But as Comrade Mao Zedong pointed out, the large-scale turbulent class struggles of a mass character have in the main come to an end. . . . The Great Cultural Revolution should also be viewed historically, scientifically, and in a down-to-earth way. Comrade Mao Zedong initiated this great revolution primarily in the light of the fact that the Soviet Union had turned revisionist and for the purpose of opposing revisionism and preventing its occurrence. As for the shortcomings and mistakes in the actual course of the revolution, they should be summed up at the appropriate time as experience and lessons so as to unify the views of the whole Party and the people of the whole country. However, there should be no haste about this. . . .

c)  Speech by Ye Jianying on September 29, 1979 Commemorating the 30th Anniversary of the Founding of the People's Republic of China

     . . . In the ten years of the Cultural Revolution which began in 1966, our country went through a fierce struggle between revolution and counterrevolution. The Cultural Revolution was launched with the aim of preventing and combatting revisionism. For a proletarian party in power, it is of course necessary to be constantly on guard against going down the revisionist road characterized by oppression of the people at home and pursuit of hegemony abroad. But the point is that, at the time when the Cultural Revolution was launched, the estimate made of the situation within the Party and the country ran counter to reality, no accurate definition was given of revisionism, and an erroneous policy and method of struggle were adopted, deviating from the principle of democratic centralism. Driven by counterrevolutionary motives, Lin Biao, the gang of four and other conspirators and careerists exploited these errors, pushed things to the extreme and formulated and pursued an ultra-Left line. They engaged in "overthrowing everything and launching an all-out civil war," usurping the Party leadership and staging a coup to seize power. They attempted to undermine the foundation of our socialist system, subvert the dictatorship of the proletariat, destroy the leadership of the Party, adulterate Marxism-Leninism-Mao Zedong Thought and plunge our country once again into blood-baths and terror. The havoc which the counterrevolutionary gang wrought for ten long years spelt calamity for our people and constituted the most severe reversal to our socialist cause since the founding of the People's Republic. Their conspiratorial activities were entirely different in nature from the errors committed by our Party. They were the most vicious enemies of the entire people, and it was impossible to settle their case through inner-Party struggle. . . .

d)  "Resolution on Certain Questions in the History of Our Party Since the Founding of the People's Republic of China" (adopted by the Party Central Committee on June 27, 1981)

     The "cultural revolution," which lasted from May 1966 to October 1976, was responsible for the most severe setback and the heaviest losses suffered by the Party, the state and the people since the founding of the People's Republic. It was initiated and led by Comrade Mao Zedong. His principal theses were that many representatives of the

bourgeoisie and counterrevolutionary revisionists had sneaked into the
Party, the government, the army and cultural circles, and leadership in
a fairly large majority of organizations and departments was no longer
in the hands of Marxists and the people; that Party persons in power
taking the capitalist road had formed a bourgeois headquarters inside
the Central Committee which pursued a revisionist political and organizational line and had agents in all provinces, municipalities and
autonomous regions, as well as in all central departments; that since
the forms of struggle adopted in the past had not been able to solve
this problem, the power usurped by the capitalist-roaders could be
recaptured only by carrying out a great cultural revolution, by openly
and fully mobilizing the broad masses from the bottom up to expose
these sinister phenomena; and that the cultural revolution was in fact
a great political revolution in which one class would overthrow
another, a revolution that would have to be waged time and again. . . .
These erroneous "Left" theses, upon which Comrade Mao Zedong based himself in initiating the "cultural revolution," were obviously inconsis-
tent with the system of Mao Zedong Thought, which is the integration of
the universal principles of Marxism-Leninism with the concrete practice
of the Chinese revolution.  These theses must be thoroughly distin-
guished from Mao Zedong Thought.  As for Lin Biao, Jiang Qing and others, who were placed in important positions by Comrade Mao Zedong, the
matter is of an entirely different nature.  They rigged up two counterrevolutionary cliques in an attempt to seize supreme power and, taking
advantage of Comrade Mao Zedong's errors, committed many crimes behind
his back, bringing disaster to the country and the people. . . .
    Chief responsibility for the grave "Left" error of the "cultural
revolution," an error comprehensive in magnitude and protracted in
duration, does indeed lie with Comrade Mao Zedong.  But after all it
was the error of a great proletarian revolutionary.  Comrade Mao Zedong
paid constant attention to overcoming shortcomings in the life of the
Party and state.  In his later years, however, far from making a
correct analysis of many problems, he confused right and wrong and the
people with the enemy during the "cultural revolution."  While making
serious mistakes, he repeatedly urged the whole Party to study the
works of Marx, Engels and Lenin conscientiously and imagined that his
theory and practice were Marxist and that they were essential for the
consolidation of the dictatorship of the proletariat.  Herein lies his
tragedy.  While persisting in the comprehensive error of the "cultural
revolution," he checked and rectified some of its specific mistakes,
protected some leading Party cadres and non-Party public figures and
enabled some leading cadres to return to important leading posts.  He
led the struggle to smash the counterrevolutionary Lin Biao clique.  He
made major criticisms and exposures of Jiang Qing, Zhang Chunqiao and
others, frustrating their sinister ambition to seize supreme leadership.  All this was crucial to the subsequent and relatively painless
overthrow of the gang of four by our Party.  In his later years, he
still remained alert to safeguarding the security of our county, stood
up to the pressure of the social-imperialists, pursued a correct
foreign policy, firmly supported the just struggles of all peoples,
outlined the correct strategy of the three worlds and advanced the
important principle that China would never seek hegemony.  During the
"cultural revolution" our Party was not destroyed, but maintained its
unity.  The State Council and the People's Liberation Army were still
able to do much of their essential work.  The Fourth National People's
Congress . . . was convened and it determined the composition of the

State Council with Comrades Zhou Enlai and Deng Xiaoping as the core of its leadership. The foundation of China's socialist system remained intact and it was possible to continue socialist economic construction. Our country remained united and exerted a significant influence on international affairs. All these important facts are inseparable from the great role played by Comrade Mao Zedong as their respected and beloved great leader and teacher.

e) "Build Socialism with Chinese Characteristics," Article on the 90th Anniversary of Mao Zedong's Birth (26 December, 1983)

Comrade Mao Zedong was a great Marxist and a great proletarian revolutionary, strategist, and theorist. By integrating Marxism-Leninism with the specific practice of China's revolution, he performed eternally indelible feats for the founding and development of our party and the PLA, for the success of the cause of liberating various Chinese nationalities, and for the development of the cause of socialism. He made major contributions to the liberation of the oppressed nations of the world and to the cause of human progress. . . .

. . . Working with other veteran proletarian revolutionaries, Comrade Mao Zedong elimiated various practical and theoretical errors involving deviating from Marxism and turning Marxism into dogma, overcame numerous difficulties, and gradually formulated as well as exercised leadership over the implementation of the line, guiding principles, and policies which proceeded from China's real situation and which helped turn the revolution from a failure into a success. Only thus could we achieve great success in China's revolution.

During the socialist construction period, Comrade Mao Zedong continued to make major contributions to integrating the universal truths of Marxism-Leninism with China's specific practice. During the initial 7 years after the founding of the PRC, proceeding from China's basic socioeconomic characteristics, Comrade Mao Zedong and our party creatively opened up a path of socialist transformation suited to China's conditions. . . . In his speech "On Ten Major Relations" published in April 1956, Comrade Mao Zedong put forth the question of exploring a path of socialist construction suited to our national conditions. . . .

. . . These ideas proceeded from our country's concrete conditions and have been proved correct through the test of practice. They constitute the basic aspects of the living soul of Mao Zedong Thought, that is, they are reflections in socialist construction of the principles of seeking truth from facts, the mass line, and maintaining independence and keeping the initiative in our own hands. They have enriched and helped develop the theory of scientific socialism.

An important reason for Comrade Mao Zedong's mistakes of his later years is that he violated the ideological line of being realistic, which he himself always advocated. Our country's socialist cause experienced grave setbacks on two occasions, namely, during the "Great Leap Forward" period and the "Great Cultural Revolution." Then, not only was the new search for a path of socialist construction suited to our national conditions hindered, but many originally correct things were also criticized as errors. It was not until the 3rd Plenary Session of the 11th CPC Central Committee that order was brought out of chaos, a great historical change of our party was brought about, and the Marxist-Leninist ideological, political, and organizational lines were reestablished. . . .


Source:  a)  BR, August 26, 1977, pp. 38-39.
         b)  BR, December 29, 1978, p. 173.
         c)  BR, October 5, 1979, p. 15.
         d)  BR, July 6, 1981, pp. 20-21, 23-24.
         e)  Foreign Broadcast Information Service, China Report:  Red
             Flag, no. 24 (December 26, 1984), pp. 8-11.

## V.  FOREIGN RELATIONS AND NATIONAL DEFENSE

### 1.  Introduction and Suggested Readings

China in the Modern World   For over a century China has simultaneously faced three foreign policy problems.  The first problem is
strategic, avoiding both isolation and dependence.  The second is
diplomatic, gaining international recognition and respect as a full
member of the community of nations.  The third is military, protecting
national borders from external threat.

China's plight was probably most acute in the late 19th and early
20th centuries.  (See the chronologies of Sino-Soviet [V.2], Sino-
Japanese [V.3], and Sino-American relations [V.4] on pages 76-94.)  The
foreign powers treated China as a semi-colony, depriving it of
sovereign powers (such as collection of maritime customs and
prosecution of foreigners who committed crimes in the country).  Militarily, China was weak, the object of periodic episodes of "gunboat
diplomacy."  Strategically, it had to choose between isolation in the
face of a foreign "united front" or extreme dependence on one power.
There was some improvement under the Nationalists -- customs autonomy
was restored in the early 1930s and extraterritoriality ended in the
early 1940s -- but that progress came in the context of a major
Japanese invasion and anxious reliance on the United States.

With the Communist victory in 1949, the problems of foreign policy
persisted (see chronologies cited above).  International recognition
had to be gained anew.  New strategic choices had to be made.  And a
revolutionary army had to be transformed into a national defense force.
Although the United States did not initially view a "Communist China"
in a completely negative light, the outbreak of the Korean War in June
1950 led to a 20-year US diplomatic, strategic, and military
containment of the PRC.

Foreign Policy Strategy   Since 1949 China's foreign relations
have gone through three major phases.  In the 1950s Beijing "leaned" to
the side of the socialist camp (especially the Soviet Union) for trade,
economic assistance, and national security.  However, soon Mao and
other Chinese leaders became suspicious of Moscow's foreign policy
line.  They also resented the dependency involved in the relationship
and came to doubt whether the Soviet economic model could be adapted to
China.

The Sino-Soviet conflict began as early as 1956 and was public by
the early 1960s.  China adopted a foreign policy posture of opposition
to both the United States and the Soviet Union.  More isolated interna-
tionally, Beijing sought closer ties with the growing number of Third
World countries, chose Japan as its major trading partner, and began
developing nuclear weapons.  This second "anti-imperialist" stage of
Chinese foreign policy was most intense during the turmoil of the
Cultural Revolution.

With the Soviet invasion of Czechoslovakia in 1968 and a bloody incident on the Sino-Soviet border in early 1969, Chinese foreign policy entered yet another phase which has gone through many permutations over the past 16 years. The essence of this policy was the discarding, by Mao and Zhou, of the dual adversary strategy of the 1960s. The initial thrust of the policy was a de facto tilt towards the United States which developed from the Nixon trip to China in 1971 until the last years of the Carter administration. During these years, although the Chinese criticized both the Soviet Union and the United States, they seemed to be edging towards some type of strategic cooperation with Washington. With the Soviet invasion of Afghanistan and the Vietnamese invasion of Kampuchea, Sino-Soviet relations hit a low point.

Moreover, after Mao's death in 1976, the strategic elements of China's foreign policy took on an economic dimension. In the late 1970s and early 1980s, there was a dramatic increase in China's economic contacts with the world. China welcomed foreign investment, accepted foreign loans, and became an active member of the international economic community.

By 1981-82 the Chinese strategic, but not the economic, posture seemed to change. Beijing attacked both superpowers, had a series a bitter exchanges with the United States over Taiwan, and resumed talks with the Soviet Union. Some commentators spoke of an attempt by the Chinese leadership to achieve equidistance in their relations with Washington and Moscow.

However, as of the beginning of 1984, Sino-American relations seem to have achieved a certain degree of stability. Although there is more talk of trade and investment and less of strategic cooperation, the Reagan-Zhao visits and difficulties in the Sino-Soviet talks have improved the atmosphere of Sino-American relations.

Growing International Status    The change in China's strategic position facilitated its emergence as a full member of the international community. Gaining diplomatic recognition was a slow process (see chronological list of recognizing countries [V.9] on pages 103-104). In late 1949 and early 1950, all the Soviet-bloc countries and 15 European and Asian nations recognized the new regime. With the beginning of the Korean War and the American containment policy, the situation remained frozen till 1955. Over the course of the next decade a number of new Third World nations and France defied American opposition and recognized Beijing. After the turmoil of the Cultural Revolution (1966-69), as the United States was moving toward China strategically, all but a handful of countries have extended recognition. In 1971 China replaced the Nationalists in the United Nations. With the normalization of US-China relations in 1979 and China's entry into the World Bank, International Monetary Fund, the Olympics, etc., the process is now virtually complete.

The Chinese Military    China has the world's largest standing army, with about 4 million persons under arms and a much larger militia force in reserve. As early as 1927, the Communist Party began building armed forces to survive in a militarized political environment. By 1949 the People's Liberation Army (PLA) had grown to over 2.3 million soldiers, and its five major component armies had defeated the Nationalists in civil war and had occupied various parts of China. The PLA, which now includes other service arms as well, has two principal tasks: preserving China's national security and, when necessary, insuring domestic stability. To fulfill the former goal, China has occasionally crossed its borders to fight limited wars (in Korea in the early 1950s, in India in 1959 and 1962, and in Vietnam in 1979). The late 1960s, the period of greatest Cultural Revolution turmoil, was the principal instance of PLA intervention in domestic politics to preserve order.

The PLA, as the chart (V.10) on page 105 indicates, is under the dual supervision of the Party's Military Commission and the government's ministry of national defense and central military commission. PLA headquarters includes three general departments -- staff, logistics, and political -- and a number of specialized service arms. The country is geographically divided into military regions and military districts. The PLA leadership (see list [V.11] on page 106) is in the midst of a generational succession as veteran leaders of the revolution are replaced by officers whose central career experience has been the tumultuous politics of post-1949 China.

There are three types of ground force units. First are well-equipped main force units, administered by the military regions but controlled by the Military Commission. Military districts (usually equivalent to provinces) have charge over the second type, local force units which have border defense and internal defense functions. Third, units such as communes, factories, and mines maintain militia units. The disproportionate deployment of main force units in the Shenyang, Beijing, Lanzhou, and Urumqi Military Regions in the north and the Guangzhou and Kunming Military Regions in the south reflects China's concern about the USSR and its Vietnamese ally. (See table [V.12] on page 107.)

China's leaders have long debated the assets and liabilities of a "labor-intensive" army. In the wake of the Korean War, the PLA began with extensive Soviet help the modernization and professionalization of China's conventional forces. As China moved away from the Soviet economic model in the late 1950s, there was simultaneous deemphasis of military modernization. Revived was the strategy of "people's war," whereby an enemy is "lured in deep" and then overwhelmed by large numbers of politically conscious soldiers with only basic weapons. China did not eschew high technology completely -- a small nuclear arsenal was developed to provide a deterrence floor.

The "people's-war" strategy remained basically the orthodoxy for the rest of the Maoist era, though there were variations (military expenditures rose substantially during the period of Lin Biao's ascendancy but declined once Zhou Enlai and his economic planners regained influence). Following Mao's death, national defense was designated one of the "four modernizations," and the importance of "weapons" (relative to "men") has increased steadily. Technical training has received new encouragement and, as in the civilian sector, there is an emphasis of promoting technically proficient cadres.

However, the army's showing in Vietnam in 1979, corroborated by external estimates and limited foreign observation, suggests that the PLA's arsenal is inferior to those of the US and USSR (see table [V.13] on page 108). Nonetheless, the leadership has decided that modernization of China's conventional forces (to replace the equipment purchased from the Soviets in the 1950s) should be commensurate with general economic growth. Total military expenditures, the CIA estimates, amount to 5-10% of the GNP and represents about 15% of the nation's budget. There have been occasional signs of China interest in purchasing military equipment from the US and other western nations. However, quickfix purchases of advanced military technology from abroad will be constrained not only by the cost involved, but by the leadership's determination to remain basically militarily self-reliant. Still, for the foreseeable future, the PLA will be able to provide China with basic yet limited security.

## Suggested Readings

Barnett, A. Doak. China and the Major Powers in East Asia. Washington, DC: The Brookings Institution, 1977. A detailed analysis of China's relations with Japan, the United States, and the Soviet Union, focusing on the early 1970s. Discusses the possible emergence of a stable balance of power in North Asia.

Ch'en, Jerome. China and the West. Bloomington: Indiana University Press, 1979. A study of China's social and cultural contacts with the West from the early 19th century through the late 1930s and the consequences for China's modernization.

Clubb, O. Edmund. China and Russia: The Great Game. New York: Columbia University Press, 1971. A history of the clash of Russian and Chinese civilizations, in the 20th century and before.

Gittings, John. The Role of the Chinese Army. London: Oxford University Press, 1967. Analyzes the emergence of the People's Liberation Army.

_____. The World and China, 1922-1972. New York: Harper & Row, 1974. Examines the development of the CCP's view of the world, combining both Marxist-Leninist and Chinese elements.

Griffith, Samuel B., II. The Chinese People's Liberation Army. New York: McGraw-Hill, 1967. The history of the Chinese military.

Gurtov, Melvin and Hwang, Byong-Moo. China Under Threat: The Politics of Strategy and Diplomacy. Baltimore: The Johns Hopkins University Press, 1980. A study of the crises in Chinese foreign relations since the Korean War, emphasizing the domestic political context.

Harding, Harry. China and the U.S.: Normalization and Beyond. New York: Foreign Policy Association and China Council of The Asia Society, 1979. Discusses the issues now facing the US as it develops its relationship with China.

Isaacs, Harold R. Scratches on Our Minds. White Plains, NY: M. E. Sharpe, Inc., 1980. A classic study, published first in 1958, of the evolution of American images of China, both positive and negative.

Jansen, Marius B. Japan and China: From War to Peace, 1894-1972. Chicago: Rand McNally, 1975. A history of China and Japan from the first Sino-Japanese War to the normalization of PRC-Japanese relations.

Jones, DuPre, ed. China: U.S. Policy Since 1945. Washington, DC: Congressional Quarterly, Inc., 1980. An excellent source of analysis, chronology, documents, and statistics.

Lee, Chae-jin. Japan Faces China: Political and Economic Relations in the Postwar Era. Baltimore: Johns Hopkins Press, 1976. A thorough analysis of Sino-Japanese relations through normalization in 1972.

Nelsen, Harvey W. The Chinese Military System: An Organizational Study of the People's Liberation Army. Revised edition. Boulder, CO: Westview Press, 1981. A scholarly examination of the Chinese military from an organizational perspective.

Oksenberg, Michel, and Robert B. Oxnam, eds. Dragon and Eagle, United States-China Relations: Past and Future. New York: Basic Books, Inc., 1978. Essays on the historical context of contemporary US-China relations.

Schaller, Michael. The United States and China in the Twentieth Century. New York: Oxford University Press, 1979. An interpretive history of US-China relations.

Solomon, Richard H., ed. The China Factor: Sino-American Relations and the Global Scene. Englewood Cliffs, NJ: Prentice-Hall, 1981. China's role in the issues of American foreign policy.

Whitson, William. The Chinese High Command: A History of Communist Military Politics, 1927-71. New York: Praeger, 1971. An extensive scholarly treatment of Communist military history, focusing on the factional divisions within the military and their impact on politics in general.

Yahuda, Michael. Towards The End of Isolationism: China's Foreign Policy After Mao. London: MacMillan Press, 1983. An overview of China's recent foreign policy from the perspectives of both geopolitics and domestic society.

## 2. Chronology of Sino-Soviet Relations

17th-18th    Russian migration eastwards, spearheaded by the Cossacks,
centuries:   leads to military confrontation between the Chinese and
             Russian troops in the 17th century.  Treaties are signed at
             Nerchinsk (1689) and Kiakhta (1727) to delineate Sino-
             Russian boundaries and to establish limited commercial and
             diplomatic exchanges.

1858-60:     Through military occupations, ratified by so-called "unequal
             treaties," Russia takes all the land north of the Amur River
             and east of the Ussuri River.  This land was later called
             the Maritime Province, and has been a source of Chinese
             hostility towards Russia to the present day.

late 19th    Although China manages to maintain most of its territories
century:     in the westernmost province of Xinjiang, Russian interest in
             East Asia increases through the late 19th century, particu-
             larly with the building of the Trans-Siberian Railway in the
             1890s.

1900-05:     Russia occupies part of Manchuria in the wake of the Boxer
             Rebellion of 1900.  This becomes a major cause of the
             Russo-Japanese War which resulted in the Russian defeat by
             Japan in 1905.

1917-20:     The Bolshevik Revolution of 1917 stirs considerable interest
             among Chinese students and intellectuals, particularly in
             the year 1919 when the Versailles Treaty cedes former German
             concessions in China to the Japanese (thus casting doubts on
             Western liberalism and Wilsonian idealism).

1920-27:     Comintern agents assist in the development of the Chinese
             Communist Party (CCP).  But the major thrust of Soviet
             policy developed by Stalin is to build Sun Yat-sen's
             Nationalist Party into a strong political and military
             movement allied with the Soviet Union.  Stalin helps foster
             a CCP-Nationalist alliance, the first "united front," which
             lasts until 1927.  In April of that year, Chiang Kai-shek
             begins the "White Terror" in Shanghai and other cities,
             arresting or killing many of his Communist allies and
             terminating the short-lived united front.

1927-35:     In the CCP underground in Shanghai, Stalin's influence
             remains strong.  But Mao Zedong works independently to build
             a peasant-based guerrilla movement in southeastern China.
             During the Long March (1934-35), Mao emerges as the leader
             of the CCP.

1935-36:     Fearing encirclement by Japan and Germany, the Comintern
             called upon the CCP and other Communist Parties to form
             "united fronts" with other nationalistic forces.  Having
             retreated to the Yan'an area in northwest China, the CCP
             gradually adopts the united front policy.  When Chiang
             Kai-shek is kidnapped by a recalcitrant general in Xian in

December 1936, the CCP initially favors executing him.
However, ultimately Zhou Enlai helped to negotiate his
release and these talks provide the basis for the second
united front with the Kuomintang. Soviet policy is to
condemn the kidnappers and support Chiang. During the rest
of the Yan'an period, Mao creates a strong and independent
movement in the northwest, as the anti-Japanese "second
united front" with the Nationalists gradually deteriorates.
From 1937-39 the USSR provides Chiang with over 4,000
advisers and over $250 million in aid. During the Second
World War, small numbers of Soviet agents are stationed in
Yan'an, while most diplomatic and military negotiations in-
volve the Soviets with the Chinese Nationalists.

1945:    In the Yalta Agreement and subsequent negotiations, Stalin
         pledges to deal only with the Nationalists. Soviet troops
         are permitted into Manchuria for possible involvement in the
         war against Japan. After V-J Day, Soviet troops block the
         Nationalists' advance into Manchuria and strip the region of
         many military and industrial supplies. The Soviet armies
         also facilitate Communist entry into certain areas.

1946-49: Soviet troops withdraw from Manchuria in 1946, and Moscow
         remains aloof during the Chinese civil war. In 1949 Stalin
         admits his surprise over the rapid CCP military success, and
         Moscow extends diplomatic recognition to the newly estab-
         lished People's Republic of China (PRC) in October 1949.

1950:    Sino-Soviet Treaty of Friendship, Alliance, and Mutual
         Assistance is signed. During the 1950s, the Soviets provide
         limited loans to the PRC and send 10,000 technical advisers
         to assist in China's economic development.

late     Beginnings of the Sino-Soviet split. In 1956 the Chinese
1950s:   criticize "de-Stalinization" movement and support Gomulka's
         Poland. They also disapprove of the Soviet use of force in
         suppressing the Hungarian revolt and of Khrushchev's policy
         of "peaceful coexistence" with the United States. Soviets
         are reluctant to provide PRC with nuclear weaponry, and do
         not support the PRC in the Quemoy-Matsu Crisis (1958) and
         the Sino-Indian border conflict (1959).

1960-63: Full-scale Sino-Soviet split. Led by Mao, the Chinese de-
         nounce the Soviet foreign policy line and the Soviets with-
         draw all technical advisers from the PRC in 1960. Chinese
         criticize Soviet handling of the Cuban Missile Crisis and
         signing of Nuclear Test Ban Treaty. The Soviets remain
         neutral during the Sino-Indian War of 1962. The two sides
         compete for influence among other Communist Parties and
         emerging Third World countries. Sino-Soviet trade declines
         sharply.

1966-68: Soviets criticize Cultural Revolution as the work of "Mao
         Zedong and his group." After the Soviet embassy is besieged
         in Beijing, Soviet and Chinese diplomats are withdrawn from
         each country. Both countries increase troop strength along

the Sino-Soviet border. In August 1968 the Soviet Union invades Czechoslovakia, saying later that it was obligated to do so because "socialism" had been fundamentally attacked.

1969: In March armed clashes develop between Soviet and Chinese troops over an island on the Ussuri River.

1970-75: While the propaganda battle continues, both sides increase troop strengths along the Sino-Soviet border, to the point that each side has about one million troops. Both sides pursue rapprochement with the United States. China fears that the US will either "collude" with the Soviet Union or "appease" its policy of "superpower hegemonism." South Vietnam falls (April 1975), and North Vietnam emerges as a Soviet-leaning power on China's border.

1976: In the wake of Mao Zedong's death, Moscow eases anti-Chinese propaganda as a gesture to the new leadership, but China's propaganda offensive against the Soviets continues unabated.

1977: China's leadership holds to the Zhou-Mao strategy of the early 1970s. Moscow resumes its verbal attacks in April, calling China a "threat to world peace." In October, after eight years of talks, the two countries reach a limited agreement on rules of navigation on the Ussuri River.

1978: In February the Soviets make a major proposal for the improvement of relations with China. The Chinese reject the offer in March. As Sino-Vietnamese relations deteriorate (over the issues of Cambodia and the overseas Chinese in Vietnam), China charges the Soviet Union with responsibility for the deterioration. As part of its effort to build an anti-Soviet "global united front," China concludes a Peace and Friendship Treaty with Japan (August) and agrees to normalize relations with the United States (December). Vietnam and the Soviet Union conclude a treaty of friendship and cooperation, and Vietnam invades Cambodia (November).

1979: Deng Xiaoping visits the United States (January-February); Moscow accuses him of making "slanderous" remarks about its role in the world. On February 17 the PRC invades Vietnam, and withdraws by March 16 after Vietnam agrees to negotiations. In April China announces that it will not renew the 1950 treaty of friendship with the Soviet Union but calls for talks to reduce bilateral tensions. Amid propaganda charges and countercharges, the talks begin in September. The Soviet Union invades Afghanistan (December).

1980: In the wake of the Soviet invasion, US Defense Secretary Brown visits China (January). Each side pledges "parallel action" to deal with the challenge; China vows to continue aid to the Afghan rebels; the US encourages Chinese aid for Thailand should it be invaded by Vietnam; and the US offers to sell China non-lethal military equipment. China refuses to resume the recessed Sino-Soviet talks (January). To protest the Soviet invasion of Afghanistan, China joins the

Olympic boycott (February). China tests an intercontinental ballistic missile with a range that includes all points within the Soviet Union (May).

1981:     Moscow charges that the US liberalization of arms sales policy vis-a-vis China is a sign of deepening Sino-American "conspiracy" and a "serious threat to Southeast Asia." In response to news reports that the US and China have engaged in joint monitoring of Soviet missile tests, Moscow claims that the Chinese are becoming "voluntary agents of the imperialist intelligence services" (June). As Sino-American tensions over the Taiwan issue increase, the Soviet Union proposes to China that the two sides resume talks on improving relations, stalled since early 1980 (September). Amid continuing mutual recriminations, the Chinese put the Soviets off saying that "adequate preparations should be made before negotiations can be resumed."

1982:     Trade agreement is signed during April in Beijing; trade expected to increase 45% to its highest point since 1963. Chinese reject Leonid Brezhev's comments affirming China's socialist status and calling for an improvement in Sino-Soviet relations (May). In September Vice Premier Wan Li claims that the Chinese seek to settle problems with the Soviet Union. He also discloses that talks had been held with the Russians in August. Amid growing rumors, formal talks are held in October at the deputy foreign minister level between Leonid Ilyichev and Qian Qichen. It is agreed to hold the talks in each capital, alternately. In November, with the death of Brezhnev, the Chinese express some optimism regarding the future of Sino-Soviet relations.

1983:     In March the new foreign minister Wu Xueqian expresses concern regarding the transfer of Soviet SS-20 missiles from Europe as the second round of Sino-Soviet talks take place in Moscow. The Chinese continue to stress the three obstacles to any normalization in Sino-Soviet relations: the Vietnamese occupation of Kampuchea, the Soviet occupation of Afghanistan, and the concentration of Soviet troops on the Chinese border. However, one Soviet official indicates that the two countries had agreed to increase two-way trade to one billion dollars by 1983. In a June visit to Yugoslavia, Hu Yaobang suggests that unless Soviet policy changes in regard to Kampuchea, there could be a confrontation between the two nations. Sino-Soviet propoganda attacks heat up to their highest level since 1982. In October the third round of Sino-Soviet talks open with the Chinese emphasizing the SS-20 issue — suggesting the addition of a fourth obstacle in Sino-Soviet relations. However, talk of increased trade continues.

1984:     The year begins with sharp attacks on the Soviet Union in the Chinese press. In February, however, the Chinese send a high-ranking delegation led by Vice Premier Wan Li to Yuri Andropov's funeral; the Chinese foreign minister had led the delegation to Brezhev's funeral. In the same month, a trade

agreement is signed providing for 1.16 billion dollars of
two-way trade.    In March the fourth round of Sino-Soviet
talks is completed and Deputy Prime Minister Arkhipov's
visit to China is set for May.    In April a Soviet friendship
delegation meets with its Chinese counterparts.    However, in
early May, soon after the Reagan visit, the Arkhipov visit
is suddenly postponed by Moscow.    The official explanation
given is that greater time was needed to prepare for the
trip.

## 3. Chronology of Sino-Japanese Relations

1868:    With the Meiji Restoration Japan begins its program of modernization through selective borrowing from the West. In the process it begins to move out of the orbit of China, its nominal suzerain, from which it drew cultural inspiration in previous centuries.

1870s:    Japan establishes control over the Ryukyu Island group (nominally under Chinese domain), and begins to put pressure on Chinese-controlled Taiwan and Korea.

1894-95:    Sino-Japanese War. Japan soundly beats China, annexes Taiwan, severs Korea from Chinese control, and shocks Chinese political leaders and intellectuals into a realization of the country's weakness. In the wake of the defeat, Chinese students begin going to Japan to study.

1902:    Establishment of Anglo-Japanese Alliance.

1905:    Russo-Japanese War. Japan defeats Russia, the first loss by a Western power to an Asian one. Japan inherits the Liaodong Peninsula, previously held by Russia, and begins construction of the South Manchurian Railway. The flow of Chinese students to Japan increases to more than 10,000 per year.

1910:    Japan annexes Korea.

1915:    With the European powers preoccupied with World War I, Japan presents the Chinese government of Yuan Shikai with the notorious Twenty-One Demands, which, if accepted, would have given Japan a greatly enhanced position in China. Leads to a nationalistic protest.

1919:    Japan's attempt to assume German rights in Shandong province arouses intense nationalistic protest in China — the May Fourth Movement.

1920s:    Japan pursues a generally moderate policy towards China, but remains protective of its interests in Manchuria and willing to intervene militarily if provoked.

1931-33:    Japan gradually takes control of northeast China, first by occupying Fengtian, Jilin, and Heilongjiang provinces in the months following the Mukden (Shenyang) Incident (September 1931); second, by occupying Jehol province in early 1933 and threatening north China. In 1932 Japan establishes the puppet state of Manchukuo, with the last Qing emperor (Henry Pu-yi) as its nominal leader. The Japanese occupation provokes another round of Chinese nationalism, but Chiang Kai-shek is unwilling to commit his forces to resist the aggression.

1935:    The Japanese military forces the end of the formal Nationalist presence in North China and the Nationalists later consent to autonomous political bodies more amenable to Japanese pressure. This provokes new anti-Japanese protest under the banner of the December 9th Movement.

1936: In the midst of gradual preparations to challenge Japan, Chiang is kidnapped in Xian. He moves closer to a policy of resistance in a united front with the CCP.

1937: War with Japan begins in August after a military incident at Marco Polo Bridge outside Beijing on July 7. The second united front with the Communists is consummated. Japan captures Nanjing (the Nationalist capital) in December.

1938: The Japanese take the central China city of Wuhan, thus assuming complete control of the main transportation arteries of lowland China and driving the Nationalists into west China.

1939-44: The conflict persists, usually at low levels, with the Japanese trying in vain to eliminate guerrilla resistance from the CCP and others and to build political support through puppet governments. The Nationalist-CCP united front gradually dissolves as the Communists extend their influence throughout north China.

1945: Japan surrenders; Taiwan comes under Nationalist control; the CCP and the Nationalists begin the contest for control of occupied China.

1950: The victorious CCP regards American-occupied Japan as a source of potential danger and signs a defense pact with the Soviet Union specifically directed at American-supported Japan. Chinese fears are confirmed when, after the start of the Korean War, Japan becomes the principal US staging area.

1951-52: Japan and the US conclude peace and security treaties. As part of the latter, Japan is bound to conclude a peace treaty and establish diplomatic relations with the Nationalists on Taiwan.

1952-57: China tries to develop trade, cultural, and political ties with a variety of groups in Japan in the hope that they would pressure Tokyo to be more independent of Washington.

1957-60: In response to Prime Minister Kishi's strengthening of Japan's ties with Taiwan, China creates insurmountable obstacles to trade, supports left-wing parties opposed to the ruling Liberal Democratic Party, and calls for the end to the US-Japan security treaty.

1960-62: In the wake of the Great Leap Forward and the withdrawal of Soviet technical aid, China turns to Japan as an economic alternative, dropping previous political conditions. Trade grows with "friendly" Japanese firms and through a more formal barter agreement.

1964:       Japan and China exchange trade missions. But when a
            Japanese company seeks Japanese Export-Import Bank backing
            for the sale of a synthetic textile factory, Taiwan objects
            and Japan backs down. Trade grows to $310 million.

1965:       Prime Minister Sato affirms a dual policy of maintaining
            relations with Taiwan and promoting contact with the PRC.

1966-68:    Trade grows to $621 million in 1966, then declines during
            the turmoil of the Cultural Revolution; Japanese corres-
            pondents and businessmen are harrassed or expelled.

1969-71:    As the US withdraws from Vietnam and returns Okinawa to
            Japan, China fears that a pro-Taiwan Japan is moving to fill
            the military vacuum. Tokyo's view, expressed in November
            1969, that Taiwan was "important" and Korea "essential" to
            Japanese security prompts a Chinese propaganda campaign
            against Japanese "remilitarization." China refuses to trade
            with Japanese firms that have business interests in Taiwan
            or South Korea (1970). In July 1971 Richard Nixon angers
            Japan by beginning rapprochement with China without
            informing Japan. Sino-Japanese trade rises to $900 million.

1972:       China sends a trade mission to Japan, the first in six
            years; two-way trade reaches $1.1 billion. Kakuei Tanaka
            becomes prime minister of Japan (July) and travels to
            Beijing (September) to normalize relations. Japan recog-
            nizes China, says that it "understands and respects" China's
            claim that Taiwan is a part of China, and develops informal
            mechanisms to continue relations with Taiwan.

1973:       China ends the trade restrictions imposed in 1970 (March),
            and diplomatic relations begin formally (April). Trade
            soars to just over $2 billion, and agreement is reached on a
            three-year trade pact which includes Japanese most-favored-
            nation treatment of China (August).

1974:       Japan and China sign a civil air agreement (April) and a
            shipping agreement (November). Trade reaches $3.3 billion.

1975:       A fishery agreement is concluded (August). Trade climbs to
            $3.8 billion.

1976-77:    With the death of Mao Zedong and its aftermath, Sino-
            Japanese trade drops to around $3 billion.

1978:       An eight-year trade agreement is concluded whereby China
            will send coal and oil to Japan in return for technology and
            finished goods, to total $10 billion. The two countries
            finally conclude a Treaty of Peace and Friendship that
            includes a clause opposing "hegemonism" (August). The trade
            agreement is extended by five years and $20 billion (Septem-
            ber). Throughout the fall Japanese firms reach a number of
            major business deals with China. Deng Xiaoping visits Japan
            to sign the Peace and Friendship Treaty; television coverage
            of the trip exposes Chinese to the Japanese standard of

living (October).  Two-way trade equals $5.1 billion.

1979:  Unsure of its ability to finance a major import program,
China suspends 22 major contracts with Japanese firms, worth
$2.5 billion (February).  The target value of the trade
agreement is more than doubled (March).  Because the
Japanese Export-Import Bank extends $1.7 billion in credits,
China restores 21 of the suspended contracts (May).  In
December Prime Minister Ohira visits China and reaches
agreement on a $1.5 billion Japanese government loan to
China and on joint exploration and exploitation of oil and
natural gas in the Bohai Gulf.  Total trade is $6.7 billion.

1980:  Hua Guofeng makes a state visit to Japan (May).  Late in the
year China announces suspension of construction on three
petrochemical plants and the second stage of the Baoshan
steel mill (near Shanghai), in which Japanese firms have
substantial interest.  Two-way trade climbs over $9 billion.

1981:  China announces that it is cancelling the four projects
postponed in late 1980, and postponing completion of the
first stage of Baoshan (January).  The total cancellation
amounts to around $1.5 billion and threatens to damage
Sino-Japanese relations even though China promises to pay
compensation.  China announces the resumption of the
petrochemical projects and asks Japan for a $2.68 billion
loan (April).  Japan offers a $1.3 billion loan package to
revive the first stage of the Baoshan steel mill and one
petrochemical plant.  China accepts in principle and, in
September agrees to compensate Japanese firms for costs
involved in the cancellations.  Gu Mu travels to Tokyo for
talks.  Both sides see no major issues separating them.
Two-way trade for the year is 10.4 billion dollars; 24% of
China's total trade.

1982:  In May Zhao Ziyang visits Japan.  He proposes terms for the
further development of Sino-Japanese trade and economic
cooperation.  In July relations take a turn for the worse as
the Chinese attack a revised history text which they feel
distorts the history of Japan's war in China.  The Chinese
Foreign Ministry presents this as violating the spirit of
the Sino-Japanese 1972 joint statement and warns of revived
Japanese militarism.  The textbook controversy is settled
during the fall and discussions held regarding the expansion
of economic relations between the two countries.  Amidst all
this controversy, Japanese loans to China are increased but
two-way trade drops to 8.8 billion dollars.

1983:  In February Susumu Nikaido comes to Beijing to brief the
Chinese on Japanese Prime Minister Nakasoni's talks in the
United States and South Korea.  Premier Zhao and Foreign
Minister Wu warn that Japan should consider the concerns of
her neighbors when building Japan's military might.  In
February Minister Chen Muhua arrives in Japan to discuss
increased economic cooperation.  In April and May two more
Japanese loan packages are announced.  In October an oil

platform pact is announced.  Hu Yaobang visits Japan in late November.  Year-end trade figures indicate a rise back to 10 billion dollars in two-way trade.

1984:      In March Japanese Prime Minister Yasuhiro Nakasone is warmly welcomed in Beijing.  He discusses a broad range of strategic issues and pledges 2.1 million dollars in credits to help finance capital construction.

4. <u>Chronology of Sino-American Relations</u>

1784: First American ship, the "Empress of China," calls at Chinese port; Sino-American trade begins, mainly in US food crops (maize, sweet potato, peanuts, tobacco) and Chinese arts, crafts, and textiles.

1811: First American missionary arrives in China. Their ranks grow rapidly in the latter half of the century to about 8,000 in 1925.

1844: Treaty of Wangxia (Wang-hsia) signed by the United States and China, granting America same rights imposed upon China by Britain after the Opium War (1839–42) -- extraterritoriality, most-favored-nation treatment, and establishment of commercial centers, churches, and hospitals in five ports.

1850: Beginning of two decades of substantial Chinese immigration into the United States.

1861: US Secretary of State Seward sends Anson Burlingame as a first minister to China with instructions to cooperate with other foreign powers in assuring equal economic opportunity for all.

1864: Roughly 10,000 Chinese are recruited to work on the first transcontinental railroad across the United States.

1868–70: Anson Burlingame conducts a worldwide tour to help revise treaties with foreigners in the hope of bringing "the shining banners of Western civilization" to China.

1872–81: A total of 120 Chinese students travels to the United States.

1882: Congress passes and President Arthur signs into law a bill to suspend Chinese immigration for ten years.

1892: Congress promulgates Geary Act, another exclusion law, which also requires Chinese to register and carry identification.

1899–
1900 Secretary of State John Hay plays the leading role in having Western powers endorse the "Open Door Policy," which upholds the "equality of economic opportunity" for foreigners, and promises to protect the "territorial and administrative integrity" of China.

1900: America provides 2,100 men for an Allied force which suppresses the Boxer Rebellion and occupies the city of Beijing. In 1901 the United States is granted part of the indemnity paid by China because of the Boxer Rebellion. US later returns the money to China in the form of scholarships for selected Chinese to study in America.

1902:    US exports to China reach $25 million, and investments total $19.7 million.

1905:    Students in China initiate boycotts of American goods, protesting US immigration restrictions.

1912:    US is first Western power to recognize the newly proclaimed Republic of China.

1915:    By this time 1,200 Chinese students are studying in US universities.

1917-18: High tide of Chinese student interest in America prompted by Woodrow Wilson's idealism, and of Chinese hopes for an end to foreign imperialism through "self-determination." John Dewey lectures at Beijing (Peking) University and wins many adherents to his philosophy of pragmatism.

1919:    Widespread anger and protests by Chinese students and intellectuals concerning the Versailles Treaty, which ceded former German concessions in China to the Japanese. This "May Fourth Movement" engendered much hostility against the United States and turned many eyes towards Russia, which had just experienced its October Revolution.

1921-22: At initiative of US, treaty powers hold Washington Conference to work out postwar settlement of Far East territorial claims; Japan obliged to withdraw from Chinese territory.

1928:    US recognizes Nanjing (Nanking) government of Chiang Kai-shek and restores tariff autonomy to China.

early
1930's   Beset with problems at home and wary of foreign involvement, the US does little to halt the Japanese penetration of China. The Silver Purchase Act (1934), passed for domestic political reasons, seriously complicates Nationalist efforts to rebound from the Great Depression.

1937-41: Although formally neutral in the war between China and Japan, the US provides China with economic aid and diplomatically takes an increasingly anti-Japanese line.

1941:    Claire Chennault organizes "Flying Tigers" to aid the Chinese against the Japanese. Pearl Harbor bombed, bringing the US into war as China's ally. Chiang Kai-shek becomes "Supreme Commander of the China

Theater" and General "Vinegar Joe" Stilwell is named his chief of staff.

1943: US formally rescinds extraterritoriality in China. US insists, at Moscow Conference of the Allied Powers, that China be included as one of the Big Four. Madame Chiang Kai-shek tours United States and addresses Congress. US later grants China a $300 million "morale-booster" loan.

1944: Chiang forces resignation of General Stilwell, who is replaced by General Albert Wedemeyer. Ambassador Patrick Hurley arrives in China on a mission to maximize the war effort (in the face of complaints of Chiang's laxness), and to negotiate improved relations between the Nationalist government and the Chinese Communist Party.

1945: War with Japan ends. At US urging, Chiang and Mao Zedong sign a ceasefire agreement, but internal fighting continues. US troops involved in minor skirmishes with Communists. General George Marshall, architect of the "Marshall Plan" to aid Europe, arrives in China to try to effect a coalition government between the Nationalists and the Communists.

1947: Marshall Mission fails; the civil war intensifies. Congress approves $400 million aid bill for Nationalists (total postwar aid amounts to $2.5 billion). Wedemeyer report (made public in 1949) bluntly indicts Nationalist government for its failures; US continues to support Chiang.

1949: Government of the People's Republic of China (PRC) established. Nationalists abandon mainland and flee to Taiwan. State Department "White Paper" on China ascribes Nationalist defeat to corruption and incompetence. US follows interim policy of withholding recognition from new government while attempting to disassociate itself from the Nationalists and wait for the "dust to settle."

1950: With increasing harassment of Americans in China, US withdraws all official personnel, closes embassy and consulates. North Korean invasion of South Korea. Truman reverses policy and orders the US Seventh Fleet into Taiwan Straits to prevent any Communist attack. China enters Korean War as UN forces (over half of which are US troops) approach the Yalu River and Chinese territory. US freezes Chinese assets in the US and begins a trade embargo.

1953: Korean Armistice; several thousand US troops remain in South Korea.

1954: In December US and Nationalist government sign Mutual Defense Treaty, ratified by Congress in February 1955.

1955:    US-PRC ambassadorial-level talks begin in Geneva, later to be moved to Warsaw where they continue intermittently for 15 years.  State Department rejects Chinese proposal that Dulles and Zhou Enlai meet to discuss "Taiwan and other problems," citing continued imprisonment of 13 Americans in Beijing.

1956:    In speech to the National People's Congress, Zhou states that "traditional friendships" between the American and Chinese people will eventually lead to US diplomatic recognition of China.

1958:    Chinese precipitate crisis by shelling Nationalist-held offshore islands of Quemoy and Matsu.

1962:    China begins a series of warnings against US intrusion into or over Chinese territory in connection with war in Vietnam.

1965:    American bombing of North Vietnam provokes strong PRC reaction in anti-US statements and increased aid to Hanoi.

1966:    Senate Foreign Relations Committee holds hearings on US-China relations.  President Johnson declares the "US will persist in efforts to reduce tensions between the two countries" (US and PRC). At the United Nations, Ambassador Goldberg announces support of Italian proposal to take a fresh look at seating China in the UN.

1969:    Secretary of State Rogers implies United States is prepared to accept principle of "peaceful coexistence" with PRC.  US eases restrictions on American travel to China for scholars, journalists, students, scientists, and members of Congress.  US suspends Seventh Fleet patrols of Taiwan Straits.  Trade restrictions eased, permitting foreign subsidiaries of US companies to trade with the PRC in non-strategic goods.  Sino-Soviet border conflicts encourage Beijing to explore rapprochement with non-Communist powers.

1970:    Mao Zedong tells American journalist Edgar Snow that he would welcome a visit by President Nixon to Beijing. US-PRC talks resume in Warsaw but cancelled after two meetings by Chinese in protest over US invasion of Cambodia.  US announces it will support entry of PRC into UN as long as it is not at the Nationalists' expense.  Selective licensing of direct exports to China authorized.

1971:    State Department abolishes travel restrictions to China. US table tennis team invited to Beijing in April.  In July Henry Kissinger travels secretly to Beijing; a few days later President Nixon announces he will visit China in 1972 to seek "normalization of relations between the two countries." UN votes to seat People's Republic of China and expel Nationalists' representative (October).

1972: President Nixon makes his trip to Beijing, and Shanghai Communique is issued (see pages 95-96). The US acknowledges and does not challenge that all Chinese maintain that "there is but one China and that Taiwan is a part of China"; agrees to progressively reduce its forces and military installations on Taiwan "as the tension in the area diminishes," but states its interest in "a peaceful settlement of the Taiwan question by the Chinese themselves."

1973: Liaison offices are established in Beijing and Washington, and exchanges between the US and PRC gradually increase.

1974-76: Sino-American relations lose momentum for a variety of reasons. Succession conflicts in both the US (Watergate and the 1976 election) and in China (the deaths of Zhou and Mao) make normalization of relations impossible. Because of the recession and political factors, trade declines to $336 million in 1976 after hitting a peak of almost $1 billion in 1974. China criticizes US-Soviet detente and wonders what role the US will play in Asia after the fall of South Vietnam (1975). President Ford visits China in December 1975 without concrete result.

1977: At the beginning of his administration, President Jimmy Carter reaffirms that normalization of US-PRC relations is US policy. In August Secretary of State Vance visits Beijing for an "exploratory" exchange of views with Chinese officials. One month later, Vice Premier Deng Xiaoping terms the trip a "setback" in Sino-American relations, but also notes the PRC's recognition of "special conditions" in the US relationship with Taiwan.

1978: In May National Security Adviser Zbigniew Brzezinski visits Beijing to discuss strategic and bilateral issues. In July President Carter's science adviser Frank Press leads a delegation of government science administrators to China. On December 15, after five months of secret negotiations, President Carter announces the normalization of relations between the US and the PRC. Mutual recognition is extended, and diplomatic relations are to begin on January 1, 1979. Formal US relations with Taiwan are ended, but trade and cultural relations are to continue. The US reiterates its interest in a "peaceful resolution of the Taiwan question" (see pages 97-98).

1979: China begins a campaign for "peaceful reunification" of Taiwan with the mainland. Vice Premier Deng Xiaoping visits the United States on a nine-day tour (January-February). Agreements are signed on a variety of scientific and cultural exchanges; American consulates are to be established in Shanghai and Guangzhou, Chinese ones in Houston and San Francisco. The two sides state different points of view on the Soviet Union. When the PRC invades Vietnam in mid-February, the US calls for a withdrawal of Chinese troops. On March 2 the US and China initial an agreement settling the issue of frozen Chinese assets and blocked American claims, deadlocked for 30 years. After amendments that provoke Chinese criticism, Congress passes and President Carter signs (April 10) the Taiwan Relations Act, which establishes the American Institute in Taiwan to handle future relations, and specifies future US obligations to the island (see pages 98-100). In May the US and China sign the claims-assets agreement and initial a trade agreement. In the absence of an agreement on Chinese textile exports, the US unilaterally imposes quotas. The US-PRC trade pact is signed (July). In August Vice President Mondale visits China. He offers $2 billion in Export-Import Bank credits over five years, signs an expanded cultural agreement and a preliminary hydropower agreement. The US Supreme Court upholds President Carter's authority to terminate the mutual defense treaty with Taiwan (December).

1980: In the context of the Soviet invasion of Afghanistan, Defense Secretary Brown visits China. Both sides agree to take coordinated, parallel actions vis-a-vis Pakistan and Thailand (threatened by Vietnam). The US offers to sell China selected non-lethal military equipment. Congress approves the US-PRC trade agreement, thus granting most-favored-nation treatment to China (January). The two sides agree to take separate but "mutually reinforcing" actions to counter the Soviet invasion of Afghanistan, and reach final agreement on cooperation in developing China's hydroelectric power (March). Vice Premier Geng Biao visits Washington and selected military installations, and the US allows China to purchase air-defense radar, helicopters, and transport planes, and authorizes American companies to build electronics and helicopter factories in China (May). China protests the US sale of defensive military equipment to Taiwan (June). The US and China conclude a textile agreement (July). Republican presidential candidate Ronald Reagan elicits protests from Beijing by suggesting that he would restore official relations with Taiwan (August). The two sides sign agreements on establishment of consulates, airline and maritime service, and textile import quotas (September). The US grants Taiwan's representatives the privileges and immunities normally accorded diplomats, provoking a PRC protest (October).

1981: February  After suggestions that it might upgrade relations with Taiwan, the Reagan Administration announces that it will honor the "solemn undertakings" made by the United States at the time of normalization.

The PRC downgrades relations with the Netherlands after Holland sells a submarine to Taiwan. China's action is seen as a signal to the US not to supply Taiwan with advanced military equipment.

June  After a three-day visit to Beijing, Secretary of State Alexander Haig reveals that the US will consider on a case-by-case basis the sale of lethal weapons to the PRC.  Haig is said to feel that there is "no urgency" for the US to sell advanced fighter aircraft to Taiwan.  US Government sources report that the US and the PRC have cooperated in secretly monitoring Soviet missile tests.

September  The US and China sign a new, two-year cultural exchange agreement.  Beijing renews and elaborates its proposal to Taipei on reunification, by which it would tolerate the political, economic, and military status quo on the island in return for Nationalist recognition of PRC sovereignty.  Taipei immediately rejects the offer.

November  China steps up its warnings to Washington not to sell advanced fighters to Taiwan.

1982:  January  Assistant Secretary of State John Holdridge travels to Beijing to inform the Chinese government that the US will not upgrade the fighter aircraft sold to Taiwan.  Negotiations begin on the future of US arms sales to the island.

April  Ronald Reagan sends letters to Vice Chairman Deng Xiaoping and Premier Zhao, enunciating the basic American approach to US-China relations.

May  Vice President Bush visits Beijing in an effort to remove the obstacles to a settlement of the Taiwan arms issue.

August  On the 17th, the US and PRC governments issue a joint communique in which the PRC terms peaceful reunification a "fundamental policy"; the US pledges that arms sales to Taiwan will not increase in "quality or quantity" and ultimately decline (see pages 101-102).

December  Vice Minister of Foreign Affairs Zhang Wenjin appointed ambassador to the United States.

1983:  February  Secretary of State Schultz, in Beijing for four days, meets with Deng Xiaoping, Zhao Ziyang, Wu Xueqian, and Zhang Aiping; he is lectured by the Chinese on US stand on Taiwan, including arms sales and restrictions on imports of textiles.

April  Chinese embassy in Washington lodges strong protest against the US decision to grant asylum to

tennis star Hu Na and cancels 19 sports and cultural
exchanges.

**May**  Malcolm Baldrige, US Secretary of Commerce, visits
China and pledges to facilitate technology transfer.

**June**  President Reagan approves sale to China of
computers and other high technology items and moves
China into Category V for friendly nations.  The
administration also announces sale of US$530 million in
military equipment to Taiwan; the Chinese reaction is
restrained.  The Chinese government demands that Pan
American World Airways end flights to China following
the restoration of services to Taiwan.  Zhao Ziyang, in
a speech to the 6th NPC, reasserts China's membership in
the Third World and notes that the relationship with the
US "falls far short of what could have been achieved."

**July**  Deng Xiaoping appeals for talks on the
reunification of Taiwan with the mainland, guaranteeing
that the island would be able to keep its own armed
forces. On July 30 the United States and China reach an
agreement regarding textile imports to the United
States.

**August**  US Senator Henry M. Jackson (D. Wash.), after
meeting with Deng Xiaoping, says that relations between
China and the US are improving and should be expanded.
In Beijing two groups headed by Occidental Petroleum
Corporation of Los Angeles sign contracts to drill for
oil in the South China Sea.

**September**  Chinese Foreign Minister Wu Xueqian, in a
speech in New York, calls on the US to cease "official
and semiofficial" relations with Taiwan and says that
Taiwan is the principal obstacle to improved
Sino-American relations.  Textile manufacturers in the
US charge that China has granted "government subsidies"
to its textile products exports and ask the US
government to levy a "countervailing duty" to offset the
subsidies.  US Defense Secretary Weinberger arrives in
Beijing on an official visit and announces that the US
is prepared to sell China anti-aircraft weapons,
anti-tank guns, and other defensive arms.  Weinberger
subsequently announces that the United States and China
have agreed to revive a program of military cooperation
beginning in 1984.

**October**  Foreign Minister Wu Xueqian arrives in
Washington for an official visit.

**November**  China lodges a strong protest with Washington
over a US congressional resolution calling for a
peaceful solution to the problem of Taiwan and a bill
adopted by Congress urging President Reagan and
Secretary of State Schultz to support the Republic of

China in its bid to retain membership in the Asian
Development Bank.  Hu Yaobang, during a visit to Japan,
suggests that President Reagan's planned trip to China
in April may have to be cancelled.  The White House
issues a statement declaring that the support given to
the Nationalist Government in Taiwan in the two
congressional measures was contrary to administration
policy.  New guidelines for technology exports to China
are officially published.  A Chinese diplomat seeking
political asylum forces a Pan Amercian Boeing 747 to
land in Chicago.

December  China announces that it will uphold its
long-term grain trade agreement with the US.  President
Reagan adopts tighter controls over imports of textiles.

1984:  January  Premier Zhao Ziyang visits the United States
and meets with President Reagan.  The major theme
stressed by Zhao during his visit is the strength of
China's commitment to its new "open-door" policy.  The
Taiwan issue is discussed, but downplayed.

March  Zhang Pin, son of China's defence minister and
the foreign affairs director of the Science, Technology
and Defence Industry Commission, heads a four-man
delegation to the United States which discusses arms and
technology transfers.  Treasury Secretary Donald Regan
visits China.

April/May  President Reagan visits China and holds talks
on a broad range of bilateral and global issues.
Although the Chinese censor some of his public remarks,
the reception in Beijing is generally warm.  Agreements
are signed on the development of nuclear power, taxation
of American businesses in China, and cultural exchanges.

5. <u>The Shanghai Communique, February 27, 1972</u>

. . . The U.S. side stated: Peace in Asia and peace in the world require efforts both to reduce immediate tensions and to eliminate the basic causes of conflict. The United States will work for a just and secure peace: just, because it fulfills the aspirations of peoples and nations for freedom and progress; secure, because it removes the danger of foreign aggression. The United States supports individual freedom and social progress for all the peoples of the world, free of outside pressure or intervention. The United States believes that the effort to reduce tensions is served by improving communication between countries that have different ideologies so as to lessen the risks of confrontation through accident, miscalculation or misunderstanding. Countries should treat each other with mutual respect and be willing to compete peacefully, letting performance be the ultimate judge. No country should claim infallibility and each country should be prepared to re-examine its own attitudes for the common good. . . .

The Chinese side stated: Wherever there is oppression, there is resistance. Countries want independence, nations want liberation and the people want revolution — this has become the irresistible trend of history. All nations, big or small, should be equal; big nations should not bully the small and strong nations should not bully the weak. China will never be a superpower and it opposes hegemony and power politics of any kind. The Chinese side stated that it firmly supports the struggles of all the oppressed people and nations for freedom and liberation and that the people of all countries have the right to choose their social systems according to their own wishes and the right to safeguard the independence, sovereignty and territorial integrity of their own countries and oppose foreign aggression, interference, control and subversion. All foreign troops should be withdrawn to their own countries. . . .

There are essential differences between China and the United States in their social systems and foreign policies. However, the two sides agreed that countries, regardless of their social systems, should conduct their relations on the principles of respect for the sovereignty and territorial integrity of all states, non-aggression against other states, non-interference in the internal affairs of other states, equality and mutual benefit, and peaceful coexistence. International disputes should be settled on this basis, without resorting to the use or threat of force. The United States and the People's Republic of China are prepared to apply these principles to their mutual relations.

With these principles of international relations in mind the two sides stated that:

Progress toward the normalization of relations between China and the United States is in the interests of all countries;

Both wish to reduce the danger of international military conflict;

Neither should seek hegemony in the Asia-Pacific region and each is opposed to efforts by any other country or group of countries to establish such hegemony; and

Neither is prepared to negotiate on behalf of any third party or to enter into agreements or understandings with the other directed at other states.

Both sides are of the view that it would be against the interests of the peoples of the world for any major country to collude with another against other countries, or for major countries to divide up the world into spheres of interest.

The two sides reviewed the long-standing serious disputes between China and the United States. The Chinese side reaffirmed its position: The Taiwan question is the crucial question obstructing the normaliza- tion of relations between China and the United States; the Government of the People's Republic of China is the sole legal government of China; Taiwan is a province of China which has long been returned to the motherland; the liberation of Taiwan is China's internal affair in which no other country has the right to interfere; and all U.S. forces and military installations must be withdrawn from Taiwan. The Chinese Government firmly opposes any activities which aim at the creation of "one China, one Taiwan," "one China, two governments," "two Chinas," and "independent Taiwan" or advocate that "the status of Taiwan remains to be determined."

The U.S. side declared: The United States acknowledges that all Chinese on either side of the Taiwan Strait maintain there is but one China and that Taiwan is a part of China. The United States Government does not challenge that position. It reaffirms its interest in a peaceful settlement of the Taiwan question by the Chinese themselves. With this prospect in mind, it affirms the ultimate objective of the withdrawal of all U.S. forces and military installations from Taiwan. In the meantime, it will progressively reduce its forces and military installations on Taiwan as the tension in the area diminishes.

The two sides agreed that it is desirable to broaden the under- standing between the two peoples. To this end, they discussed specific areas in such fields as science, technology, culture, sports and journalism, in which people-to-people contacts and exchanges would be mutually beneficial. Each side undertakes to facilitate the further development of such contacts and exchanges.

Both sides view bilateral trade as another area from which mutual benefit can be derived, and agreed that economic relations based on equality and mutual benefit are in the interest of the peoples of the two countries. They agree to facilitate the progressive development of trade between their two countries.

The two sides agreed that they will stay in contact through various channels, including the sending of a senior U.S. representative to Peking from time to time for concrete consultations to further the normalization of relations between the two countries and continue to exchange views on issues of common interest.

The two sides expressed the hope that the gains achieved during this visit would open up new prospects for the relations between the two countries. They believe that the normalization of relations between the two countries is not only in the interest of the Chinese and American peoples but also contributes to the relaxation of tension in Asia and the world.

Source:   Excerpted from BR, March 3, 1972, pp. 4-5.

## 6. Normalization of US-China Relations, December 15-16, 1978

### The Joint Communique

The United States of America and the People's Republic of China have agreed to recognize each other and to establish diplomatic relations as of January 1, 1979.

The United States of America recognizes the Government of the People's Republic of China as the sole legal government of China. Within this context, the people of the Unites States will maintain cultural, commercial, and other unofficial relations with the people of Taiwan.

The United States of America and the People's Republic of China reaffirm the principles agreed on by the two sides in the Shanghai communique and emphasize once again that:

--Both wish to reduce the danger of international military conflict.

--Neither should seek hegemony in the Asia-Pacific region or in any other region of the world and each is opposed to efforts by any other country or group of countries to establish such hegemony.

--Neither is prepared to negotiate on behalf of any third party or to enter into agreements or understandings with the other directed at other states.

--The Government of the United States of America acknowledges the Chinese position that there is but one China and Taiwan is a part of China.

--Both believe that normalization of relations is not only in the interest of the Chinese and American peoples but also contributes to the cause of peace in Asia and the world.

The United States of America and the People's Republic of China will exchange ambassadors and establish embassies on March 1, 1979.

### The United States' Statement

As of January 1, 1979, the United States of America recognizes the People's Republic of China as the sole legal government of China. On the same date, the People's Republic of China accords similar recognition to the United States of America. The United States thereby establishes diplomatic relations with the People's Republic of China.

On that same date, January 1, 1979, the United States of America will notify Taiwan that it is terminating diplomatic relations and that the mutual defense treaty between the United States and the Republic of China is being terminated in accordance with the provisions of the treaty. The United States also states that it will be withdrawing its remaining military personnel from Taiwan within four months.

In the future, the American people and the people of Taiwan will maintain commercial, cultural, and other relations without official government representation and without diplomatic relations.

The Administration will seek adjustments to our laws and regulations to permit the maintenance of commercial, cultural, and other nongovernmental relationships in the new circumstances that will exist after normalization.

The United States is confident that the people of Taiwan face a peaceful and prosperous future. The United States continues to have an interest in the peaceful resolution of the Taiwan issue and expects that the Taiwan issue will be settled peacefully by the Chinese people themselves.

The United States believes that the establishment of diplomatic relations with the People's Republic will contribute to the welfare of the American people, to the stability of Asia where the United States has major security and economic interests and to the peace of the entire world.

## China's Statement

As of January 1, 1979, the People's Republic of China and the United States of America recognize each other and establish diplomatic relations, thereby ending the prolonged abnormal relationship between them. This is an historic event in Sino-United States relations.

As is known to all, the Government of the People's Republic of China is the sole legal government of China and Taiwan is a part of China. The question of Taiwan was the crucial issue obstructing the normalization of relations between China and the United States. It has now been resolved between the two countries in the spirit of the Shanghai communique and through their joint efforts, thus enabling the normalization of relations so ardently desired by the people of the two countries.

As for the way of bringing Taiwan back to the embrace of the motherland and reunifying the country, it is entirely China's internal affair.

At the invitation of the U.S. Government, Teng Hsiao-p'ing, Deputy Prime Minister of the State Council of the People's Republic of China, will pay an official visit to the United States in January 1979, with a view to further promoting the friendship between the two peoples and good relations between the two countries.

Source: BR, December 22, 1978, pp. 8-12.

## 7. The Taiwan Relations Act of 1979

## Declaration of Policy

. . . Sec. 2. (b) It is the policy of the United States--

(1) to preserve and promote extensive, close, and friendly commercial, cultural, and other relations between the United States and the people on Taiwan, as well as the people on the China mainland and all other peoples of the Western Pacific area;

(2) to declare that peace and stability in the area are in the political, security, and economic interests of the United States, and are matters of international concern;

(3) to make clear that the United States decision to establish diplomatic relations with the People's Republic of China rests upon the expectation that the future of Taiwan will be determined by peaceful means;

(4) to consider any effort to determine the future of Taiwan by other than peaceful means, including by boycotts or embargoes, a threat to the peace and security of the Western Pacific area and of grave

concern to the United States;

(5) to provide Taiwan with arms of a defensive character; and

(6) to maintain the capacity of the United States to resist any resort to force or other forms of coercion that would jeopardize the security, or the social or economic system, of the people on Taiwan.

(c) Nothing contained in this Act shall contravene the interest of the United States in human rights, especially with respect to the human rights of all the approximately eighteen million inhabitants of Taiwan. The preservation and enhancement of the human rights of all the people on Taiwan are hereby reaffirmed as objectives of the United States.

## Implementation of US Policy with Regard to Taiwan

Sec. 3. (a) In furtherance of the policy set forth in section 2 of this Act, the United States will make available to Taiwan such defense articles and defense services in such a quantity as may be necessary to enable Taiwan to maintain a sufficient self-defense capability.

(b) The President and the Congress shall determine the nature and the quantity of such defense articles and services based solely upon their judgment of the needs of Taiwan, in accordance with procedures established by law. Such determination of Taiwan's defense needs shall include review by the United States military authorities in connection with recommendations to the President and Congress.

(c) The President is directed to inform Congress promptly of any threat to the security or the social or economic system of the people of Taiwan and any danger to the interests of the United States arising therefrom. The President and the Congress shall determine, in accordance with constitutional process, appropriate action by the United States in response to any such danger.

## Application of Laws

Sec. 4. (a) The absence of diplomatic relations shall not affect the application of the laws of the United States with respect to Taiwan, and the laws of the United States shall apply with respect to Taiwan in the manner that the laws of the United States applied with respect to Taiwan prior to January 1, 1979. . . .

## The American Institute in Taiwan

Sec. 6. (a) Programs, transactions, and other relations conducted or carried out by the President or any other agency of the United States Government with respect to Taiwan shall, in the manner and to the extent directed by the President, be conducted and carried out by and through--

(1) The American Institute in Taiwan ["Institute" hereafter], a nonprofit corporation incorporated under the laws of the District of Columbia, or

(2) such comparable successor nongovernmental entity as the President may designate. . . .

(b) Whenever the President or any agency of the United States Government is authorized or required by or pursuant to the laws of the United States to enter into, perform, enforce, or have in force an agreement or transaction relative to Taiwan, such agreement or transaction shall be entered into, performed, and enforced, in the manner and extent directed by the President, by or through the Institute.

(c) To the extent that any law, rule, regulation, or ordinance of the District of Columbia, or of any State or political subdivision thereof in which the Institute is incorporated or doing business, impedes or otherwise interferes with the performance of the functions of the Institute pursuant to this Act, such law, rule, regulation, or ordinance shall be deemed to be prempted by this Act. . . .

## Taiwan Instrumentality

Sec. 10. (a) Whenever the President or any agency of the United States Government is authorized or required by or pursuant to the laws of the United States to render or provide to or receive or accept from Taiwan, any performance, communication, assurance, undertaking, or other action, such action shall, in the manner and extent directed by the President, be rendered or provided to, or received or accepted from, an instrumentality established by Taiwan which the President determines has the necessary authority under the laws applied by the people on Taiwan to provide assurances and to take other actions on behalf of Taiwan in accordance with the Act.

(b) The President is requested to extend to the instrumentality established by Taiwan the same number of offices and complement of personnel as were previously operated in the United States by the governing authorities on Taiwan recognized as the Republic of China prior to January 1, 1979.

(c) Upon the granting by Taiwan of comparable privileges and immunities with respect to the Institute and its appropriate personnel, the President is authorized to extend with respect to the Taiwan instrumentality and its appropriate personnel, such privileges and immunities (subject to appropriate conditions and obligations) as may be necessary for the effective performance of their functions. . . .

## Definitions

Sec. 15. For the purposes of this Act--

(1) the term "laws of the United States" includes any statute, rule, regulation, ordinance, order, or judicial rule of decision of the United States or any political subdivision thereof; and

(2) the term "Taiwan" includes, as the context may require, the islands of Taiwan and the Pescadores (Penghu), the people on those islands, corporations and other entities and associations created or organized under the laws applied on those islands, and the governing authorities on Taiwan recognized by the United States as the Republic of China prior to January 1, 1979, and any successor governing authorities (including political subdivisions, agencies, and instrumentalities thereof). . . .

Source: Public Law No. 96-98, 93 Stat. 14.

8. <u>US-China Communique on Taiwan, August 17, 1982</u>

I.    In the joint communique on the Establishment of Diplomatic Relations on January 1, 1979, issued by the Government of the United States and the Government of the People's Republic of China, the United States of America recognized the Government of the People's Republic of China as the sole legal Government of China, and it acknowledged the Chinese position that there is but one China and Taiwan is a part of China.  Within that context, the two sides agreed that the people of the United States would maintain cultural, commercial, and other unofficial relations with the people of Taiwan.  On this basis, relations between the United States and China were normalized.

II.    The question of United States arms sales to Taiwan was not settled in the course of negotiations between the two countries on establishing diplomatic relations.  The two sides held differing positions, and the Chinese side stated that it would raise the issue again following normalization.

Recognizing that this issue would seriously hamper the development of United States-China relations, they have held further discussions on it, during and since the meetings between President Ronald Reagan and Premier Zhao Ziyang and between Secretary of State Alexander M. Haig Jr. and Vice Premier and Foreign Minister Huang Hua in October 1981.

III.    Respect for each other's sovereignty and territorial integrity and noninterference in each other's internal affairs constitute the fundamental principles guiding United States-China relations.  These principles were confirmed in the Shanghai Communique of February 28, 1972, and reaffirmed in the Joint Communique on the Establishment of Diplomatic Relations which came into effect on January 1, 1979.  Both sides emphatically state that these principles continue to govern all aspects of their relations.

IV.    The Chinese Government reiterates that the question of Taiwan is China's internal affair.  The Message to Compatriots in Taiwan issued by China on January 1, 1979, promulgated a fundamental policy of striving for peaceful reunification of the motherland.

The nine-point proposal put forward by China on September 30, 1981, represented a further major effort under this fundamental policy to strive for a peaceful solution to the Taiwan question.

V.    The United States Government attached great importance to its relations with China, and reiterates that it has no intention of infringing on Chinese sovereignty and territorial integrity, or interfering in China's internal affairs, or pursuing a policy of "two Chinas" or "one China, one Taiwan."  The United States Government understands and appreciates the Chinese policy of striving for a peaceful resolution of the Taiwan question as indicated in China's Message to Compatriots in Taiwan issued on January 1, 1979, and the nine-point proposal put forward by China on September 30, 1981.  The new situation which has emerged with regard to the Taiwan question also provides favorable conditions for the settlement of United States-China differences over the question of United States arms sales to Taiwan.

VI.    Having in mind the foregoing statements of both sides, the United States Government states that it does not seek to carry out a long-term policy of arms sales to Taiwan, that its arms sales to Taiwan will not exceed, either in qualitative or in quantitative terms, the level of those supplied in recent years since the establishment of diplomatic relations between the United States and China, and that it intends to reduce gradually its sales of arms to Taiwan, leading over a period of time to a final resolution.  In so stating, the United States acknowledges China's consistent position regarding the thorough settlement of this issue.

VII.    In order to bring about, over a period of time, a final settlement of the question of United States arms sales to Taiwan, which is an issue rooted in history, the two governments will make every effort to adopt measures and create conditions conducive to the thorough settlement of this issue.

VIII.    The development of United States—China relations is not only in the interests of the two peoples but also conducive to peace and stability in the world.  The two sides are determined, on the principle of equality and mutual benefit, to strengthen their ties in the economic, cultural, educational, scientific, technological and other fields and make strong, joint efforts for the continued development of relations between the governments and peoples of the United States and China.

IX.    In order to bring about the healthy development of United States—China relations, maintain world peace and oppose aggression and expansion, the two governments reaffirm the principles agreed on by the two sides in the Shanghai Communique and the Joint Communique on the Establishment of Diplomatic Relations.  The two sides will maintain contact and hold appropriate consultations on bilateral and international issues of common interest.

Source:  New York Times, August 18, 1982.

9. Chronological List of Countries Recognizing the PRC

1949:  Union of Soviet Socialist Republics, Bulgaria, Romania, Hungary, Czechoslovakia, Democratic Republic of Korea, Poland, Yugoslavia, Mongolia, German Democratic Republic, Albania, Burma, India

1950:  Pakistan, United Kingdom, Sri Lanka, Norway, Denmark, Israel,* Afghanistan, Finland, Sweden, Democratic Republic of Vietnam, Switzerland, Netherlands, Indonesia*

1955:  Nepal

1956:  Egypt, Syria, Yemen

1958:  Cambodia, Iraq, Morocco, Sudan

1959:  Guinea

1960:  Ghana,* Cuba, Mali, Somalia

1961:  Senegal,* Tanzania (originally Tanganyka)

1962:  Laos, Algeria, Uganda

1963:  Kenya, Burundi,* Zanzibar (later merged with Tanganyka to form Tanzania)

1964:  Tunisia, France, Congo, Central African Republic, Zambia, Benin (originally Dahomey)*

1965:  Mauritania

1968:  South Yemen

1970:  Canada, Equatorial Guinea, Italy, Ethiopia, Chile

1971:  Nigeria, Kuwait, Cameroon, San Marino, Austria, Sierra Leone, Turkey, Iran, Belgium, Peru, Lebanon, Rwanda, Iceland, Cyprus

1972:  Argentina, Mexico, Malta, Mauritius, Greece, Guyana, Togo, Japan, German Federal Republic, Maldives, Malagasy, Luxembourg, Jamaica, Zaire, Chad, Australia, New Zealand

1973:  Spain, Upper Volta

1974:  Guinea Bissau, Gabon, Malaysia, Trinidad and Tobago, Venezuela, Niger, Brazil, Gambia

1975:  Botswana, Philippines, Mozambique, Bangladesh, Thailand, Sao Tome and Principe, Fiji, Western Samoa, Comoros

1976:  Cape Verde, Surinam, Seychelles, Papua New Guinea

1977:  Liberia, Barbados, Jordan

1978:   Oman, Libya

1979:   United States, Djibouti, Portugal, Ireland

1980:   Colombia, Zimbabwe, Ecuador, Kiribasi

1982:   Vanuata, Angola

1983:   Lesotho, Ivory Coast, Antigua


*Note:   Israel extended recognition but diplomatic relations were never established. China-Senegal relations were not established until 1972. China's relations were broken with Burundi in 1965, with Ghana and Benin (Dahomey) in 1966, and with Indonesia in 1967. Relations were resumed with Burundi in 1971, and with Benin and Ghana in 1972.


Source:   For the 1949-1964 period, adapted from A. M. Halpern, Policies Toward China: Views from Six Continents (New York: McGraw-Hill, 1965), pp. 496-497; for later years, CQ and BR.

## 10.  Structure of the People's Liberation Army

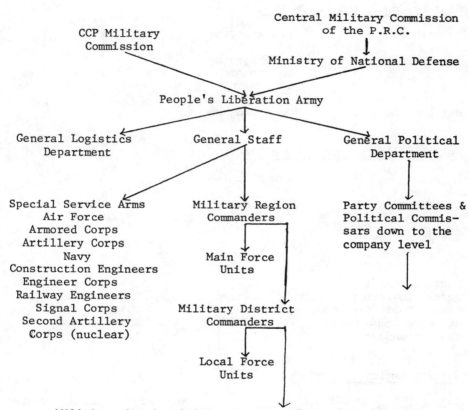

Militia units in cities, communes, factories, mines, etc., under the dual control of the Party and PLA at the relevant level.

## 11. Major Military Leaders

### Minister of National Defense

Zhang Aiping

### Military Commission of the CCP

Chairman: Deng Xiaoping

Vice Chairmen: Nie Rongzhen
Xu Xiangqian
Ye Jianying

Secretary General: Yang Shangkun

### Central Military Commission of the PRC

Chairman: Deng Xiaoping

Vice Chairmen: Nie Rongzhen           Yang Shangkun
Xu Xiangqian            Ye Jianying

### PLA Headquarters

Chief of Staff:                              Yang Dezhi
General Logistics Department Director:       Hong Xuezhi
General Political Department Director:        Yu Qiuli
Air Force Commander:                         Zhang Tingfa
Navy Commander:                              Liu Huaqing

### Military Region Commanders

| | | | |
|---|---|---|---|
| Beijing: | Qin Jiwei | Lanzhou: | Zhang Weishan |
| Chengdu: | Wang Chenghan | Nanjing: | Xiang Shouzhi |
| Fuzhou: | Yang Chengwu | Shenyang: | Li Desheng |
| Guangzhou: | You Taizhong | Urumqi: | Xiao Quanfu |
| Jinan: | Rao Shoukun | Wuhan: | Zhou Shihong |
| Kunming: | Zhang Zhixiu | | |

Source: _China Directory_ (Tokyo: Radiopress, Inc., 1984), pp. 270-312.

## 12. Deployment of PLA Ground Forces

| Military Region | Component Military Districts | Main Force Divisions | | Local Force Divisions |
|---|---|---|---|---|
| | | Infantry | Armored | |
| Beijing | Hebei<br>Inner Mongolia<br>Shanxi | 25 | 4 | 15 |
| Shenyang | Heilongjiang<br>Jilin<br>Liaoning | 18 | 3 | 16 |
| Lanzhou | Gansu<br>Ningxia<br>Qinghai<br>Shaanxi | 9 | 1 | 4 |
| Jinan | Shandong | 9 | 1 | 7 |
| Nanjing | Anhui<br>Jiangsu<br>Zhejiang | 10 | 1 | 12 |
| Fuzhou | Fujian<br>Jiangxi | 6 | | 7 |
| Wuhan | Henan<br>Hubei | 10 | 2 | 8 |
| Guangzhou | Guangdong<br>Guangxi<br>Hainan Island | 12 | | 12 |
| Chengdu | Sichuan<br>Tibet | 8 | | 6 |
| Kunming | Guizhou<br>Yunnan | 6 | | 2 |
| Urumqi | East Xinjiang<br>North Xinjiang<br>South Xinjiang | 6-10 | — | 8-9 |

Source: International Institute for Strategic Studies, The Military Balance 1982-1983, cited in China Facts, p. 117.

13. <u>Force Levels of the Chinese Military</u>

<u>Total Regular Forces</u>                                          4,000,000

       Army                                               3,150,000
       Navy                                                 360,000
       Air Force                                            490,000


<u>Ships and Submarines</u>

       Submarines (conventional attack)                         103
       Submarines (nuclear attack)                                2
       Submarines (nuclear with SLBMs)                            1
       Destroyers                                                10
       Frigates                                                  29
       Large Patrol Ships                                         8
       Missle Craft                                             230
       Coastal Craft                                            709
       Submarine Chasers                                         88
       Minesweepers                                              23
       Large Landing Ships                                       61
       Other Amphibious Types                                   449


<u>Aircraft</u>

       Bombers                                                  700
       Fighters/Ground Attack                                   500
       Fighters/Interceptors                                  4,000
       Reconnaissance                                           130


Source: <u>The Military Balance</u>, 1982–1983, pp. 78–81, 94, cited in
       Martin Lasater, <u>Taiwan: Facing Mounting Threat</u> (Washington,
       DC: Heritage Press, 1984), p. 10.

VI.   ECONOMIC DEVELOPMENT AND FOREIGN TRADE

## 1.  Introduction and Suggested Readings

The Economy Since 1949    The Communist Party in 1949 faced an
economy on the brink of collapse.  Two decades of war had ravaged the
small industrial sector and reduced the food supply.  Hyperinflation
had devalued the currency; commercial links between urban and rural
areas were disrupted; and communications were in disrepair.  Thus, the
first task for the regime was economic rehabilitation.  During the
first few years of the Communist regime, private enterprise was
permitted in the rural and urban areas in order to put the economy back
on its feet.

In 1953 the leadership felt that the economic situation had
stabilized enough to permit the launching of the First Five-Year Plan.
The plan was based on the Soviet model in both its organizational
nature and economic priorities.  Heavy industry received the lion's
share of investment and consumption was curtailed to permit the
accumulation of capital.  Light industry and agriculture received
little financial support from the state.  Organizationally, private
enterprise in the urban areas was replaced by state ownership and
agricultural collectivization in the countryside was accelerated.  The
economic system was managed from Beijing by a highly centralized plan
implemented by national ministries.

By 1956 the Chinese leadership was rethinking the applicability of
the Soviet model, some seeking greater investment in agriculture and a
certain degree of decentralization.  Mao, along with the majority of
the Party's top leadership, had other ideas.  The result was the Great
Leap Forward of 1958 to 1961.  Under this plan heavy industry would
grow at an even more accelerated pace -- but still at the expense of
agriculture.  The rural sector would provide the capital for heavy
industry as well as its own developmental needs by yet greater
production.  The key to the program's success was the communes.  These
organizations, with their emphasis on egalitarianism and their ability
to mobilize large numbers of peasants, were intended to provide greater
rural productivity and savings.  Moreover, their claim to be a yet
higher stage of socialist development made them ideologically appealing
to many within the leadership, most prominently Mao.

The Great Leap Forward was a disaster.  Millions may have died due
to food shortages.  Communist support among the peasantry clearly
suffered.  From 1961 to 1966, the Party leadership engaged in a
dramatic salvage operation.  The authority of the communes was
weakened, private plots were restored, and the peasantry was paid
according to work performed.  In the economy as a whole there was talk
of decentralization, and a larger share of the state's investment funds
was directed into agriculture.

However, beneath these changes in the economy, cleavages among the leaders of China were developing. Mao was becoming concerned about the social and ideological effects of the new economic strategy. Others, while not indifferent to this issue, felt that economic construction had to continue to take first priority. By 1966 Mao's concerns had become so profound that he promoted the Cultural Revolution.

Unlike the Great Leap Forward, the Cultural Revolution was not concerned primarily with economic issues. However, many of its ideological and social currents clearly touched the economy. Naturally, the turmoil was disruptive, particularly in respect to the nation's transportation network. More specifically, worker morale in urban and rural areas was damaged by what was perceived as an arbitrary and unfair wage system which did not reflect seniority or provide raises for ten years. Finally, the nativist mood severely limited regularized economic relations with foreign countries. Despite efforts by Zhou Enlai and Deng Xiaoping to reverse some of the currents of the Cultural Revolution in the early 1970s, any basic change had to await Mao's death in September 1976.

Amid these kaleidoscopic changes, how did the Chinese economy perform in the aggregate over the nearly three decades from 1949 to 1976? The table (VI.2) on page 117 and the more detailed table (VI.3) on page 118 demonstrate four major points.

First, China has generally experienced strong, sustained economic growth. Over the 1952-1978 period, average annual growth rates were 6% for gross national product, 11% for industry, and 2% for agriculture. If 1970 is taken as the base year, the annual growth rates were 7% for GNP, 9% for industry, and 3% for agriculture. These rates compare favorably with other large developing countries.

Second, poor performance in agriculture has inhibited growth. Given only a 2% growth rate, the food supply has held even with population growth. Though China is currently a net food exporter, it has imported grain since the early 1960s to insure sufficient reserves (see table [VI.5] on page 120).

Third, economic growth has been interrupted by three periods of recession. By far the most severe was in 1959-62, when bad weather, withdrawal of Soviet aid, and dislocations caused by the Great Leap Forward led to absolute declines in GNP, industrial production, and agricultural production. There was another dip in 1967, due mainly to disruptions of the Cultural Revolution, and a period of stagnation in 1975-76 caused by the political conflict preceding Mao's death.

Fourth, despite the strong economic growth overall, living standards have not improved. The lack of attention to demand in production planning and problems in the planning system in general have contributed to waste and the stockpiling of unmarketable goods.

Post-Mao Economic Policy    Under the banner of the "four modernizations," Mao's successors pledged to reduce China's backwardness in industry, agriculture, national defense, and science and technology by the end of this century. The annual growth targets initially proposed were very ambitious: over 10% in industry and over 4% in agriculture. Rapid mechanization of agriculture and a broad expansion of heavy industrial plant -- in part through foreign imports -- were the central features of the strategy.

By late 1978 the leadership realized that the new goals were inappropriate to China's resources and conditions. It embarked on a policy of "readjustment" to rectify a number of problems. One of these was a serious decline in labor productivity, due to a variety of factors including stagnation in personal income, insufficient managerial capability, and planning difficulties. As a solution, economic planners have tried to raise consumption capabilities and opportunites by shifting investment priorities. As investment in capital construction has gradually stabilized, personal incomes have grown, especially in the countryside. Furthermore, the government has sought to shift investment funds away from heavy industry towards agriculture (to increase the food supply), light industry (for exports and to satisfy pent-up consumer demand), and transportation and energy resources. Importing foreign technology continues, but within the context of China's ability to pay. Growth targets recently have been more modest: in 1983, for example, both agricultural and industrial output were to rise at about 4%, with production in light industry to exceed slightly that in heavy industry. According to Chinese sources, the actual rate of growth of heavy industrial output was 13%, and 8.4% for light industry. Growth in industrial output in 1984 is expected to exceed 5%.

The leadership realizes that investment in energy resources is an essential guarantee of continued economic growth. From 1976 to 1983, every 1% of increase in industrial output required a 1.35% rise in the energy supply. Potentially, China has abundant resources of coal (the primary fuel source), oil (increasingly important in the 1970s), and hydroelectric power. But the capacity to exploit these resources has been lacking, and supply has stagnated in recent years (see table [VI.6] on page 120). Aggravating the situation is a low ratio of efficiency in fuel utilization (in the 25-30% range). In the short term the government has spurred a conservation effort; for the long term it plans to use foreign technology to exploit offshore oil and onshore coal, and develop a nuclear power capability. Implementing these plans, which will mean China's closer involvement in the international economy and substantial joint venture arrangements, or possibly, foreign private investment in China, will not be an easy matter.

The post-Mao leadership has also experimented with changing the relationship between state-owned and collective enterprises and, increasingly after 1978, allowing very small private businesses to be organized. China's industrial economy has a dualistic structure, with a large number of state-owned enterprises under the control of central and lower level governments, and a much larger number of collective enterprises. The state-owned enterprises receive the bulk of available capital, are responsible for most of the output, and have a close relationship with the government. Until recently, state-owned enterprises remitted all their profits to the government, which in turn provided grants to underwrite any new investment. These remittances constitute the largest share of the state's revenue base, and economic construction (capital investment) has been the largest item of government expenditure (as the tables on the state budget [VI.8-9] on pages 121-123 demonstrate). The regime's relationship with collective enterprises has been less direct and more ideological. In politically radical periods, rural small-scale industries have been praised for their contributions to self-sufficient rural development, while some urban ones have been restricted on the grounds that they represent vestiges of "capitalism." In more pragmatic periods, questions are raised about the efficiency of rural enterprises while urban ones are encouraged in order to fill gaps left by state-owned units and reduce urban unemployment.

The current leadership has returned to the approach of past periods of pragmatism, even to the point of legitimizing individual entrepreneurship. It has also questioned whether the close relationship between the government and state-owned enterprises, copied from the Soviet Union in the 1950s, is suited to China's conditions. To better link investment and performance, a number of experiments were tried during 1979 and 1980. Material incentives to increase efficiency and profitability were created by allowing many enterprises to retain a portion of their after-tax profits for reinvestment, bonuses, and worker services. Bank loans became a growing source of funds for new investment and means to encourage improvements in managerial and technical skills. For, if an enterprise did not use borrowed money efficiently, it would be less likely to get more. Instead of relying primarily on administrative mechanisms to distribute goods, planners allowed a greater role for market forces.

These limited experiments with market socialism were controversial. As in the political sphere, implementation of the reforms was shaped, and in some cases driven off course, by existing arrangements. Lower levels used their new freedom to increase rather than restrain new investment, and an irrational price system made it difficult to measure which enterprises were truly efficient. As profit deliveries to the government declined, due to the new policy of allowing some enterprises to retain part of their earnings, the central deficit rose dramatically to RMB 17 billion in 1979 — 15.4% of total revenues -- and RMB 12.1 billion in 1980 — 10.5% of budgeted revenues. (Source: Lowell Dittmer, "China in 1981: Reform, Readjustment, Rectification," Asian Survey, vol. XXII, no. 1, January 1982, pp. 33-46.) The deficit was exacerbated by the steep increase in 1979 in the prices paid by the government for agricultural output. A greater number of investments at the local level and the provision of a 5 yuan subsidy to each urban worker to counteract rising consumer prices fed an inflationary spiral. In late 1980, in an effort to curb inflation, the government reduced central investments, halted further extension of the enterprise profit-sharing reforms, ended the bank loan reforms, and increased price controls on consumer goods. The result was a further expansion of the central deficit as industrial output and profitability declined. From the second half of 1981, controls on profits were relaxed once more and enterprises allowed to retain a portion of their after-tax profits. In 1983 this system of contracted profit payments to the government was supplemented by taxes on capital, sales, and income.

Despite these various adjustments, problems remain. Tension between central and local governments over relative shares of enterprise profits and influence over management remains an undercurrent in all policy revisions. The government continues to be frustrated by its inability to control local-level investment once enterprises are allowed to retain a portion of their earnings. Yet, profit sharing in some form seems necessary if production is to increase. Real future progress in industrial reform hinges upon a major reworking of the price system, a delicate task in any economy.

Finally, while anxious to maintain central control over the largest, most profitable enterprises, state policymakers seem willing to relax control over medium- and small-sized enterprises. Whether the government will be able to achieve economic growth by introducing a more market-oriented approach into some industrial firms, while retaining a centrally planned system in other enterprises, is yet to be demonstrated.

In the agricultural sector, the post-Mao leadership has been very successful in linking incentives to performance. In order to raise output and incomes, the government has improved rural-urban terms of trade, expanded private plots, liberalized crop management, and generally allowed the lowest levels more freedom in production decisions. No longer is there a stigma attached to making money, and rural producers have taken full advantage of the change in climate.

Under the new "responsibility system," individuals, households, or work groups are assigned parcels of land in return for their delivery of a certain amount of output to the government. After fulfilling the terms of the contact, the individual, household, or group is free to consume or sell any remaining output. The significant change which the "responsibility system" has introduced is to make the peasant household the level at which income is determined, a role previously played (since 1962) by the production team. The land worked by the peasant household remains collective property, however, and cannot be sold by the individual although a tenure of 15 years is now guaranteed. Introduction of the "responsibility system" has been matched by easier credit terms and an increase in purchase prices for some items. The result has been a rise in productivity, the re-introduction of non-agricultural activities such an animal husbandry, fishery, or forestry (called "side-line" activities by the Chinese), crop diversification, and larger incomes.

Despite the apparent success of the agricultural reforms in raising productivity and incomes, there is resistance to the program by those worried about the creation of a gap between rich and poor households and restoration of class divisions in the countryside. There is also concern among some central leaders that the state plan will be weakened by giving peasant producers too much independence. Peasant reaction to the reforms also varies depending upon the extent to which they perceive that instituting individual responsibility will rob them of the benefits of collectivized activities, such as large-scale construction or water conservation projects.

The Role of Foreign Trade   China's international trade has increased gradually over the years, dropping only during the periods of recession noted above (see table [VI.10] on page 123). Although China is not pursuing a development strategy of export-led growth like Singapore and South Korea, it shares their status as a "newly industrializing country" in that its exports are primarily industry-related commodities (see table [VI.11] on page 124). On the import side, China depends on international markets for advanced technology, supplemental food supplies, and agricultural raw materials. This dependence, and Sino-Soviet emnity since 1960, have caused a dramatic change in China's list of trading partners, with Japan and the West replacing the Soviet-bloc countries, the principal partners of the 1950s (see tables [VI.12a and 12b] on pages 125-126).

The United States embargoed trade with China from 1950 to mid-1971. Commerce jumped in 1973 and 1974, primarily because of American wheat and cotton exports, then fell for three years for political and economic reasons. From 1977 to 1980, two-way trade between the United States and China rapidly developed, doubling every year. In 1981 two-way trade increased more modestly, from 4.8 to 5.4 billion, and then fell in 1982 to 5.1 billion and in 1983 to 4.4 billion. Despite the generally upward trend in trade relations between the United States and China, and in China's international trade relations in general, the process of developing foreign trade has not been a smooth one for post-Mao China (see tables VI.14-16 on pages

128-129).

In 1978, as part of the ten-year plan launched by Hua Guofeng, China went on a buying spree, contracting to purchase plant and technology from abroad in quantities far exceeding financial capabilities. During the first six months of 1979, reevaluation of China's domestic economic plans and foreign trade practices resulted in the cancellation of $2.6 billion in contracts with Japanese companies and institution of a moratorium on the signing of new purchasing contracts with foreign firms. Six months later, the Japanese contracts were restored and the importance to China of foreign trade and investment relations was underlined by the announcement of a new law governing joint ventures.

In 1980 foreign trade increased dramatically, at least in part due to the decentralization of foreign trade decision-making authority from central trade bureaus to individual production enterprises. This decentralization was a part of the larger reform program, noted above. The result was an enthusiastic scramble by Chinese enterprises to purchase items from abroad. For the government, however, decentralization decreased its ability to control the flow of foreign exchange or to set trade plans. In response, in early 1981, the Chinese government again cancelled contracts with foreign suppliers and moved to reinstate central control over the trading of various commodities. While total two-way trade declined in 1982, the effect on some countries (such as the US where the volume of two-way trade fell from 5.4 to 5.1 billions) was not dramatic.

The United States remains China's third largest trading partner, after Japan and Hong Kong. While grain is the predominant US export to China, fertilizers, logs, and lumber are sold in large quantities. The Reagan administration's decision in June 1983 to loosen export restrictions on high technology items, and continued Chinese interest in boosting their modernization effort by importing technology, may lead to future expansion in trade in that area. United States imports from China are led by petroleum products and textiles. The latter have been a continuing sore spot in Sino-American relations. Pressure from US textile producers for protectionist restrictions on Chinese imports, and the Reagan administration's announcement in December 1983 of general support for implementing tighter controls, may limit future expansion of US textile purchases. In contrast, business relations between the US and China show some potential in the field of energy exploration. Foreign oil companies are being allowed to participate in joint oil exploration ventures, and at least one American company is involved in a coal mining operation in China.

Several factors still restrict the development of China's international trade. The composition of Chinese exports (primarily agricultural products and light manufactured goods) limits the scope of international demand. Demand for Chinese products is also subject to the effect of future world recessions (oil is the only possible exception, but the extent and quality of China's reserves is still uncertain). Limited demand and the need to import grain restrict the foreign exchange China has available for purchasing foreign technology. To deal with this problem, China is increasingly encouraging joint ventures, compensation trade, and concessionary aid. Indeed, in 1984 China plans to purchase 1 billion worth of foreign technology, financed in large part by loans from international lending organizations.

Since 1980, when China became a member of the World Bank and the International Monetary Fund (replacing Taiwan), the country's integration into the international financial system has increased. In 1981 a special domestic investment bank was created to channel loans from the World Bank to China's enterprises, and the Bank provides funding for other projects as well. China has applied to become a member of the Asian Development Bank, but approval hinges on resolution of the question of Taiwan's status (already a member) should China be admitted. In December 1983 China agreed to participate in the Multi-Fibre Arrangement (MFA) which, as part of the General Agreement on Tariffs and Trade (GATT), governs international textiles trade. The quota terms which China receives under the MFA is an important source of conflict in China's trade relations with the European Economic Community. Finally, China is encouraging foreign investment by opening special economic zones (SEZ) in Guangdong and Fujian provinces and Shanghai municipality. In 1984 similar status is extended to fourteen other areas in China. Foreign entrepreneurs are eligible for tax breaks and loans from the Bank of China if they invest in the special zones. A variety of arrangements are available to foreign investors in these areas including wholly owned or joint ventures, compensation trade, licensing, leasing, or co-production. The zones are viewed by the Chinese as a way to attract foreign capital and technology and to train personnel (see table VI.17 on page 130).

These innovations are a radical departure from the cash-and-carry approach of the Maoist era. While designed to support the domestic modernization drive, they also increase China's contact and enmeshment with the capitalist world. Like the technology-based developmental strategy as a whole, China's increasing integration into the international economic system could become a politically explosive issue domestically if it does not produce favorable results soon.

## Suggested Readings

Barnett, A. Doak. China's Economy in Global Perspective. Washington, DC: The Brookings Institution, 1981. An exhaustive analysis of China's economic program and the implications for the international trade, technology, food, and energy systems.

Baum, Richard, ed. China's Four Modernizations: The New Technological Revolution. Boulder, CO: Westview Press, 1980. A collection of essays on the problems and prospects facing China as it pursues economic modernization. The acquisition and absorption of foreign technology is given special attention.

China Business Review. Published bimonthly by the National Council for US-China Trade, Washington, DC. The most authoritative and up-to-date source of information on China's economy and foreign trade.

CIA Reference Aids. Include a number of reports and statistical data on the Chinese economy. See page 2 for ordering information.

Dittmer, Lowell. "China in 1981: Reform, Readjustment, Recitification," Asian Survey, vol. XXII, no. 1 (January 1982), pp. 33-46.

Eckstein, Alexander. China's Economic Revolution. New York: Cambridge University Press, 1977. A general analysis of China's economic heritage, development policies, and performance.

Feintech, Lynn D. China's Modernization Strategy and the United States. Washington, DC: Overseas Development Council, 1981. A brief review, with particular emphasis on financing issues.

Gray, Jack, and Gordon White, eds. China's New Development Strategy. London: Academic Press, 1982. A collection of 13 essays on post-Mao reforms in education, politics and law, industry and agriculture.

Hsiao, Gene T. The Foreign Trade of China: Policy, Law, and Practice. Berkeley and Los Angeles: University of California Press, 1977. A specialized yet thorough treatment.

Lardy, Nicholas R. Agriculture in China's Modern Economic Development. Cambridge: Cambridge University Press, 1983. A detailed study of agricultural planning and pricing policies since 1949 and prospects for success of the current reforms.

U.S. Congress, Joint Economic Committee. China Under the Four Modernizations: Retrenchment, Reform, and Reappraisal. Washington, DC: Government Printing Office, 1982. One of a series of compendia on the Chinese economy, providing detailed analysis of economic policy and performance by government and academic economists.

Woodard, Kim. The International Energy Relations of China. Stanford: Stanford University Press, 1980. An exhaustive examination of China's energy development and the implications for world markets.

## 2. Trends in Aggregate Performance

Index: 1949 = 100

| Year | Net Material Product at Constant Prices | Agricultural Shares in NMP | Industrial Shares in NMP |
|------|------|------|------|
| 1949 | 100.0 | n/a | n/a |
| 1952 | 169.8 | 58 | 20 |
| 1957 | 259.8 | 47 | 28 |
| 1962 | 222.3 | n/a | n/a |
| 1965 | 335.4 | 46 | 36 |
| 1970 | 500.4 | 41 | 40 |
| 1975 | 656.5 | 39 | 45 |
| 1977 | 692.9 | 37 | 45 |
| 1978 | 778.7 | 36 | 46 |
| 1979 | 833.2 | 183 | 715 |
| 1980 | /a | n/a | n/a |

/a State Statistical Bureau Communique on Fulfillment of the 1980
National Economic Plan, April 1981, gives the increase at constant
prices over 1979 as 6.9%.

Source: World Bank, China: Socialist Economic Development, Annex A
(1981), p. 99. n/a = not available.

### 3. Economic Indicators (1977-1982)

|  | 1977 | 1978 | 1979 | 1980 | 1981 | 1982 |
|---|---|---|---|---|---|---|
| **GNP** | | | | | | |
| billion yuan | 307.4 | 349.8 | 391.4 | 424.1 | 443.2 | 476.9 |
| billion U.S.$ | 165.5 | 207.8 | 251.7 | 283.0 | 259.9 | 260.7 |
| **Population (year-end)** | | | | | | |
| million | 945.2 | 958.9 | 970.92 | 982.55 | 994.0 | 1,008.3 |
| **Per capita GNP** | | | | | | |
| yuan | 266.6 | 303.5 | 337.8 | 366.0 | 388.0 | 473.0 |
| U.S.$ | 175.0 | 217.0 | 259.0 | 288.0 | 261.5 | 258.6 |
| **Total gross value of industrial & agricultural output value** | | | | | | |
| billion yuan | 553.1 | 616.1 | 668.6 | 716.7 | 749.0 | 806.0 |
| billion U.S.$ (1980 prices) | 299.0 | 365.9 | 430.0 | 478.4 | 439.3 | 440.7 |
| **Gross value of industrial output** | | | | | | |
| billion yuan | 372.9 | 419.9 | 455.6 | 497.4 | 517.8 | 556.0 |
| billion U.S.$ (1980 prices) | 201.6 | 249.3 | 293.3 | 332.0 | 303.7 | 304.0 |
| of which: | | | | | | |
| Heavy industry | | | | | | |
| billion yuan | — | 240.1 | 258.5 | 263.9 | 251.5 | 274.8 |
| billion U.S.$ | — | 142.6 | 166.2 | 176.2 | 147.5 | 150.2 |
| Light industry | | | | | | |
| billion yuan | — | 179.8 | 197.1 | 233.4 | 266.3 | 281.2 |
| billion U.S.$ | — | 106.8 | 126.8 | 155.8 | 156.2 | 153.8 |
| **Gross value of agricultural output** | | | | | | |
| billion yuan | 180.2 | 196.2 | 213.0 | 218.7 | 231.2 | 250.0 |
| billion U.S.$ (1980 prices) | 97.4 | 116.5 | 137.0 | 146.0 | 135.6 | 136.7 |

Note: Exchange rate is 1.826 yuan equals one dollar.

Source: Chu-yuan Cheng, "Economic Development in Mainland China Since the 12th Party Congress," The American Asian Review, vol. 1, no. 1 (Spring 1983), p. 50.

4. <u>Major Indicators of the Sixth Five-Year Plan (1980-1985)</u>

| | 1980 (Actual) | 1985 (Planned) | Percentage increase % | Annual growth % |
|---|---|---|---|---|
| 1. Population million | 982.55 | 1060 | 7.88 | 1.5 |
| 2. Gross output of industry & agriculture billion yuan | 715.9 | 871.0 | 21.67 | 4.0 |
| 3. Gross value of agriculture billion yuan | 218.7 | 266.0 | 21.67 | 4.0 |
| 4. Gross value of industry billion yuan | 497.2 | 605.0 | 21.67 | 4.0 |
| Light industry | 233.4 | 298.0 | 27.63 | 5.0 |
| Heavy industry | 263.9 | 307.0 | 16.00 | 3.0 |
| 5. Major products | | | | |
| Grains (millions tons) | 320.52 | 360.0 | 12.3 | 2.4 |
| Cotton (million tons) | 2.707 | 3.6 | 33.0 | 5.8 |
| Sugar (million tons) | 2.57 | 4.3 | 67.3 | 10.8 |
| Coal (million tons) | 620.0 | 700.0 | 12.9 | 2.4 |
| Electricity (billion KWH) | 300.6 | 362 | 20.4 | 3.8 |
| Steel (million tons) | 34.2 | 39 | 5.1 | 1.0 |
| Oil (million tons) | 105.95 | 100.0 | — | — |
| Cotton yarn (million tons) | 2.93 | 3.59 | 22.8 | 4.2 |
| 6. State revenue billion yuan | 108.5 | 127.4 | 17.4 | 3.2 |
| 7. State expenditures | 121.2 | 130.4 | 7.6 | 1.4 |
| 8. Total wage billion yuan | 77.3 | 98.3 | 27.2 | 4.9 |
| 9. Foreign trade billion yuan | 56.3 | 85.5 | 51.8 | ɔ/ |
| Exports | 27.2 | 40.2 | 47.6 | 8.ɹ |
| Imports | 29.1 | 45.3 | 55.5 | 9.2 |
| 10. College students | | | | |
| Admitted (1,000) | 280 | 400 | 42.2 | 7.3 |
| Enrolled (million) | 1.14 | 1.30 | 13.6 | 4.3 |

Source: Chu-yuan Cheng, "Economic Development in Mainland China Since the 12th Party Congress," <u>The American Asian Review</u>, vol 1, no. 1 (Spring 1983), p. 56.

5. <u>China's Import of Grain</u> (thousand metric tons)

| | 1979 | 1980 | 1981 | 1982 I | 1982 II |
|---|---|---|---|---|---|
| Total | 10,855 | 13,673 | 13,204 | 3,287 | 5,303 |
| Argentina | 913 | 655 | 126 | 73 | 173 |
| Australia | 3,063 | 2,146 | 1,184 | 586 | --- |
| Canada | 2,743 | 2,628 | 3,141 | 635 | 1,090 |
| U.S. | 3,995 | 8,037 | 8,084 | 1,968 | 4,040 |
| Other | 141 | 197 | 669 | 25 | --- |

Source: <u>China Facts</u>, p. 215.

6. <u>Energy Supply</u>

| | Coal (mn tons) | Oil (mn tons) | Natural Gas (bn cubic m) | Hydropower (bn kWh) | Total (mn tons of coal equiv.) |
|---|---|---|---|---|---|
| 1970 | 354.0 | 30.7 | 2.9 | 20.5 | 305.0 |
| 1975 | 482.2 | 77.1 | 8.9 | 47.6 | 481.8 |
| 1976 | 483.5 | 86.8 | 10.2 | 45.6 | 498.3 |
| 1977 | 550.7 | 93.6 | 12.1 | 47.7 | 558.3 |
| 1978 | 617.9 | 104.0 | 13.7 | 44.6 | 621.5 |
| 1979 | 635.5 | 106.1 | 14.5 | 50.1 | 640.2 |
| 1980 | 620.1 | 105.9 | 14.3 | 58.2 | 632.1 |
| 1981 | 620 | 101.2 | 12.7 | 65.6 | 632.0* |
| 1982 | 650 | 102 | 10.8 | 74.4** | 668.2** |
| 1983 | 715 | 106.1 | 12.2 | 86.4 | 713 |

Source: <u>China Facts</u>, p. 167; except * which is from <u>BR</u>, May 9, 1983, p. 5; 1983 and ** are from Foreign Broadcast Information Service, <u>Daily Report: China</u> (Springfield, VA: National Technical Information Service, May 1, 1984), p. K-6.

7. <u>Energy Consumption by Sectors of the Economy, 1980-85</u> (mn tons of coal equivalent)

| | 1980 | 1981 | 1982 | 1983 | 1984 | 1985 |
|---|---|---|---|---|---|---|
| Metallurgy | 97.8 | 88.9 | 88.4 | 87.2 | 85.9 | 84.3 |
| Other heavy industry | 129.0 | 121.9 | 120.7 | 119.5 | 117.2 | 115.6 |
| Light industry | 54.5 | 58.9 | 63.6 | 68.7 | 74.2 | 80.1 |
| Agriculture | 26.3 | 26.0 | 26.1 | 26.5 | 26.6 | 26.9 |
| Transport | 30.9 | 30.0 | 30.0 | 29.9 | 29.6 | 29.4 |
| Residential-commercial | 95.7 | 95.2 | 95.0 | 94.9 | 94.7 | 94.6 |

Source: <u>China Facts</u>, p. 169.

8. <u>The National Budget</u>: Revenues (in million yuan) /a

| | 1977 | 1978/b | 1979 | 1980 | 1981 | 1982 (estimate) | 1983 (forecast) |
|---|---|---|---|---|---|---|---|
| <u>Total Revenue</u> | <u>87,450</u> | <u>112,110</u> | <u>110,330</u> | <u>108,523</u> | <u>108,946</u> | <u>110,690</u> | <u>123,200</u> |
| Enterprise profit remittances /c | n/a | 57,200 | 49,290 | 43,524 | 35,368 | 31,100 | 32,390 |
| Of which: Industrial enterprise profit remittances | 32,814 | 44,100 | n/a | 44,920 | /d | n/a | n/a |
| Taxes | n/a | 51,900 | 53,780 | 57,170 | 62,989 | 67,950 | 72,970 |
| Of which: Industrial-commercial tax | 40,090 | 45,200 | n/a | 50,135 | /d | n/a | n/a |
| Agricultural tax | n/a | 2,800 | n/a | 2,767 | /d | n/a | n/a |
| Treasury bonds /e | -- | -- | -- | -- | /f | n/a | n/a |
| Foreign loans | n/a /g | 200 | 3,530 | 4,301 | 7,308 ⎫ | 7,440 | 5,400 |
| Other /h | n/a | 2,800 | 3,730 | 3,528 | 3,281 ⎭ | | 8,440/i |

/a  Consolidated budgetary accounts of all levels of government.
/b  Individual components are based on percentage breakdowns in State Statistical Bureau (1982), p. 396, and are rounded off to the nearest Y100 million.
/c  These come entirely from state-owned units.  Starting in 1980 the profit remittances of state-owned industrial enterprises are larger than the total for all state-owned units, meaning that non-industrial state enterprises were subsidized on a net basis.
/d  Preliminary figures for these items in 1981 were:  industrial enterprise profit remittances Y41,114 million, industrial-commercial tax receipts Y53,905 million, and agricultural tax receipts Y2,811 million.
/e  No treasury bonds were issued before 1981.
/f  A total of Y4,866 million worth of treasury bonds were sold in 1981, but this amount was not formally included in the accounts of any year as budgetary revenue.
/g  Foreign loans in 1977 most likely were very small.
/h  Derived as a residual.  Includes depreciation funds handed over to central authorities, averaging somewhat more than Y2 billion each year in 1978-1983.
/i  Including a new category of revenue called "construction funds for key projects in energy and transport."

Source:  Reprinted by permission of Westview Press from <u>China's Financial System</u>:  <u>The Changing Role of Banks</u> by William Byrd, pp. 147-48.  Copyright 1983 by Westview Press, Boulder, Colorado.  n/a = not available.

9. **The National Budget: Expenditures** (in million yuan) /a

| | 1977 | 1978 | 1979 | 1980 | 1981 | 1982 (estimate) | 1983 (forecast) |
|---|---|---|---|---|---|---|---|
| Total Expenditure | 84,350 | 111,100 | 127,390 | 121,273 | 111,497 | 113,690 | 126,200 |
| Capital construction | 30,088 | 45,192 | 51,470 | 41,939 | 33,063 | 30,270 | 36,180 |
| Of which: Financed by foreign loans | n/a /b | n/a /b | 7,090 | 7,300 | 7,308 | 5,000 | 5,400 |
| Modernization of existing enterprises and new product development | n/a /c | n/a /c | 7,200 | 8,045 | 6,530 | 6,070 | 6,570 |
| Additional circulating funds for enterprises /d | n/a /c | n/a /c | 5,200 | 3,671 | 2,284 | 2,300 | 2,250 |
| Aid to agriculture | 5,068 | 7,695 | 9,010 | 8,210 | 7,368 | 7,650 | 7,750 |
| Education, culture, public health, and science | 9,020 | 11,266 | 13,210 | 15,626 | 17,136 | 19,000 | 20,400 |
| Defense | 14,910 | 16,784 | 22,270 | 19,384 | 16,797 | 17,870 | 17,870 |
| Administration | 4,332 | 4,908 | 5,690 | 6,679 | 7,088 | 8,000 | 8,500 |
| Other /e | n/a | n/a | 13,340 | 17,719 | 21,231 | 22,530 | 26,680 |
| Budget Surplus /f | 3,100 | 1,010 | -17,060 | -12,750 | -2,551 | -3,000 | -3,000 |

/a  Consolidated budgetary accounts of all levels of government.
/b  Only small amounts of state-budgeted capital construction investment were financed by foreign loans in 1977 and 1978.
/c  Total spending on existing enterprises (not just the two categories given here) was Y13,680 million in 1977 and Y16,780 million in 1978.
/d  The 1979 figure also includes appropriations of credit funds for banks; later figures apparently do not.
/e  Derived as a residual, it includes expenditures like repayments of principal and interest on foreign loans, payment of interest on domestic loans from the PBC, social relief, and employment creation.
/f  Deficits are indicated by a minus sign.

Source:  Reprinted by permission of Westview Press from China's Financial System: The Changing Role of Banks by William Byrd, pp. 149-50. Copyright 1983 by Westview Press, Boulder, Colorado.  n/a = not available.

10. **Balance of Foreign Trade** (million US$)

| Year | Total Trade | | | | Communist Countries | | | | Non-Communist Countries | | | |
|---|---|---|---|---|---|---|---|---|---|---|---|---|
| | Total | Exports | Imports | Balance | Total | Exports | Imports | Balance | Total | Exports | Imports | Balance |
| 1950 | 1,210 | 620 | 590 | 30 | 350 | 210 | 140 | 70 | 860 | 410 | 450 | -40 |
| 1951 | 1,900 | 780 | 1,120 | -340 | 975 | 465 | 515 | -50 | 920 | 315 | 605 | -290 |
| 1952 | 1,890 | 875 | 1,015 | -140 | 1,315 | 605 | 710 | -105 | 575 | 270 | 305 | -35 |
| 1953 | 2,295 | 1,040 | 1,255 | -215 | 1,555 | 670 | 885 | -215 | 740 | 370 | 370 | 0 |
| 1954 | 2,350 | 1,060 | 1,290 | -230 | 1,735 | 765 | 970 | -205 | 615 | 295 | 320 | -25 |
| 1955 | 3,035 | 1,375 | 1,660 | -285 | 2,250 | 950 | 1,300 | -350 | 785 | 425 | 360 | 65 |
| 1956 | 3,120 | 1,635 | 1,485 | 150 | 2,055 | 1,045 | 1,010 | 35 | 1,065 | 590 | 475 | 115 |
| 1957 | 3,055 | 1,615 | 1,440 | 175 | 1,965 | 1,085 | 880 | 205 | 1,090 | 530 | 560 | -30 |
| 1958 | 3,765 | 1,940 | 1,825 | 115 | 2,380 | 1,280 | 1,100 | 180 | 1,385 | 660 | 725 | -65 |
| 1959 | 4,290 | 2,230 | 2,060 | 170 | 2,980 | 1,615 | 1,365 | 250 | 1,310 | 615 | 695 | -80 |
| 1960 | 3,990 | 1,960 | 2,030 | -70 | 2,620 | 1,335 | 1,285 | 50 | 1,370 | 625 | 745 | -120 |
| 1961 | 3,015 | 1,525 | 1,490 | 35 | 1,685 | 965 | 715 | 250 | 1,335 | 560 | 775 | -215 |
| 1962 | 2,670 | 1,520 | 1,150 | 370 | 1,410 | 915 | 490 | 425 | 1,265 | 605 | 660 | -55 |
| 1963 | 2,775 | 1,575 | 1,200 | 375 | 1,250 | 820 | 430 | 390 | 1,525 | 755 | 770 | -15 |
| 1964 | 3,220 | 1,750 | 1,470 | 280 | 1,100 | 710 | 390 | 320 | 2,120 | 1,040 | 1,080 | -40 |
| 1965 | 3,880 | 2,035 | 1,845 | 190 | 1,165 | 650 | 515 | 135 | 2,715 | 1,385 | 1,330 | 55 |
| 1966 | 4,245 | 2,210 | 2,035 | 175 | 1,090 | 585 | 505 | 80 | 3,155 | 1,625 | 1,530 | 95 |
| 1967 | 3,915 | 1,960 | 1,955 | 5 | 830 | 485 | 345 | 140 | 3,085 | 1,475 | 1,610 | -135 |
| 1968 | 3,785 | 1,960 | 1,825 | 135 | 840 | 500 | 340 | 160 | 2,945 | 1,460 | 1,485 | -25 |
| 1969 | 3,895 | 2,060 | 1,835 | 255 | 785 | 490 | 295 | 195 | 3,110 | 1,570 | 1,540 | 30 |
| 1970 | 4,340 | 2,095 | 2,245 | -150 | 860 | 480 | 380 | 100 | 3,480 | 1,615 | 1,865 | -250 |
| 1971 | 4,810 | 2,500 | 2,310 | 190 | 1,085 | 585 | 500 | 85 | 3,725 | 1,915 | 1,810 | 105 |
| 1972 | 6,000 | 3,150 | 2,850 | 300 | 1,275 | 740 | 535 | 205 | 4,725 | 2,410 | 2,315 | 95 |
| 1973 | 10,300 | 5,075 | 5,225 | -150 | 1,710 | 1,000 | 710 | 290 | 8,590 | 4,075 | 4,515 | -440 |
| 1974 | 14,080 | 6,660 | 7,420 | -760 | 2,435 | 1,430 | 1,010 | 420 | 11,645 | 5,230 | 6,415 | -1,185 |
| 1975 | 14,575 | 7,180 | 7,395 | -215 | 2,390 | 1,380 | 1,010 | 370 | 12,185 | 5,800 | 6,385 | -585 |
| 1976 | 13,275 | 7,265 | 6,010 | 1,255 | 2,345 | 1,240 | 1,105 | 135 | 10,930 | 6,025 | 4,905 | 1,120 |
| 1977 | 15,055 | 7,955 | 7,100 | 855 | 2,520 | 1,370 | 1,150 | 225 | 12,530 | 6,580 | 5,950 | 630 |
| 1978 | 20,435 | 10,120 | 10,315 | -195 | 3,095 | 1,560 | 1,535 | 25 | 17,340 | 8,560 | 8,780 | -220 |
| 1979 | 28,165 | 13,785 | 14,380 | 595 | 3,555 | 1,700 | 1,855 | -155 | 24,610 | 12,085 | 12,525 | -440 |
| 1980 | 39,195 | 19,780 | 19,415 | 365 | 4,025 | 2,035 | 1,990 | 45 | 35,170 | 17,745 | 17,425 | 320 |
| 1981 | 38,587 | 21,643 | 17,944 | 3,698 | 2,515 | 1,243 | 1,272 | -28.5 | 37,072 | 20,400 | 16,673 | 3,727 |
| 1982 | 38,440 | 22,359 | 16,081 | 6,278 | 2,622 | 1,355 | 1,267 | 88.0 | 35,818 | 21,004 | 14,814 | 6,190 |

Source: 1950-77 data (exports f.o.b., imports c.i.f.) are drawn from CIA, China: A Statistical Compendium, (Springfield, VA: National Technical Information Service, NTISSUB/E/282-011, July 1979), p. 13; 1978-80 data (both exports and imports f.o.b.) from CIA, National Foreign Assessment Center, China: International Trade, First Quarter, 1981 (Springfield, VA: National Technical Information Service, August 1981), pp. 6-10; 1981-82 data from BN, December 1983, pp. 10-11. Data are rounded to the nearest $5 million for 1980 and earlier.

- 123 -

## 11. Commodity Composition of Foreign Trade, 1982[1]

| | $ million | % of Total | | $ million | % of Total |
|---|---|---|---|---|---|
| **IMPORTS** | | | **EXPORTS** | | |
| **Total** | **16,081** | **100** | **Total** | **22,359** | **100** |
| **Foodstuffs & live animals** | **3,485** | **22.0** | **Foodstuffs & live animals** | **3,635** | **16.0** |
| Live animals | 2 | 01.01 | Live animals | 384 | 1.7 |
| | | | Meat and fish | 783 | 3.5 |
| Cereals and cereal preps. | 2,477 | 15.0 | Cereal and cereal preps. | 577 | 2.6 |
| Fruits and vegetables | 99 | 0.6 | Fruits and vegetables | 1,000 | 4.5 |
| Animal feedstuffs | 35 | 0.2 | Coffee, tea, and spices | 339 | 1.5 |
| Misc. food preps. and products | 817 | 5.0 | Tobacco | 53 | 0.23 |
| Beverages and tobacco | 55 | 0.3 | Other foodstuffs | 499 | 2.2 |
| **Crude materials** | **2,270** | **14.0** | **Crude materials** | **7,239** | **32.0** |
| Oilseeds and oilnuts | 82 | 0.5 | Hides and skins, undressed | 73 | 0.3 |
| Crude rubber | 310 | 2.0 | Oilseeds and oilnuts | 253 | 1.0 |
| Textile fibers | 1,174 | 7.0 | Textile fibers | 488 | 2.2 |
| Metalliferous ores | 66 | 0.4 | Crude fertilizer & minerals | 289 | 1.3 |
| Crude fertilizers & minerals | 69 | 0.4 | Metalliferous ores | 140 | 0.63 |
| Misc. materials | 569 | 3.5 | Crude animal & vegetable materials | 476 | 2.1 |
| | | | Coal and coke | 580 | 2.6 |
| Mineral fuels and products | 157 | 0.9 | Petroleum products | 4,820 | 22.0 |
| | | | Fixed vegetable oils | 82 | 0.4 |
| | | | Other materials | 38 | 0.1 |
| **Chemicals** | **1,938** | **12.0** | **Chemicals** | **1,302** | **6.0** |
| Elements and compounds | 450 | 3.0 | Elements and compounds | 588 | 2.6 |
| Dyestuffs | 125 | 0.8 | Medicines | 198 | 0.8 |
| Manufactured fertilizers | 548 | 3.0 | Manufactured fertilizers | 7 | 0.3 |
| Other chemicals | 815 | 5.0 | Other products | 509 | 2.8 |
| **Semi-manufactured goods** | **4,027** | **25.0** | **Semi-manufactured goods** | **5,218** | **23.0** |
| Paper and paperboard | 189 | 1.0 | Paper | 173 | 0.8 |
| Textile yarn and fabrics | 1,145 | 7.0 | Textile yarn and fabrics | 3,153 | 14.0 |
| Mineral manufactures | 106 | 0.6 | Mineral manufactures | 467 | 2.0 |
| Iron and steel | 1,833 | 11.0 | Iron and steel | 267 | 1.9 |
| Other products | 754 | 5.0 | Other products | 1,158 | 5.2 |
| **Machinery and equipment** | **3,401** | **21.0** | **Machinery and equipment** | **756** | **4.0** |
| Non-electric machinery | 1,637 | 10.0 | Non-electric machinery | 311 | 1.4 |
| Electrical machinery | 870 | 6.0 | Electric machinery | 341 | 1.5 |
| Transport equipment | 894 | 6.0 | Transport equipment | 104 | 0.5 |
| **Misc. manufactured goods** | **669** | **4.0** | **Misc. manufactured goods** | **4,140** | **18.0** |
| Furniture | 9 | 0.6 | Furniture | 209 | 0.9 |
| Clothing | 49 | 0.3 | Clothing | 2,441 | 11.0 |
| Precision instruments | 326 | 2.0 | Precision instruments | 136 | 0.6 |
| Other | 285 | 2.0 | Other | 1,354 | 6.1 |
| **Other** | **134** | **0.8** | **Other** | **69** | **0.3** |

[1]Figures are rounded to nearest million. Because of rounding, components may not add to totals shown in bold. Totals may not compare exactly with direction of trade data in table "Trade by Area and Selected Countries." Direction of trade figures is revised monthly as partner countries make their trade statistics available. Commodity data, however, are updated only annually.

Source: BN, December 1983, p. 9.

## 12. Direction of Foreign Trade

a) Leading Trade Partners, 1959 & 1982 (in million US$)

| 1959 | | 1982 | |
|------|------|------|------|
| Country | Total Trade | Country | Total Trade |
| USSR | 2,054 | Japan | 8,583.4 |
| East Germany | 221 | Hong Kong | 7,309.5 |
| Hong Kong | 201 | United States | 5,186.9 |
| Czechoslovakia | 195 | FRG | 1,462.7 |
| West Germany | 191 | Canada | 1,170.5 |
| United Kingdom | 121 | Australia | 1,103.0 |
| Indonesia | 111 | Singapore | 1,079.0 |
| Poland | 99 | Romania | 755.3 |
| Malaya/Singapore | 88 | France | 714.5 |
| Hungary | 84 | Italy | 582.4 |

Source: 1959 data adapted from Alexander Eckstein, Communist China's Economic Growth and Foreign Trade (New York: McGraw-Hill, 1966), pp. 94, 280-85, 291. 1982 data from BN, December 1983, p. 12.

b) Trade by Areas and Selected Countries, 1982 (in million US$)

|  | Total | Balance |
|---|---|---|
| Total (all countries) | 38,440.4 | 6,278.1 |
| Non-Communist Countries | 35,818.3 | 6,190.1 |
| East Asia & Pacific | 9,801.5 | 1,023.1 |
|   Australia | 1,103.0 | -525.6 |
|   Japan | 8,583.4 | 1,583.4 |
| North America | 6,357.4 | -1,477.0 |
|   U.S. | 5,186.9 | -637.1 |
|   Canada | 1,170.5 | -839.9 |
| Western Europe | 4,780.9 | -101.3 |
|   France | 714.5 | 43.9 |
|   FRG | 1,462.7 | -242.5 |
|   Italy | 582.4 | 161.8 |
|   U.K. | 473.5 | 116.5 |
| Southeast Asia | 10,911.8 | 4,743.0 |
|   Malaysia | 407.0 | 148.9 |
|   Singapore | 1,079.0 | 598.2 |
| South Asia | 588.6 | 92.6 |
|   Sri Lanka | 48.3 | 31.6 |
|   Pakistan | 293.3 | -10.3 |
| Middle East | 1,494.4 | 1,210.8 |
|   Kuwait | 191.6 | 165.8 |
|   Syria | 176.3 | 105.7 |
| North Africa | 334.1 | 99.2 |
|   Egypt | 115.6 | -5.4 |
|   Tunisia | 53.2 | -14.7 |
| Sub-Saharan Africa | 632.2 | 354.6 |
|   Nigeria | 41.3 | 41.3 |
|   Sudan | 78.0 | 13.0 |
| Latin America | 917.6 | 245.2 |
|   Argentina | 129.5 | -112.5 |
|   Brazil | 400.7 | 277.9 |
| Hong Kong | 7,309.5 | 3,443.7 |
| Communist Countries | 2,622.1 | 88.0 |
|   U.S.S.R. | 307.8 | -22.6 |
|   Eastern Europe | 1,540.4 | 142.0 |
|   Czechoslovakia | 145.2 | 20.5 |
|   GDR | 203.7 | 2.1 |
|   Romania | 755.3 | 54.7 |

Source: BN, December 1983, p. 11.

## 13. <u>Highlights of US Trade with China</u>

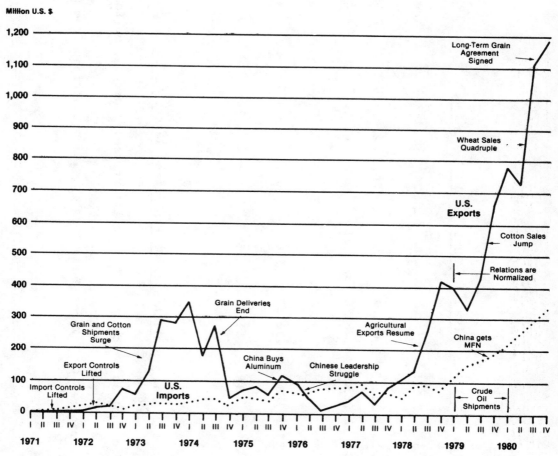

Data are from US Department of Commerce and show both
exports and imports on an f.o.b. basis.

Source:  <u>BN</u>, June 1981, p. 17.

14. US-China Trade, 1978-1983 (million US$)

| | 1978 | 1979 | 1980 | 1981 | 1982 | 1983 | 1984 (projected) |
|---|---|---|---|---|---|---|---|
| US Exports (fas)* | 823.6 | 1,716.5 | 3,749.0 | 3,598.6 | 2,904.5 | 2,163.2 | 3,000 |
| US Imports (customs value)* | 324.1 | 548.5 | 1,039.2 | 1,830.0 | 2,215.9 | 2,217.5 | 2,500 |
| TOTAL | 1,147.7 | 2,265.0 | 4,788.2 | 5,428.6 | 5,120.4 | 4,380.7 | 5,500+ |
| US Trade Surplus(+)/ Deficit(-) | 499.5 | 1,168.0 | 2,709.8 | 1,768.6 | 688.6 | -54.3 | 500 |
| US Two-way Trade as % of China's Total Trade ** | 5% | 8% | 13% | 15% | 13% | 10% | 11-12% |

* approximately equivalent to fob; see Highlights of US Export and Import Trade, Bureau of the Census, U.S. Department of Commerce (FT 990)

** US imports and exports (fob/fob) as percent of China's imports and exports (fob/fob)

Source: U.S. Department of Commerce; CBR, March-April 1984, p. 19; projections from CBR, January-February 1984, p. 37.

15. **US-China Trade:  Selected Exports to China** (million US$)

| Commodity | Jan-Oct 1982 | Jan-Oct 1983 |
|---|---|---|
| wheat | 983.7 | 206.1 |
| corn | 131.1 | 158.1 |
| soybeans | 63.2 | 0 |
| logs & lumber | 190.7 | 184.6 |
| raw cotton | 176.2 | 1.1 |
| chemical elements · & compounds | 43.8 | 44.3 |
| fertilizers | 121.2 | 129.3 |
| synthetic resins & rubber | 196.5 | 72.1 |
| paper & paperboard | 30.4 | 37.2 |
| textile yarns & fabric | 124.1 | 13.3 |
| aluminum & alloys | 0.3 | 46.0 |
| hand tools | 3.0 | 16.4 |
| coal cutting, mining & well-drilling machinery | 41.2 | 35.8 |
| metal-working machinery | 2.0 | 18.1 |
| office machinery & computers | 30.4 | 41.0 |

Source:  National Committee for US-China Trade, 1983.

16. **US-China Trade:  Selected Imports from China** (million US$)

| Commodity | Jan-Oct 1982 | Jan-Oct 1983 |
|---|---|---|
| clothing & accessories | 527.5 | 663.3 |
| textile yarns & fabrics | 208.2 | 197.8 |
| footwear | 34.3 | 27.3 |
| textile fibers, raw | 14.8 | 12.3 |
| petroleum products | 323.5 | 327.6 |
| crude petroleum | 42.6 | 34.6 |
| non-ferrous metals | 42.6 | 27.4 |
| non-ferrous ores & concentrates | 20.5 | 7.7 |
| non-metallic minerals | 34.1 | 27.2 |
| metal manufactures | 44.2 | 50.1 |
| chemical elements & compounds | 56.8 | 37.5 |
| medicines & pharmaceuticals | 15.0 | 18.8 |
| glassware & pottery | 26.8 | 29.2 |
| art & antiques | 16.8 | 23.3 |
| vegetables & fruit | 44.6 | 46.3 |
| tea & maté | 8.3 | 8.1 |

Source:  National Committee for US-China Trade, 1983.

17. Foreign Joint Equity Ventures in China by Country and Region
(million US$) (US firms lead all other countries with 34 percent
of the total value of foreign investment in Chinese joint
ventures.)

| | Number of Ventures | | Investment | | |
|---|---|---|---|---|---|
| | In export zones | Outside export zones | Foreign side | Chinese side | Total value |
| Hong Kong | 6 | 27 | $78.9 | $73.4 | $152.3 |
| U.S. | 2 | 17 | $102.6 | $123.6 | $226.2 |
| Japan | 1 | 11 | $19.6 | $34.8 | $54.4 |
| U.K. | 1 | 4 | $31.2 | $90.8 | $122.0 |
| Philippines | 1 | 3 | $32.8 | $34.0 | $66.8 |
| Norway | 1 | 1 | $20.9 | $21.7 | $42.5 |
| W. Germany | -- | 2 | $0.3 | $0.4 | $0.7 |
| France | -- | 2 | $0.3 | $0.7 | $1.0 |
| Belgium | -- | 1 | $8.0 | $12.0 | $20.0 |
| Switzerland | -- | 1 | $4.0 | $12.0 | $16.0 |
| Sweden | -- | 1 | $6.0 | $6.0 | $12.0 |
| Thailand | -- | 1 | $0.3 | $0.5 | $0.8 |
| Australia | -- | 1 | $0.2 | $0.2 | $0.5 |
| Other | 2 | 3 | $0.1 | $0.1 | $0.2 |
| TOTAL | 14 | 75 | $305.2 | $410.2 | $715.4 |

Source:  CBR, September-October 1983, p. 28.

VII.  MATERIAL WELFARE, EDUCATION, AND PUBLIC HEALTH

## 1.  Introduction and Suggested Readings

All the characteristic problems of very poor societies plagued China in 1949.  Distribution of wealth and income was quite unequal and most people were at or below subsistence level.  Malnutrition, starvation, and infectious diseases were widespread.  As a result, only 80 out of every 100 infants survived to their first birthday; the average life expectancy was between 35 and 40 years of age.  Social services were minimal and concentrated in urban areas.  The ratio of patients to doctors trained in modern science was around 35,000:1.  There were only 17 million primary school students, 20% of the total age group.  Only a million of those could expect to get any secondary education.  And probably a substantial majority of adults were illiterate.

How has post-1949 economic development (outlined in the previous chapter) affected the welfare of the Chinese people?  The Communist Party has undeniably ended the mass poverty that it found when it took power in 1949.  Through institutional and technological change, through expanding production and improving distribution, the regime has for the most part laid a floor of subsistence so that very few people must relive the horrors of the past.  Public health services have reduced serious infectious diseases.  Basic education is now available to many instead of the very few.

But progress beyond subsistence has come slowly to China's growing population.  Consequently, Party leaders have continually argued over whether poverty or inequality is the greater political liability, and over how to rectify the situation.  One group, led by Mao Zedong before his death, has held that inequality breeds political alienation, which in turn breeds economic stagnation.  It has advocated reducing the gap -- in material goods, in education, in health care, etc. -- between the relative "haves" and the relative "have-nots."  It favors fostering political consciousness to spur productivity.  The other group, epitomized by Deng Xiaoping, believes that this egalitarianism has only perpetuated backwardness.  It believes that all will benefit to some degree from rapid economic growth, but that those who are more productive should receive a greater material reward.

Material Welfare  Estimating the quality of life in China is not an easy task since statistical information is limited and of uncertain validity and reliability.  Per capita GNP has risen slowly over the past 30 years, declining after the Great Leap Forward and rising more rapidly in the years following Mao's death.  Per capita supplies of basic necessities -- grain, cotton cloth, processed sugar, for example -- grew rapidly in the early 1950s and then stagnated until after Mao's death.  Data on average food consumption (table [VII.2] on page 137) indicate a diet limited in both quantity and quality.

The post-Mao leadership has admitted that there is a good bit of

variation around these national averages.   It was revealed in March
1979, for example, that about 100 million people (10% of the population) suffered from malnutrition.   Only rough estimates of the extent
of social inequality are available at this point.   The tables (VII.3)
on pages 137-138 provide Chinese government and World Bank measures of
income inequality.   They suggest that China has been fairly successful
in limiting income inequality within urban and rural communities,
though less successful in reducing disparity between city and
countryside.   It is clear, however, that the material incentives now
being used to spur productivity will widen the gaps that still exist,
with unpredictable political and social consequences.

A recent province-by-province comparison of industrial and
agricultural output value indicates wide disparities in levels of
development (see table [VII.4] on page 139).   The major cities and
provinces of the east and northeast (Shanghai, Tianjin, Beijing
municipalities; Liaoning, Jiangsu and Heilongjiang provinces), where
economic development began before the communist victory in 1949, remain
the leading areas in value of output.   Most striking is Shanghai
municipality, where per-capita output value is twice as high as in
Tianjin and Beijing and 18 times that of Guizhou province.   Shanghai
thus continues to play a primary role in the national economy, just as
it did pre-1949.

More detailed information on urban wages and family budgets suggests some of the sources of inequality in cities.   For the individual,
occupation and seniority level are the key factors.   Senior cadres,
professionals, and technicians receive substantially higher monthly
incomes than juniors in their own field or ordinary workers.   For
families, the proportion of workers to non-workers in the household is
crucial.   The size of the family work force is even more important in
the countryside, and ranks with natural conditions as the chief
determinants of rural income.   The disparity in wages and consumption
between urban and rural areas is shown in the tables on pages 140-142.
The table on page 142 presents agricultural income earned from
collective work and sideline activities.   Introduction of the
"responsibility system" in rural areas has allowed private income to
increase.   Private income as a percentage of collective income still
varies between areas, however.   The post-1978 economic reforms are
contributing to greater diversity in sources of income and, while
raising income levels in general, also are increasing inequality in
earnings.

It would be incomplete, however, to concentrate only on income as
a measure of inequality.   Foreign observers and the Chinese themselves
have pointed out that those in positions of power have special access
to material goods and social services, and can, if they choose, use
their posts for personal or family gain.   This form of corruption --
its prevalence is unknown -- lends a definite political cast to
inequality caused by economic factors.

Education   How best to use scarce educational resources has been
an issue of continuing controversy in China.   Quality and quantity have
been competing goals.   On the one hand, economic development requires
increasing numbers of technicians and managers.   On the other, spread-
ing basic knowledge is essential to rural development and fostering
upward mobility.   The rival priorities are evident in the evolution of
the educational system (see outline [VII.9] on pages 143-144) and
enrollment statistics (see table [VII.10] on page 145).

The pre-Cultural Revolution approach emphasized training technical

specialists. Middle school and college enrollments grew at a faster
rate than primary school enrollments. The Cultural Revolution attacked
this focus on expertise: schools were closed for varying lengths of
time from 1966 on, with universities not reopening until 1970. The
approach that then emerged stressed the expansion of primary and
secondary enrollments, especially in the rural areas, and the selection
of university students on the basis of political commitment rather than
tested academic ability. The post-Mao leadership has reemphasized
expertise. Expanding higher education is the highest priority, uni-
versalizing middle school education is now a goal for the long term,
and entrance exams have been restored as a screening device.
Short-term colleges and "TV universities" have been opened and the
government has encouraged the creation of rotational training programs
for cadres. Graduate degree programs have been reintroduced and the
number of students sent abroad greatly increased. By the end of 1982,
approximately 6,000 Chinese government-sponsored students and research
scholars and 3,500 privately sponsored students were studying in the
United States alone (BN, December 1983, p. 7).

An educational balance sheet reveals pluses and minuses in both
quality and quantity. Primary education is now nearly universal, and
secondary education has expanded considerably. The adult literacy rate
is said to be about 85%. However, rural schools still lag behind their
urban and suburban counterparts, and closing that gap does not seem to
be a high priority of current policy. The Cultural Revolution turmoil
and the enrollment policies adopted after 1970 are said to have caused
a decline in school discipline. In contrast to the interest in
expanding opportunities for higher education, tighter standards,
demographic trends, and introduction of the "responsibility system" in
rural areas have caused primary and secondary enrollments to decline.

Concerning quality, the higher education system has over the past
30 years trained a corps of specialists in fields appropriate to
modernization -- science, engineering, teaching, and medicine (see
table [VII.12] page 147). But here the Cultural Revolution took a
tremendous toll, damaging or destroying the careers of older specialists and preventing the training of younger ones. The revival of the
higher education system will remedy this shortage of skilled manpower
only over the long term. To further deal with the problem of lack of
specialized skills, senior high schools in many provinces are focusing
upon vocational training.

If one uses aggregate enrollment statistics to measure equality of
educational opportunity, the following becomes clear:

--As noted above, primary education has become increasingly
accessible, with about 93% of the age group in school.

--Secondary education has become increasingly accessible (middle
school enrollments were about 10% of primary school enrollments in
1957, 13% in 1965, 25% in 1974, 39% in 1977, and 38% in 1980), but
total enrollments declined in 1980 and 1981.

--As secondary education expanded to 1980, university education
became relatively less accessible (enrollments for the latter were 7%
of the former in 1957, 4% in 1965, and around 1% in 1974 and 1977).
That trend, which actually continued during the Cultural Revolution,
has now been reversed to a limited extent (the ratio was 2.1% in 1980).

--Primary school enrollments have more than doubled since 1957.
The probability of the average primary school student getting into
university is somewhat better at present (around 1 in 128 in 1980),
after decreasing opportunities from 1957 to the late 1970s.

But these general trends mask an underlying question: whether specific groups -- for example, urban youth, particularly children of officials and the well educated -- are getting better access to scarce secondary and higher education resources. The renewed emphasis on academic admissions criteria, especially for university, would seem to favor these groups. Mao's mid-1960's belief that elite groups held a disproportionate share of college enrollments, at a time when the number of high school graduates was growing, was a partial basis for his Cultural Revolution attack on the educational system. The current leadership's emphasis on improving quality may create similar political discontent among those who have gained and would stand to gain from the Maoist stress on education for all.

    <u>Health Care</u>   As with education, medical services have expanded gradually, but not without political conflict over how they are distributed. The number of hospital beds and doctors has increased over time (see tables [VII.13 and 14] on pages 147-148), with public health campaigns to combat specific problems supplementing the more formal medical institutions. This combination has brought about the "modernization" of China's health problems. Infectious and endemic diseases are now fairly rare. According to Chinese estimates, life expectancy is now 67 years for men and 69 for women; infant mortality is around one-tenth of its 1949 rate. As in the industrial world, cancer and cardiovascular problems are now the main cause of death. Although epidemiological statistics for one district of Beijing are not representative of the country as a whole, they do demonstrate the dimensions of the transformation (see table [VII.15] on page 148).

    Despite this progress, there has been substantial political controversy over which groups should receive what level of medical services. Public health work before 1966 tended to focus on the urban areas, although some progress was made in rural health care. With the launching of the Cultural Revolution, the countryside was given special emphasis. Subsequently, health services spread much more broadly, so that by 1979 each of the country's 2,000 counties had at least one general hospital, and each of the 55,000 communes had at least one clinic. By 1981 urban and rural areas were served by over 2 million medical and health personnel, more than three times the number in 1950 (see table [VII.14] on page 148). The total number of hospital beds increased from less than 100,000 to more than 2 million during the same period (see table [VII.13] on page 147).

    But this quantitative improvement came at the expense of quality of care, especially in the cities. Upgrading urban hospitals and improving the skills of medical personnel -- especially paramedics and full doctors trained after 1966 -- are now of high priority. It remains to be seen whether there will be sufficient resources (scarce to begin with) to maintain and improve services in the countryside, where peasants have become used to basic health care.

    Evaluating the quality of life in China depends in large measure on the yardstick employed. If the standard is the dark days of the 1940s, then there has been substantial progress. Basic subsistence and services are available to the great majority of the population, an accomplishment which many developing countries have yet to achieve. How to meet the needs of the poorest 10-20% of the population, whose nutrition, education, and health levels are significantly lower than the rest of the population, will be an immense challenge. Even if the standard is the still spartan existence of China's cities and wealthier communes, then a large proportion of the population has a long way to go. If one judges by the expectations of Chinese themselves, there can only be a tentative verdict. Those who experienced China at its pre-1949 worst seem fairly content. Less satisfied are those for whom the past is only their parents' reminiscences, who have lived the contradiction between socialism's promise and its mixed performance. Unless the "four modernizations" soon bring them palpable rewards, they may be unwilling to sacrifice for an uncertain future.

## Suggested Readings

Ch'en Pi-chao. Population and Health Policy in the People's Republic of China. Washington, DC: The Smithsonian Institution, 1976. A detailed and useful introduction to institutions and policies in the public health and population control fields.

Eberstadt, Nick. Poverty in China. Bloomington: Indiana University International Development Institute, 1980. An evaluation of the PRC's success in raising the level of human welfare, in the context of performance of other developing countries and prior claims of China's progress.

Fingar, Thomas, ed. Higher Education in the People's Republic of China. Stanford: Stanford University Northeast Asia-United States Forum on International Policy, 1980. A thorough review of the structure of the contemporary Chinese university system.

Henderson, Gail E. and Myron S. Cohen. The Chinese Hospital. New Haven: Yale University Press, 1984. A report on health care and hospital life by a sociologist and physical who worked for five months in a Chinese hospital.

Lampton, David M. The Politics of Medicine in China. Boulder, CO: Westview Press, 1977. A detailed analysis of health care as an issue of political conflict.

Lofstedte, Jan-Inger. Chinese Educational Policy: Changes and Contradictions, 1949-1979. Atlantic Highlands, NJ: Humanities Press, 1980. Describes the evolution of education policy in the PRC, with emphasis on primary and secondary levels.

Montaperto, Ronald N., and Jay Henderson, eds. China's Schools in Flux. White Plains, NY: M. E. Sharpe, 1979. A report on China's primary and secondary school systems during the post-Cultural Revolution transition.

Orleans, Leo, ed. Science in Contemporary China. Stanford: Stanford University Press, 1980. A field-by-field report of the state of the art of Chinese science.

Pepper, Suzanne. "Chinese Education After Mao: Two Steps Forward, Two Steps Back and Begin Again?" The China Quarterly, no. 81 (March 1980), pp. 1-65. A comprehensive analysis of the post-Mao educational system and the contrast with its predecessor.

Seybolt, Peter J., ed. Revolutionary Education in China: Documents and Commentary. White Plains, NY: International Arts and Science Press (now M. E. Sharpe), 1973. Examination of the educational system that emerged in the early 1970s.

Shirk, Susan L. Competitive Comrades: Career Incentives and Student Strategies in China. Berkeley: University of California Press, 1982. A case study of the application of Maoist educational policies in an urban high school.

Unger, Jonathan. Education Under Mao: Class and Competition in Canton Schools 1960-80. New York: Columbia University Press, 1983. An overview of educational policies in China which focuses on the demographic pressures limiting advancement in the educational system.

Wolfe, Margery, and Roxane Witke, eds. Women in Chinese Society. Stanford: Stanford University Press, 1975. A collection of ten essays by historians and anthropologists on women in both traditional and contemporary Chinese society.

2. Food Intake, 1975-1981

| | 1978 Smil | 1975-77 FAO | 1980-81 Klatt | 1981 SSB |
|---|---|---|---|---|
| **Calories per day** | | | | |
| vegetable | 2,030 | 2,153 | 2,150 | n/a |
| animal | 105 | 256 | 250 | n/a |
| TOTAL | 2,135 | 2,439 | 2,400 | 2,666 |
| **Protein grams per day** | | | | |
| vegetable | 51 | 50 | 55 | n/a |
| animal | 6 | 13 | 15 | n/a |
| TOTAL | 57 | 63 | 70 | 79 |
| **Fats, grams per day** | | | | |
| vegetable | 15 | 19 | 15 | n/a |
| animal | 10 | 21 | 20 | n/a |
| TOTAL | 25 | 40 | 35 | 41 |

Source:  V. Smil, Food Policy, May 1981; FAO, Monthly Bulletin,
November 1979; W. Klatt, "The Staff of Life:  Living Standards
in China, 1977-1981," CQ, no. 93 (March 1983), p. 45; and PRC
State Statistical Bureau, BR, June 7, 1982.  n/a = not
available.

3. Estimates of Income Inequality

a)  Chinese Government Estimates of Per Capita Income

| | |
|---|---|
| National, 1977 | 120.4 yuan |
| National, 1980 | 193.8 yuan |
| Rate of increase | 73.4% |
| | |
| Urban, 1977 | 411.5 yuan |
| Urban, 1980 | 569.9 yuan |
| Rate of increase | 38.5% |
| | |
| Rural, 1977 | 65.4 yuan |
| Rural, 1980 | 118.5 yuan |
| Rate of increase | 81.2% |
| | |
| Urban-Rural Ratio, 1977 | 6.3:1 |
| Urban-Rural Ratio, 1980 | 4.8:1 |

b)   World Bank Estimates of Urban Inequality, 1980

|  | Income Share* |
|---|---|
| Poorest 40% | 30.0% |
| Next 40% | 41.8% |
| Richest 20% | 28.2% |
| Richest 10% | 15.8% |
| Gini Coefficient | 0.16 |

c)   World Bank Estimates of Rural Inequality, 1980

|  | Income Share* |
|---|---|
| Poorest 40% | 20.1% |
| Next 40% | 60.5% |
| Richest 20% | 39.4% |
| Richest 10% | 22.8% |
| Gini Coefficient | 0.31 |

* distribution is of people ranked by household per capita income

Source:   a) Ta Kung Pao, October 8, 1981.
          b) and c) Far Eastern Economic Review, August 14, 1981.

4. Per Capita Total Industrial and Agricultural Output Value, 1981*

| Regions | Total Output Value (million yuan) | Annual Average Population (million persons) | Per-capita Output Value (yuan) |
|---|---|---|---|
| National | 749,000 | 989.39 | 757 |
| Shanghai | 64,200 | 11.55 | 5,558 |
| Tianjin | 21,800 | 7.57 | 2,880 |
| Beijing | 23,500 | 8.94 | 2,629 |
| Liaoning | 53,500 | 35.11 | 1,524 |
| Jiangsu | 67,400 | 59.74 | 1,128 |
| Heilongjiang | 34,100 | 32.22 | 1,058 |
| Jilin | 19,100 | 22.21 | 860 |
| Zhejiang | 33,100 | 38.49 | 860 |
| Hubei | 36,000 | 47.12 | 764 |
| Shandong | 54,300 | 73.46 | 739 |
| Shanxi | 17,200 | 24.93 | 690 |
| Hebei | 33,200 | 52.12 | 637 |
| Guangdong | 37,000 | 58.32 | 634 |
| Xinjiang | 7,500 | 12.93 | 580 |
| Hunan | 30,700 | 53.21 | 577 |
| Fujian | 14,000 | 25.38 | 552 |
| Shaanxi | 15,500 | 28.48 | 544 |
| Inner Mongolia | 10,200 | 18.90 | 540 |
| Gansu | 10,200 | 19.30 | 528 |
| Ningxia | 2,000 | 3.79 | 528 |
| Qinghai | 2,000 | 3.80 | 526 |
| Jiangxi | 16,800 | 32.87 | 511 |
| Henan | 36,800 | 73.42 | 501 |
| Anhui | 24,600 | 49.25 | 499 |
| Sichuan | 46,700 | 98.72 | 473 |
| Guangxi | 15,400 | 35.76 | 431 |
| Yunnan | 13,000 | 31.98 | 407 |
| Tibet | 740 | 1.86 | 398 |
| Guizhou | 8,500 | 28.02 | 303 |

* calculated according to 1980 constant prices

Source: China Facts, p. 140.

5.  <u>Urban Work Force and Wages, 1977–1981</u> (All wages are monthly
figures in yuan [in 1980 1 yuan = $0.62].  Not included are allowances
for transportation, cost of living, etc., nor bonuses paid in
factories.)

|  | 1978 | 1979 | 1980 | 1981 |
|---|---|---|---|---|
| Urban Work Force (millions) | | | | |
| Public Sector | 74.51 | 76.93 | 80.19 | 83.72 |
| Collective Sector | 20.48 | 22.74 | 24.25 | 25.68 |
| TOTAL | 94.99 | 99.67 | 104.44 | 109.40 |
| | | | | |
| Wage Bill (billion yuan) | | | | |
| Public Sector | 46.90 | 52.94 | 62.80 | 66.00 |
| Collective Sector | 10.02 | 11.72 | 14.50 | 16.00 |
| TOTAL | 56.92 | 64.66 | 77.30 | 82.00 |
| | | | | |
| Average Wage (yuan per month) | | | | |
| Public Sector | 52.5 | 58.7 | 65.2* | 67.7* |
| Collective Sector | 40.3 | 43.9 | 50.0* | 53.5* |
| TOTAL | 50.0 | 54.2 | 61.7* | 64.3* |
| | | | | |
| Average Wage (yuan per annum) | | | | |
| Public Sector | 630 | 705 | 782** | 812** |
| Collective Sector | 490 | 515 | 600** | 642** |
| TOTAL | 600 | 650 | 740** | 772** |

\*   includes food subsidy of 5 yuan
\*\* includes food subsidy of 60 yuan

Source:  Reprinted with permission from W. Klatt, "The Staff of Life:  Living
Standards in China, 1977–81," <u>CQ</u>, no. 93 (March 1983), p. 40.

6.  Urban Income and Expenditure, 1978-1981

| Income per capita (percent) yuan per month: | 1978 | 1980 | 1981 |
|---|---|---|---|
| over 50 | (5.0) | 9.3 | 18.4 |
| 25-50 | (65.0) | 67.2 | 74.1 |
| under 25 | (30.0) | 23.5 | 7.5 |
| TOTAL | 100.0 | 100.0 | 100.0 |

| Expenditure per capita (percent) | | | |
|---|---|---|---|
| Foodstuffs | 64.0 | 60.6 | 61.6 |
| Clothing | 15.1 | 18.6 | 16.1 |
| Daily necessities | 14.0 | 15.6 | 16.6 |
| Other expenditure | 6.9 | 5.2 | 5.7 |
| TOTAL | 100.0 | 100.0 | 100.0 |

| Income disparities (1980) by per capita income yuan per month: | per worker | per capita | per family |
|---|---|---|---|
| over 50 | 71.2 | 61.0 | 213.6 |
| 35-50 | 64.4 | 43.0 | 180.3 |
| 25-35 | 63.5 | 35.0 | 158.7 |
| 15-25 | 61.9 | 24.8 | 123.8 |
| under 15 | 62.4 | 15.3 | 81.1 |
| TOTAL | 63.9 | 35.8 | 157.9 |

Source:  Reprinted with permission from W. Klatt, "The Staff of Life:
         Living Standards in China, 1977-81," CQ, no. 93 (March 1983),
         p. 41; parentheses indicate author's estimate.


7.  Consumer Goods Production (million units unless otherwise
    indicated)

| | 1982 | % change 1982/81 | 1983 | % change 1983/82 |
|---|---|---|---|---|
| TV sets | 5.92 | 9.8 | 6.6 | 11.6 |
| bicycles | 24.2 | 38.0 | 28.0 | 15.7 |
| sewing machines | 12.86 | 23.8 | 11.0 | -14.4 |
| wrist watches | 33.01 | 14.9 | 36.1 | 9.5 |
| radios | 17.24 | -57.5 | 18.8 | 9.3 |
| refrigerators (thou. units) | 99.9 | 79.7 | 197.6 | 97.8 |

Source:  Adapted from CBR, January-February 1984, p. 53.

8.  Rural Income and Expenditure, 1977-1981

| | 1978 | 1978 | 1981 | 1981 |
|---|---|---|---|---|
| Sample Survey: | | | | |
| households | | n/a | | 18,529 |
| counties | | n/a | | 568 |
| provinces | | n/a | | 28 |
| | Yuan per annum | percent | Yuan per annum | percent |
| Income per capita (in cash) | 63.9 | 47.8 | 153.2 | 68.6 |
| (in kind) | 69.7 | 52.2 | 70.2 | 31.4 |
| Total | 133.6 | 100.0 | 223.4 | 100.0 |
| | | | | |
| Income per capita (collective) | 88.5 | 66.2 | 116.2 | 52.0 |
| (sideline) | 35.8 | 26.8 | 84.5 | 38.0 |
| (other) | 9.3 | 7.0 | 22.7 | 10.0 |
| Total | 133.6 | 100.0 | 223.4 | 100.0 |
| | | | | |
| Expenditure per capita: | | | | |
| purchase of commodities | 44.8 | 38.6 | n/a | n/a |
| value of own production | 68.1 | 58.7 | n/a | n/a |
| other expenditures | 3.1 | 2.7 | n/a | n/a |
| TOTAL | 116.0 | 100.0 | 190.8 | 100.8 |
| | | | | |
| Expenditure per capita: | | | | |
| staple foodstuffs | 51.4 | 44.5 | 61.1 | 32.1 |
| non-staple foodstuffs | 24.7 | 21.2 | 41.5 | 21.8 |
| other foodstuffs | 2.5 | 2.0 | 11.2 | 5.8 |
| all foodstuffs | 78.6 | 66.7 | 113.8 | 59.7 |
| clothing | 14.7 | 12.7 | 23.6 | 12.3 |
| housing | 3.7 | 3.2 | 18.7 | 9.8 |
| other necessities | 7.6 | 6.6 | 19.5 | 10.2 |
| fuel | 8.2 | 7.1 | 10.6 | 5.6 |
| cultural expenses | 3.2 | 2.7 | 4.6 | 2.4 |
| TOTAL | 116.0 | 100.0 | 190.8 | 100.0 |
| | | | | |
| Residual per capita (income unspent) | 17.6 | ---- | 32.6 | ---- |
| | | | | |
| Income disparities (yuan per annum): | | | | |
| under 150 | ---- | 65.0 | ---- | 19.7 |
| 150-300 | ---- | 32.6 | ---- | 57.7 |
| over 300 | ---- | 2.4 | ---- | 22.6 |
| TOTAL | ---- | 100.0 | ---- | 100.0 |

Source:   Reprinted with permission from W. Klatt, "The Staff of Life: Living Standards in China, 1977-81," CQ, no. 93 (March 1983), p. 48.  n/a = not available.

## 9. Outline: Evolution of the Educational System

### The Pre-Cultural Revolution Model

This model emerged gradually over the years between 1949 and 1965. It emphasized the cultivation of expertise, through examinations to evaluate performance and potential, and "key" schools at all levels for brighter students. Theoretical research was stressed in universities. Curriculm was centralized. This model was attacked vigorously during the Cultural Revolution as an elitist system that did not address adequately the educational needs of Chinese society.

Primary School:     6 years - 4 years junior and 2 years senior

Secondary School:   6 years - 3 years junior and 3 years senior

Higher Education:   Undergraduate programs, 4 to 5 years; teacher's college, 2 years; postgraduate research & training

### The Cultural Revolution Model

Following the Cultural Revolution period's initial turmoil, there was much local experimentation, especially in curriculum, and no single pattern prevailed for the country as a whole. On the whole, years of schooling were reduced. Examinations, academic criteria, teaching professionalism were downgraded, and more emphasis was placed on political criteria. Applied or practical study was stressed over advanced theoretical research. Two to three years of productive labor were required before admission to university.

Primary School:     4 to 6 years

Secondary School:   4 to 5 years, 2 to 3 years junior and 2 to 3 years senior

Higher Education:   2 to 3 years for undergraduate programs; in-service training replaces postgraduate programs

### The Post-Mao Model

Since mid-1977, the major elements of the pre-Cultural Revolution model — academic criteria, examinations, length of schooling, "key" schools, centralization of curricula, postgraduate study, theoretical research — have returned. Some aspects of the Cultural Revolution model -- the work experience requirement before university, heavy emphasis on political commitment -- were relaxed. Advanced students and scholars, many of them graduates of the pre-Cultural Revolution system, have gone overseas to study.

Primary School:     6 years

Secondary School:   6 years - 3 years junior and 3 years senior

Higher Education:    4-year undergraduate program; restoration of
                     graduate research and degree programs; overseas
                     study


    <u>Other Educational Institutions</u>   Three important, and more or less
formal, types of institutions supplement the regular educational system.   First is the variety of locally run preschool programs (nurseries, day-care centers, and kindergartens).   Second, is the large,
complex system of part-time and "half-work/half-study" schools that
provide compensatory technical or vocational education.   Third, Chinese
citizens acquire knowledge about work, society, and politics through
participation in study groups, special campaigns and conferences, and
on-the-job training.

10. <u>School Enrollments</u> (in thousands)

| Year | Primary | General Secondary | Specialized Secondary | University |
|------|---------|-------------------|-----------------------|------------|
| 1949 | 24,391 | 1,039 | 220 | 117 |
| 1950 | 28,924 | 1,305 | n/a | 137 |
| 1951 | 43,154 | 1,568 | n/a | 153 |
| 1952 | 51,100 | 2,490 | n/a | 191 |
| 1953 | 51,664 | 2,933 | n/a | 212 |
| 1954 | 51,218 | 3,587 | n/a | 153 |
| 1955 | 53,126 | 3,900 | n/a | 288 |
| 1956 | 63,464 | 5,165 | n/a | 403 |
| 1957 | 64,279 | 6,281 | n/a | 441 |
| 1958 | 86,400 | 8,520 | n/a | 660 |
| 1959 | 90,000 | n/a | n/a | 810 |
| 1960 | 90,000 | n/a | n/a | 955 |
| 1965 | 110,000 | 14,418 | n/a | 533 |
| 1972 | 127,000 | 36,000 | n/a | 200 |
| 1974 | 145,000 | 36,500 | n/a | 325 |
| 1977 | 150,000 | 58,280 | 690 | 620 |
| 1978 | 146,240 | 65,480 | 889 | 850 |
| 1979 | 146,630 | 59,050 | 1,199 | 1,020 |
| 1980 | 146,270 | 55,081 | 1,697* | 1,144 |
| 1981 | 143,330 | 48,596 | 1,550* | 1,280 |
| 1982 | 139,720 | 47,540 | 1,742** | 1,154 |
| 1983 | 135,780 | 46,873 | 2,363** | 1,207 |

* includes agricultural and professional middle schools

** includes secondary technical schools, agricultural and vocational middle schools

Source:  David M. Lampton, "Performance and the Chinese Political System," <u>CQ</u>, no. 75 (September 1978), p. 525; Suzanne Pepper, "<u>Chinese</u> Education After Mao," <u>CQ</u>, no. 81 (March 1980), p. 6; Leo A. Orleans, <u>Manpower for Science and Engineering in China</u> (Washington, DC:  Government Printing Office, 1980); <u>BR</u>, May 12, 1980, pp. 12-15; <u>BR</u>, May 18, 1981, pp. 18-19; China <u>Report</u>, p. 674; <u>BR</u>, October 3, 1983, pp. 26-27; and <u>BR</u>, May 14, 1984, p. 10.  n/a = not available.

## 11. Educational Specialization and Achievement

### Number of University Graduates in

| Year | Engi-neering | Natural Sciences | Agricul./Forestry | Medicine | Other* | Total |
|------|------|------|------|------|------|------|
| 1949 | 4,752 | 1,584 | 1,718 | 1,314 | 11,632 | 21,000 |
| 1950 | 4,711 | 1,468 | 2,477 | 1,391 | 8,953 | 18,000 |
| 1951 | 4,416 | 1,488 | 1,538 | 2,366 | 9,192 | 19,000 |
| 1952 | 10,213 | 2,215 | 2,361 | 2,636 | 14,575 | 32,000 |
| 1953 | 14,565 | 1,753 | 2,633 | 2,948 | 26,101 | 48,000 |
| 1954 | 15,596 | 802 | 3,532 | 4,527 | 22,543 | 47,000 |
| 1955 | 18,614 | 2,015 | 2,614 | 6,840 | 24,917 | 55,000 |
| 1956 | 22,047 | 3,978 | 3,541 | 5,403 | 28,081 | 63,000 |
| 1957 | 17,162 | 3,524 | 3,104 | 6,200 | 26,010 | 56,000 |
| 1958 | 17,499 | 4,645 | 3,513 | 5,393 | 40,950 | 72,000 |
| 1959 | 23,300 | 4,400 | 6,318 | 9,000 | 26,982 | 70,000 |
| 1960 | 45,000 | 8,500 | 10,800 | 14,900 | 55,800 | 135,000 |
| 1961 | 54,000 | 10,000 | 12,000 | 19,000 | 67,000 | 162,000 |
| 1962 | 59,000 | 11,000 | 20,000 | 17,000 | 71,000 | 178,000 |
| 1963 | 77,000 | 10,000 | 17,000 | 25,000 | 71,000 | 200,000 |
| 1964 | 70,000 | 11,000 | 18,000 | 23,000 | 78,000 | 200,000 |
| 1965 | 60,000 | 10,000 | 15,000 | 19,000 | 66,000 | 170,000 |
| 1966 | 29,000 | 5,000 | 7,500 | 9,000 | 32,500 | 83,000 |
| 1967 | 36,000 | 5,400 | 8,100 | 10,000 | 44,500 | 104,000 |
| 1968 | 40,000 | 6,000 | 9,000 | 11,000 | 48,000 | 114,000 |
| 1969-72 | 0 | 0 | 0 | 0 | 0 | 0 |
| 1973 | 11,300 | 1,700 | 3,200 | 3,500 | 9,300 | 29,000 |
| 1974/75 | 64,400 | 9,900 | 18,200 | 18,100 | 54,400 | 165,000 |
| 1976 | 58,500 | 9,000 | 16,500 | 16,500 | 49,500 | 150,000 |
| 1977 | 60,800 | 9,600 | 16,000 | 16,000 | 57,600 | 160,000 |
| 1978 | 61,400 | 10,000 | 16,600 | 16,600 | 61,400 | 166,000 |
| 1979 | 58,300 | 9,700 | 14,600 | 14,600 | 64,800 | 162,000 |
| Total | 937,575 | 154,672 | 234,849 | 281,218 | 1,070,686 | 2,679,000 |

* primarily teachers

Note: All figures for 1949 through 1958 and 1961 through 1963 are actual reported figures. Figures for 1966 through 1968 and 1974 through 1977 are estimates. For 1959, 1960, 1964, 1965, 1973, 1978, and 1979, only the totals are actual reported figures. For 1959, the total and the figures for agriculture and forestry, and for medicine are actual reported figures.

Source: Leo A. Orleans, Manpower for Science and Engineering in China (Washington, DC: Government Printing Office, 1980), p. 22.

## 12. Institutes of Higher Learning, 1982

|  | No. of Schools | No. of graduates | New enrolment | No. of students |
|---|---|---|---|---|
| Total | 715 | 454,814 | 311,820 | 1,133,494 |
| Universities | 32 | 51,827 | 35,239 | 125,200 |
| Polytechnic institutes | 206 | 183,830 | 106,388 | 405,619 |
| Agricultural institutes | 56 | 36,720 | 19,963 | 70,182 |
| Institutes of forestry | 10 | 4,031 | 2,280 | 7,986 |
| Medical universities | 112 | 25,964 | 29,314 | 161,869 |
| Teachers' institutes | 194 | 125,444 | 94,878 | 281,828 |
| Language institutes | 10 | 4,398 | 2,847 | 11,431 |
| Institutes of finance and economics | 36 | 9,207 | 11,267 | 37,247 |
| Institutes of political science and law | 9 | 920 | 2,595 | 9,225 |
| Institutes of physical culture | 13 | 4,904 | 2,383 | 8,349 |
| Art institutes | 27 | 2,951 | 1,731 | 4,957 |
| Institutes for nationalities | 10 | 4,618 | 2,935 | 9,601 |

Source: BR, vol. 26, no. 40 (October 3, 1983), p. 27.

## 13. Hospital Beds, 1950-1983

| Beds | 1950 | 1960 | 1970 | 1980 | 1981 | 1983 |
|---|---|---|---|---|---|---|
| Total | 99,800 | 654,779 | 1,104,984 | 1,982,176 | 2,017,088 | 2,110,000 |
| County and above | 99,800 | 600,235 | 711,865 | 1,192,393 | 1,239,001 | n/a |
| Commune | ---- | 46,272 | 367,992 | 775,413 | 763,114 | n/a |

Source: China Report, p. 684; BR, May 14, 1984, p. 10.  n/a = not available.

14.  Medical and Health Personnel, 1950-1983*

|                              | 1950    | 1960      | 1970      | 1980      | 1981      |
|------------------------------|---------|-----------|-----------|-----------|-----------|
| Total personnel              | 555,040 | 1,504,894 | 1,453,247 | 2,798,241 | 2,011,038 |
| Qualified personnel          | 42,425  | 89,781    | 235,663   | 502,022   | 638,549   |
| doctors of western medicine  | 41,400  | 81,811    | 220,992   | 447,288   | 516,498   |
| Secondary level personnel    | 118,527 | 441,837   | 685,051   | 1,174,435 | 1,180,665 |
| paramedics – western medicine | 53,400 | 168,311   | 256,053   | 443,761   | 436,196   |
| nurses                       | 37,800  | 170,143   | 259,147   | 465,798   | 474,569   |
| doctors – Chinese medicine   | 286,000 | 345,987   | 225,259   | 262,185   | 289,502   |

* In 1983 the number of total personnel and nurses increased to
3,253,000 and 596,000 respectively.  The 1983 statistics for the
other categories are not available.

Source:  China Report, p. 685; BR, May 14, 1984, p. 10.

15.  Changing Incidence of Disease in Beijing

| Cause                | Deaths per 100,000 persons | |
|----------------------|---------|---------|
|                      | 1955-59 | 1974-78 |
| Infectious Disease   | 112.9   | 17.4    |
| Cancer               | 25.6    | 67.6    |
| Heart Attacks        | 73.8    | 118.4   |
| Stroke               | 43.1    | 97.3    |
| Total Cardiovascular | 116.9   | 215.7   |

Source:  M. Gregg Bloche, "China Discovers Health Perils Accompanying
         Modernization," Washington Post, August 19, 1979; and Bloche,
         "Hypertension on the Rise in Modern China," Washington Post,
         August 20, 1979.

## 16. Women in China

Women members of the Communist Party
  (percent total)                                                           13

Women functionaries in economic, political, cultural,
  educational, and health departments, 1981 (mn)     4.7
    Percentage of total functionaries                    26
    Percentage increase since 1951                    1400

Women deputies to the National People's Congress
  (percent of total)
  1954 (1st Congress)                              12
  1978                                         21.2

Women officials from the grassroots level to the central
  government, 1981 (percent of total)            3-6

Women urban workers

| | Number | Percent of Labor Force |
|---|---|---|
| 1949 | 600,000 | 7.5 |
| 1980 | 34,000,000 | 34 |
| Beijing | | |
|   1949 | 4,887* | 3.8 |
|   1979 | 924,000 | 44 |

Women by industries, 1981 (percent of total
  workers)
  Textile industry                            55
  Light industry                           48.5
  Railways                                  25
  Heavy industry                           n/a

Peasant women in rural work, 1981 (mn)         150
Children under six years in nurseries and
  kindergartens, 1980 (percent)
  China                                    28
  Beijing, Shanghai, Tianjin, and Shandong
  and Guangdong provinces**                50+

Girls and women enrolled in schools, 1981
  (percent of total)
  Primary schools                          50
  Secondary schools                      46
  Colleges                                24

Women scientific workers
  Natural science researchers             86,000
    Percent of total                      27
  Chinese Academy of Sciences
    Women on the Scientific Council
    (membership 400)                   15
    Women researchers               5,000

\* There were no women taxi, truck, bus, or trolley drivers in Beijing before 1949; there are now about 1,600.

\*\* Childcare facilities are scarce in rural areas. Fewer than 10 percent of the 140,000 nursery or kindergarten teachers in Hebei province are trained in preschool education. Many are primary or middle school graduates or grannies.

Source: First line in table from People's Daily, December 11, 1983; everything else from China Facts, p. 466-67.

VIII.  DAILY LIFE


1. Introduction and Suggested Readings

Trying to describe the daily life of a society of 1 billion people is presumptuous at best.  Previous chapters have made apparent China's great variety and the Chinese people's range of life styles.  Most foreigners can make only general observations.

Families and Organizations    The family is an important institution in China today, though very different from what it was 30 years ago.  Reforming the family system was high on the CCP's immediate post-1949 agenda:  land reform and confiscation of firearms deprived the clan of its power, and a marriage law ended flagrant abuses against women.  Subsequently, demographic changes have caused the extended family to decline.  But Chinese today still spend much of their time as members of family units.  The family is still a principal institution for production, savings, consumption, and socialization.  And in many ways, it is perhaps more cohesive, more closely knit, and more a part of the social fabric today than it was in 1949.  The post-1949 restoration of political and economic stability made the forced breakup of families less likely.  Public health measures and better diet have increased the number of generations living at the same time.  Severe restrictions on migration within the country have discouraged family members from seeking employment away from their kin.  Because they provide a foundation of social order, facilitate savings, and instill discipline, China's approximately 200 million family units are a significant resource in fostering development.

But unlike three decades ago, Chinese now live in a world of organizations that are linked directly or indirectly to the state. Everyone is a member of a work unit or a residential unit -- in many cases the two are the same.  An individual's work unit -- danwei -- defines one's social status; sets the level of income, health care, and old-age pension; provides (in cities) ration coupons for scarce basic commodities; may regulate the purchase of durable consumer goods; authorizes marriage; and even attempts to regulate the conception of children.  One's unit often also provides a family-like social support. Organizations are responsible for a wide range of other social activities -- schools for education, medical facilities for health care, urban housing offices for living space, retail outlets for consumer goods, the police and the courts for social control, and the Communist Party and mass organizations for political indoctrination.

Women    Before 1949 women in China had only limited educational and employment opportunities, could not marry freely, and were subject to the authority of their own families and their spouse's family after marriage.  While advanced age led to greater social status for women as well as men and educational opportunities were made available to some women, particularly in wealthy or well-educated families, in general, life was delimited by the traditional priority given to males.

After 1949 the promolgation of the new marriage law in 1950 which legalized freedom of choice for both men and women, and continuing efforts to convince the population that women "hold up half the sky," did much to improve the social status of and the opportunities available to women in China. The number of women in government positions has increased dramatically in the last 30 years, although the total remains small (see table [VII.16], page 149). Only one woman, Zhou Enlai's widow Deng Yingchao, is a full member of the Politburo.

Women do, however, play a particularly active role in local level organizations, such as street committees, and in supervising the implementation of birth control policies. The All-China Women's Federation, headed by Kang Keqing, has responsibility for transmitting policies which affect women and representing women's interests to some extent. In recent years, the Federation has conducted surveys on women's domestic, professional, and social roles, but the impact of such studies on policymaking remains unclear.

Women workers predominate in certain sectors, such as textiles, light industry, and precision machine tools, and comprise an increasing percentage of the work force in the electronics industry. However, in many industries technical and higher level staff positions are still more often filled by men, while women are assigned to lower paying assembly-line or support jobs, such as operating cranes.

In the countryside, under the previous system of calculating individual income on the basis of work points, in general, a woman could earn a maximum of eight work points for a day's labor, as compared to ten for a man. Some women "shock workers" could, however, earn more. The recent "responsibility system," which sets quotas for households or work groups, provides an alternative to the disparity in total points which most women and men were eligible to earn. Under both the work point and responsibility systems, the head of household is made responsible for allocating family income, rather than directly assigning income to the individual.

In short the opportunities -- educational, social, and professional -- available to women have increased since 1949. However, problems remain: There are indications that the "responsibility system" reinforces the traditional preference in rural areas for male children, forced marriages are not unknown, a substantial proportion of the urban unemployed are women, and most importantly of all, it is not clear that intrinsic attitudes about the social role of women have been changed by the revolution.

Work   The type of work dictates much about the individual's daily life and the extent to which organizations impinge on it. In the composition of its labor force, China is still very much an agricultural country (see table [VIII.2] on page 158). Three-fourths of the labor force works in farming, one-tenth in the manufacturing sector, and the remainder in the service sector. As in many developing countries, creating new jobs in China's cities has not kept pace with even the natural increase of the urban population. As the table suggests, less than half-a-percent of the labor force has moved out of agriculture each year.

The government has taken a variety of measures over the years to minimize urban unemployment and the social problems it engenders. There have been strict controls on internal migration since the late 1950s. Beginning in the early 1960s, millions of urban middle school graduates have had to settle on communes and state farms at varying distances from their home cities for varying lengths of time. The resettlement rate rose in 1968 (to restore order after the turmoil of the Cultural Revolution) and then again in the mid-1970s (see table [VIII.3] on page 158). The post-Mao leadership deemphasized this very unpopular program, but soon faced a rise in urban unemployment -- about 20 million persons by March 1979 (20% of the urban population). The government is now permitting private citizens to establish individual and partnership enterprises, especially in handicraft and service trades, to reduce the number of young people out of work.

There is a sharp contrast between city and countryside in the organization of work. In the rural areas, the changes have been most dramatic. For example, a peasant in his or her mid-50s today has lived through several very different kinds of work environments (see chronology [VIII.4] on pages 159-160). In the immediate post-revolutionary period, the Communists carried out a policy of land reform and the norm was privately owned family farms. By the early 1950s, the CCP was encouraging cooperation among families while still recognizing peasant ownership of land and livestock. In the mid-1950's, Soviet-style collectivization was carried out with ownership of land and livestock passing to the collective (a village or number of villages), with the peasant being paid from the proceeds of common labor. In the late 1950s came the communes. Peasants were organized into multi-village work units and were often paid the same wage regardless of work done or individual productivity. By the early 1960s, the basic work unit was the multi-family team (20-40 families). Although some private family plots were allowed, most income came from the fruits of this collective labor, and was distributed to individuals according to work done after provisions had been made for expenses, reserves, and welfare services.

In 1979 yet another dramatic change took place; the so-called "responsibility" system which allows peasant production groups, households, or individuals to sign contracts for what they will produce for the state and retain the surplus for their own use (see chapter VI for more detail). As a result, the proportion of family income earned from above-contract production and non-agricultural activities has greatly increased in some areas. The role of the team in managing labor in the countryside has been reduced by the reform, and it remains uncertain whether teams receive any income from the production activities of peasant households. Once again, the family has become the basic economic and work unit in the Chinese countryside. Despite a general rise in income in rural areas, the decline in collective funds may have a critical effect on old or disabled people who previously have relied on team welfare for support.

Recently, individuals or families have been permitted to establish small private enterprises. However, in urban areas the vast majority of organizations -- factories, stores, schools, government offices, etc. -- are still "owned by the whole people" and run by the state. These tend to be large, formal organizations in which the family as an institution plays a much more limited role than in the countryside. The work week is usually six eight-hour days. Monthly wages are paid according to the relevant salary scale. In some cities, employees also receive supplemental payments to compensate for a higher cost of living. The wage program, originally set forth in the mid-1950s, called for wage increases every two to three years for most workers. In fact, no raises based on work evaluations were given from 1963 to 1977. Workers did receive bonuses, but they were not tied to skills or achievement. The result was a decline in real wages and a deadening of motivation. Wage adjustments since 1977 have increased the incomes of a majority of China's industrial workers and efforts are being made to link raises and bonuses to performance.

In sum, work creates two very different styles of life in China. In agriculture, the hours are long and irregular, and hard physical labor is the norm. In the urban areas, one's job is still quite time-consuming, but the hours are more regular and there are many exceptions to physical labor. In the countryside, production is now based on the household unit. In urban areas, most workers remain employees of collective or state-run enterprises, though an increasing number of individuals (particularly the young unemployed) are starting up very small businesses of their own. While rural inhabitants still envy the wide variety of consumer goods available in the cities, urban residents may become increasingly jealous of the high incomes earned by many peasants participating in the "responsibility" system.

Residence    City and countryside also differ considerably in the housing available to families, and in the degree of neighborhood organization. Rural dwellers usually own their own homes (but not the land on which they sit), may build new ones, and may transfer ownership to their children when they die. Depending on the family's wealth, houses range from mud huts to spacious two-story brick homes.

Urban residents must put up with more crowded conditions. They either live in traditional one-story houses or in multi-story apartment buildings. There are some enterprises that provide quarters for their employees, but many urban residents rent housing from the municipal government. The supply of urban housing has not kept pace with population growth, and families must live in very tight quarters. According to government statistics, residents of 192 municipalities have 3.6 square meters of living space per capita, a decline from the early 1950s. The government is investing more in new housing, but not enough to quickly alleviate the shortage.

Concerning community organization, rural areas are much less complex than cities. Production teams, equivalent to a small natural village or part of a large one, are the basic units. In some parts of China, the production team is composed of members with the same surname. In cities, separation of work and residence is the norm, and municipal governments have extended organizational tentacles into urban neighborhoods, both to maintain social control and to mobilize the populace (see the chart and glossary [VIII.5] on pages 161-162). Fifteen to 40 households form a residents' small group, which is under the jurisdiction of a residents' committee supervising up to several hundred households. The next level is the neighborhood committee, which controls several residents' committees and probably several thousand people. Units at each level work under the supervision of police and various administrative agencies. Direct official intervention occurs only for the most serious cases, however.

Generally speaking, the organizational networks that most affect daily life -- both work and residential, in both city and countryside -- encourage individuals to solve problems within their immediate social context.

Leisure    The demands of work and household maintenance leave Chinese relatively little time for leisure, and the quantity and quality of recreational activities have varied over time. The low point was certainly the Cultural Revolution decade (1966-76): Offerings in the arts were few and didactic, and many parks and monuments

were closed on the grounds that they might foster "feudal" thinking.
But since the fall of the "gang of four," there has been substantial
liberalization in the cultural realm.  Entertainment is no longer taboo
in the performing arts (though a political message often remains), and
the number of movies, plays, and operas -- some of which are foreign --
has greatly increased.  In the fine arts, both traditionalism and a
searching modern eclecticism are permitted.  Literature has become an
important vehicle for personal expression.  Museums and reopened
traditional cultural sites appeal to the Chinese pride in their long
past.  Spectator sports continue to be popular and are an outlet for
patriotic enthusiasm as China enters more international competitions.
Radio and, increasingly, television bring varied cultural fare into
units and households.  Limits to cultural liberalization remain,
however.  Literature and the arts has continued to be a sensitive area
politically.  In 1981 sharp criticism was directed at the screenplay
"Bitter Love," and in the fall of 1983 a more general campaign was
launched against "spiritual pollution."    While the campaign had
decelerated by early 1984, it provided a potent reminder that freedoms
in cultural expression, in social behavior, and even in personal
fashion, must be expanded gradually if they are not to alarm those
concerned that China's contact with the West may introduce
inappropriate ideas, values, and practices.

<u>Restoring Political Bonds</u>    The liberalization of culture is part
of a broader effort to recreate public confidence in the regime.  Over
the last three decades, the Communist Party lost much of its originally
broad mandate to transform the country's social and political life.
Especially among those born after 1949, there is skepticism -- how much
is impossible to measure -- about whether the government can bring a
change for the better.

The relatively low standard of living and limited career opportunities -- problems common in most developing societies -- are partly
responsible for these attitudes.  But China's unique political history
also plays a role.  A final verdict has yet to be rendered on the
Cultural Revolution era, but there is substantial evidence that it
wreaked havoc with the lives of many and created a social climate of
cynicism and anxiety.

The post-Mao leadership has taken some specific steps to reduce
its political liabilities and reknit old loyalties.  It has cancelled
class labels assigned during the social and political transformations
of the 1950s and 1960s, and forbid discrimination in employment, social
services, and political participation on the basis of class.  Revival
of legal institutions and training is seen as a way to reinstate
confidence in authority based on rules of due process rather than
arbitrary force.  And regularized popular participation is being
encouraged in many areas through introduction at the county level of
direct election of deputies to people's congresses.

On the surface, the shape of daily life in China will probably not
change radically in the foreseeable future.  The great majority of
Chinese will, as they do now, have to work hard to guarantee a standard
of living that ranges from basic subsistence to moderate comfort.  They
will continue to live in close quarters with families and neighbors,
relying on time-tested ways of maintaining social harmony.  Like others
in the modern world, they must find personal orbits in a universe of
organizations that create opportunites while imposing controls.  But
whether they have confidence in their government will depend on its
success in raising the general standard of living and guaranteeing some

measure of personal autonomy.

## Suggested Readings

Bennett, Gordon A. Huadong: The Story of a Chinese People's Commune. Boulder, CO: Westview Press, 1978. A description of the structure and daily life of one commune in South China.

Bernstein, Thomas P. Up to the Mountains, Down to the Villages: The Transfer of Youth from Urban to Rural China. New Haven: Yale University Press, 1977. An exhaustive analysis of the origins, rationale, and effectiveness of one solution to the problem of youth unemployment.

Bonavia, David. The Chinese. New York: Lippincott, 1980. Perceptive observations of life in China today by a British journalist resident in Beijing.

Butterfield, Fox. China: Alive in the Bitter Sea. New York: Times Books, 1982.

Chan, Anita, Richard Madson, and Jonathan Unger. Chen Village. Berkeley: University of California Press, 1984. A detailed study of rural life in China since the 1960s.

Chen, Jack. A Year in Upper Felicity: Life in a Chinese Village during the Cultural Revolution. New York: Macmillan, 1973. A report on a year's (1969-70) residence in a rural commune. The author, who lived in the PRC for many years, offers much detail on village life, attitudes, and relationships.

Ch'en Jo-hsi. The Execution of Mayor Yin: Stories from the Great Proletarian Cultural Revolution. Bloomington: Indiana University Press, 1978. Graphic stories of daily life in China during the late 1960s and early 1970s by a Chinese-American who lived in China during that period.

Chinese Literature (monthly). Short stories, poems, and novellas from both the traditional and modern periods. Literature is currently one of the principal modes of personal expression in China, and so is an excellent way to "get inside" contemporary Chinese life.

Croizier, Ralph C., ed. China's Cultural Legacy and Communism. New York: Praeger, 1970. A collection of essays on all aspects of culture, broadly defined. Although scholarly in approach, they have much to offer the general reader about the old and new in China and how the individual Chinese experiences the mixture.

Davis-Friedmann, Deborah. Long Life: Aging and Old Age in the Peoples's Republic of China. New Haven: Yale University Press, 1981. Scholarly examination of the place of old people in contemporary Chinese society.

Finklestein, David. "When the Snow Thaws." The New Yorker, September 10, 1979. A revealing look at the "underside" of Chinese life and the impact of the Cultural Revolution.

Frolic, B. Michael. Mao's People: Sixteen Portraits of Life in Revolutionary China. Cambridge, MA: Harvard University Press, 1980. Individual Chinese relate both their pride in much of what China has accomplished and their problems in coping with a shifting and sometimes oppressive political environment.

Johnson, Kay Ann. Women, the Family and Peasant Revolution in China. Chicago: The University of Chicago Press, 1983. A study of policy toward women in rural areas since 1949.

Liang Heng, and Judith Shapiro. Son of the Revolution. New York: Alfred A. Knopf, 1983. The turmoil of the Cultural Revolution portrayed through the experience of a young Chinese student and his family.

Lo, Ruth Earnshaw, and Katharine S. Kinderman. In the Eye of the Typhoon. New York: Harcourt Brace Jovanovich, 1980. The powerful memoir of an American woman, the widow of a Chinese intellectual, who lived in China from 1937 to 1978.

Mathews, Jay, and Linda Mathews. One Billion: A China Chronicle. New York: Random House, 1983. A thoughtful journalistic account of contemporary life in China.

Parish, William L. "The Family and Economic Change," China: The 80s Era, edited by Norton Ginsburg and Bernard A. Lalor. Boulder: Westview Press, 1984.

_____, and Martin King Whyte. Village and Family in Contemporary China. Chicago: University of Chicago Press, 1978. An important scholarly study that analyzes rural social change, and the persistence of some traditional social patterns in post-1949 China.

_____. Urban Life in Contemporary China. Chicago: University of Chicago Press, 1984. Indepth study of life in urban China by two prominent American sociologists.

Rawski, Thomas G. Economic Growth and Employment in China. Washington, DC: The World Bank, 1980. An economist's examination of China's performance in providing employment for its work force of over 400 million persons.

Schell, Orville. "The Wind of Wanting To Go It Alone," The New Yorker, January 23, 1984. A look at the countryside under the responsibility system.

Terrill, Ross, ed. The China Difference. New York: Harper & Row, 1979. A collection of essays in which 16 scholars evaluate what makes China tick after three decades of Communist rule by exploring the complexities of belief systems and social, political, and cultural life.

2. <u>Composition of the Labor Force</u> (in millions)

|  | 1957 | | 1975 | |
|---|---|---|---|---|
| Sector | Size | % | Size | % |
| <u>Agriculture</u>* | 231.53 | 84.5 | 329.04 | 76.7 |
| <u>Manufacturing and Services</u> | | | | |
| Industry and Contruction | 16.71 | 6.1 | 45.90 | 10.7 |
| Commerce, Finance, Food & Drink, Personal Services | 4.38 | 1.6 | 9.00 | 2.1 |
| Transport & Communications | 8.76 | 3.2 | 19.30 | 4.5 |
| Health, Education, & Culture | 4.65 | 1.7 | 14.15 | 3.3 |
| Government & Mass Organizations | 3.01 | 1.1 | 6.00 | 1.4 |
| Military | 3.01 | 1.1 | 3.43 | 0.8 |
| Salt & Fishing | 1.91 | 0.7 | 2.14 | 0.5 |
| Total, Manufacturing and Services | 42.47 | 15.5 | 99.96 | 23.3 |
| TOTAL | 274.00 | 100.0 | 429.00 | 100.0 |

* includes farmland capital contruction, forestry, and water conservancy

Source: Adapted from <u>The Economist</u>, February 16, 1980, p. 108.

3. <u>Transfer of Urban Youth to the Countryside</u>

| Year | Number | Year | Number |
|---|---|---|---|
| 1962-63 | 292,000 | 1972 | 646,000 |
| 1964 | 3-400,000 | 1973 | 1,123,000 |
| 1965 | 250,000 | 1974 | 2,000,000 |
| 1968 | 1,725,000 | 1975 | 2,000,000 |
| 1969 | 2,700,000 | 1976-78 | 5,000,000 |
| 1970 | 1,067,000 | 1979 | 800,000 (projected) |
| 1971 | 738,000 | | |

Source: Thomas P. Bernstein, <u>Up to the Mountains, Down to the Villages: The Transfer of Youth From Urban to Rural China</u> (New Haven: Yale University Press, 1978), pp. 25, 32; Suzanne Pepper, "Chinese Education After Mao: Two Steps Forward, Two Steps Back and Begin Again?" in <u>CQ</u>, no. 81 (March 1980), pp. 48, 57.

## 4. Rural Organization:  Chronology and Structure

Since the late 1940s, the Chinese Communist Party has led a sweeping social transformation in the Chinese countryside.  Land reform was the first stage.  Subsequently, the Party has had to address two major institutional issues:  the extent of collectivization of ownership and work, and the size of the social unit designated the "basic accounting unit" (the unit that makes work assignments, organizes production and distribution of the agricultural product, and handles its own accounting with responsibility for profits and losses).

The chart and chronology that follow outline the evolution of the ownership system, the search for the appropriate basic accounting unit, and the institutions created at various levels of rural society (sub-village, village, and multi-village marketing area).  The glossary describes the key units in the present system, as it stabilized after 1963.  The following abbreviations are used:  BAU = Basic Accounting Unit; MAT = Mutual Aid Team; LAPC = Lower Agricultural Producers' Cooperative; HAPC = Higher Agricultural Producers' Cooperative.

### a) Chronology

| Time  /  Level of Society | 1949 Land Reform | 1952 Land Reform Ends | 1955 | 1957 | 1958 | 1959 | 1963 | 1979 |
|---|---|---|---|---|---|---|---|---|
| Supra Marketing Area | | | | | Commune = BAU | | | |
| Marketing Area | | | | | | | Commune | ----> |
| Large Village/ Village Cluster | | | | HAPC = BAU | Production Brigade | = BAU | --------- | ----> |
| Small Village/ Village Section | | MAT | LAPC = BAU | Production Team | ------- | ------- | = BAU | ----> |
| Household | = BAU | = BAU | LAPC Component | Team Component | ------- | ------- | ------- | = BAU |

1949:  The household was the basic accounting unit (BAU).  Land reform (1949-52) redistributed the land, ending tenancy and larger holdings and creating a system of roughly equal holdings among owner-cultivators.  But the peasant household remained the BAU.

1952:  Mutual Aid Teams (MAT) were introduced.  Small groups of neighbors shared labor, tools, and draft animals on an informal, temporary, or seasonal basis.

1955:  Lower Agricultural Producers' Cooperatives (LAPC) began to appear as the BAU.  Members pooled land, labor, tools, and animals, and divided the agricultural product collectively, but retained ownership of their pooled assets and received shares that reflected the value of these assets.

1957: Higher Agricultural Producers' Cooperatives (HAPC) emerged as the BAU. These were "fully socialist" collectives in which all assets were pooled, ownership passed to the collective, and distribution was based on work. (LAPCs became "production teams" within the HAPCs responsible for organizing collective work.)

1958: People's communes -- a new administrative and economic unit larger in size than existing marketing systems -- were established as the BAU. HAPCs became "production brigades" within the commune.

1959: Because of difficulties in the early commune system, the brigade again became the BAU.

1963: The commune experiment was further modified: the production team was designated the BAU; communes were reduced in size to conform roughly to rural marketing areas; and "private plots" (collectivized in 1958) were restored for household use. This system remained basically intact from the early 1960s to the late 1970s. During that period, the number of communes declined (from 70,000 in the early 1960s to about 50,000 in the mid-1970s) and the average population increased.

1979: Experiments in the 1970s to make the production brigade the BAU have been replaced since 1979 by the introduction of the "responsibility system" and the designation of teams and households as the BAU.

b) Glossary

People's Commune. A local economic system of importance, usually assumed to coincide with a rural marketing area. Figures suggest an average population of 15,000, but communes near large cities or in highly productive areas are known to be much larger. The commune management (formerly revolutionary) committee administers state plans and provides unified planning for its area. It manages hospitals or clinics, middle and vocational schools, rural industry, power plants and water conservation projects, large-scale commercial agriculture, tractor stations, radio stations, stores, and banks.

Production Brigade. Composed of 100-300 households. The intermediate level of the "three-level commune management" system, with responsibility for health stations, primary schools, small industry and handicrafts, and medium-scale undertakings such as animal husbandry, orchards, and fisheries. It is served by branches of state stores and banks, and often is the equivalent of a natural village.

Production Team. Composed of 20-40 households. The lowest level of management within the commune. In larger villages, it coincides with a neighborhood and can play a major role in coordinating the work of several families.

Household. A social, residential, and work unit, normally pooling and
budgeting the income of its members. Households probably average
four to five persons, although they vary greatly in size and
structure. Under the "responsibility system" (sanctioned in
1979), the family has, once again, become a most important
production unit in the countryside.

5. Urban Neighborhood Organization

A combination of official government agencies and community organizations structure the life of city residents. Municipal administration extends down to the level of the "neighborhood" (7,000 to 14,000
households). Two levels of subordinate community organizations cover
smaller areas. Guided by the city government, they mobilize the
populace to pursue collective goals, preserve social order, and try to
deal with problems at the lowest level possible.

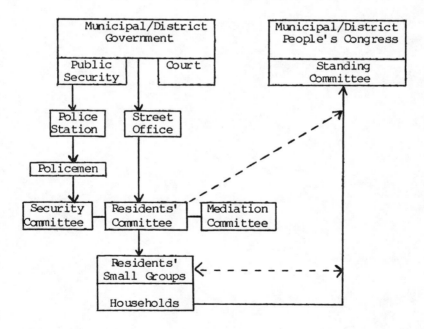

Municipal or District Government. The administrative organs of basic-
level government. In theory, government leaders are selected by
the relevant congress; in practice, personnel decisions are made
within the administration itself. Subordinate to municipal and
district governments are a number of functional departments. Most
important for urban neighborhoods are the public security department (the police) and the courts.

Street Office. A branch office of the city or district administration
at the neighborhood level. Together with the police station, it
extends state authority and activity into the neighborhood for
more direct contact with citizens and mass organizations. It
administers government programs and campaigns and may run street
factories or neighborhood hospitals and clinics.

Residents' Committees and Residents' Small Groups. These organizations
emerged in the early 1950s and have recently received new official
support. The residents' committee has jurisdiction over large
residential groupings (normally 100 to 600 households); residents'
small groups deal with smaller ones (normally 15 to 40 households). Both operate under street office leadership and supervision. Each residents' small group chooses a leader, who is
likely to serve as that group's representative on the residents'
committee. Committees and small groups work together to set up
working street committees, recruit activists, and organize the
residents to carry out activities that assist the government and
benefit the community. Public security committees which work
closely with the police, and mediation committees which try to
settle civil disputes under the supervision of the courts, are
common. Residential organizations also assume responsibilities
for child care, public sanitation, maintenance of public facilities, propagation and implementation of campaigns, household
services activities, and cultural enrichment programs.

APPENDIX: ROMANIZATION CONVERSION CHART

Below are the Chinese proper names whose <u>pinyin</u> romanization differs from previous systems used. Personal names are accompanied by their Wade-Giles equivalents. Place names appear with their Postal Atlas equivalent where it exists; for others the hyphenated Wade-Giles rendering is provided. For other terms, the Wade-Giles form is given.

## Personal Names

| Pinyin | Wade-Giles | Pinyin | Wade-Giles |
|---|---|---|---|
| Bo Yibo | Po Yi-po | Nie Fengzhi | Nieh Feng-chih |
| Chen Duxiu | Ch'en Tu-hsiu | Nie Rongzhen | Nieh Jung-chen |
| Chen Muhua | Ch'en Mu-hua | Peng Chong | P'eng Ch'ung |
| Chen Xilian | Ch'en Hsi-lien | Peng Dehuai | P'eng Te-huai |
| Chen Yi | Ch'en Yi | Peng Zhen | P'eng Chen |
| Chen Yonggui | Ch'en Yung-kui | Qin Jiwei | Ch'in Chi-wei |
| Chen Yun | Ch'en Yun | Rao Shoukun | Jao Shou-k'un |
| Deng Xiaoping | Teng Hsiao-p'ing | Sey Pidin | Saifudin |
| Deng Yingchao | Teng Ying-ch'ao | Song Renqiong | Sung Jen-ch'iung |
| Du Yide | Tu Yi-te | Su Yu | Su Yu |
| Geng Biao | Keng Piao | Wang Dongxing | Wang Tung-hsing |
| Gu Mu | Ku Mu | Wang Hongwen | Wang Hung-wen |
| Hai Rui | Hai Jui | Wang Ping | Wang P'ing |
| Han Guang | Han Kuang | Wang Renzhong | Wang Jen-chung |
| Han Xianchu | Han Hsien-ch'u | Wang Zhen | Wang Chen |
| Hong Xuezhi | Hung Hsueh-chih | Wei Guoqing | Wei Kuo-ch'ing |
| Hu Qiaomu | Hu Ch'iao-mu | Wu De | Wu Te |
| Hu Yaobang | Hu Yao-pang | Wu Kehua | Wu K'e-hua |
| Hua Guofeng | Hua Kuo-feng | Xi Zhongxun | Hsi Chung-hsun |
| Huang Huoqing | Huang Huo-ch'ing | Xiao Ke | Hsiao K'e |
| Huang Zhen | Huang Chen | Xiao Quanfu | Hsiao Ch'uan-fu |
| Ji Dengkui | Chi Teng-k'ui | Xu Shiyou | Hsu Shih-yu |
| Ji Pengfei | Chi P'eng-fei | Xu Xiangqian | Hsu Hsiang-ch'ien |
| Jiang Hua | Chiang Hua | Yang Dezhi | Yang Te-chih |
| Jiang Qing | Chiang Ch'ing | Yang Jingren | Yang Ching-jen |
| Kang Shi'en | K'ang Shih-en | Yang Shangkun | Yang Shang-k'un |
| Li Dazhao | Li Ta-chao | Yang Yong | Yang Yung |
| Li Desheng | Li Te-sheng | Ye Fei | Yeh Fei |
| Li Xiannian | Li Hsien-nien | Ye Jianying | Yeh Chien-ying |
| Lin Biao | Lin Piao | You Taizhong | Yu T'ai-chung |
| Liu Bocheng | Liu Po-ch'eng | Yu Qiuli | Yu Ch'iu-li |
| Liu Shaoqi | Liu Shao-ch'i | Yuan Baohua | Yuan Pao-hua |
| Mao Zedong | Mao Tse-tung | Yuan Shikai | Yuan Shih-k'ai |
| Ni Zhifu | Ni Chih-fu | | |

| Pinyin | Wade-Giles | Pinyin | Wade-Giles |
|--------|-----------|--------|-----------|
| Zhang Aiping | Chang Ai-p'ing | Zhang Zhixiu | Chang Chih-hsiu |
| Zhang Caiqian | Chang Ts'ai-ch'ien | Zhao Ziyang | Chao Tzu-yang |
| Zhang Chunqiao | Chang Ch'un-ch'iao | Zhou Enlai | Chou En-lai |
| Zhang Tingfa | Chang T'ing-fa | Zhu De | Chu Te |

## Place Names

| Pinyin | Postal Atlas | Pinyin | Postal Atlas |
|--------|-------------|--------|-------------|
| Baotou | Paotow | Ji'nan | Tsinan |
| Beijing | Peking | Lanzhou | Lanchow |
| Changsha | Changsha | Liaodong | Liaotung |
| Chengdu | Chengtu | Ningxia | Ninghsia |
| Daqing | Ta-ch'ing | Qingdao | Tsingtao |
| Dazhai | Ta-chai | Qinghai | Tsinghai |
| Fengtian | Fengtien | Shaanxi | Shensi |
| Fujian | Fukien | Shandong | Shantung |
| Fuzhou | Fuchow | Shanxi | Shansi |
| Gansu | Kansu | Shijiazhuang | Shihchiachuang |
| Guangdong | Kwangtung | Sichuan | Szechwan |
| Guangxi | Kwangsi | Tianjin | Tientsin |
| Guangzhou | Canton | Diaoyutai | Tiao-yu-t'ai |
| Guiyang | Kuiyang | Wuxi | Wu-hsi |
| Guizhou | Kuichow | Xi'an | Sian |
| Ha'erbin | Harbin | Xiangtan | Hsiang-t'an |
| Hangzhou | Hangchow | Xi'ning | Sining |
| Hebei | Hopei | Xinjiang | Sinkiang |
| Hefei | Hofei | Xizang | Tibet |
| Heilongjiang | Heilungkiang | Xuzhou | Hsuchow |
| Henan | Honan | Yan'an | Yenan |
| Hubei | Hupei | Yangzi | Yangtze |
| Huhehaote | Huhehot | Yinchaun | Yinchwan |
| Jiangsu | Kiangsu | Zhejiang | Chekiang |
| Jiangxi | Kiangsi | Zhengzhou | Chengchow |
| Jilin | Kirin | | |

## Other

| Pinyin | Wade-Giles | Pinyin | Wade-Giles |
|--------|-----------|--------|-----------|
| Bai | Pai | pu'tonghua | p'u-t'ung-hua |
| Dong | Tung | Zhuang | Chuang |
| Hongqi | Hung-ch'i | | |

N.B.  The apostrophe in _pinyin_ indicates syllable division in words where there might be confusion as to the proper division.  In Wade-Giles, the apostrophe indicates aspiration of the preceding consonant.